PARIS
BY BISTRO

PARIS
BY BISTRO

A Guide to Eating Well

Christine and Dennis Graf

Interlink Books

An imprint of Interlink Publishing Group, Inc.
Northampton, Massachusetts

This edition first published in 2009 by

INTERLINK BOOKS
An imprint of Interlink Publishing Group, Inc.
46 Crosby Street, Northampton, Massachusetts 01060
www.interlinkbooks.com

Library of Congress Cataloging-in-Publication Data
Graf, Christine.
Paris by bistro / by Christine Graf and Dennis Graf.
p. cm.
Includes bibliographical references and index.
ISBN 978-1-56656-740-4
1. Restaurants—France—Paris—Guidebooks. 2. Paris
(France)—Guidebooks. I. Graf, Dennis. II. Title.
TX907.5.F72P373324 2002
647.95443'61—dc21
2002011142

Printed and bound in Korea

Book design by Juliana Spear

To request our complete 40-page full-color catalog,
please call us toll free at
1-800-238-LINK, visit our website at **www.interlinkbooks.com**, or write to
Interlink Publishing
46 Crosby Street, Northampton, Massachusetts 01060
e-mail: info@interlinkbooks.com

CONTENTS

ACKNOWLEDGMENTS

To all of the people who have so generously shared their enthusiasm for Paris and their insights into bistros with us, including Lisa Bernard, Amy Boggio, Lucy Brennan, Susan Cole, Christine Estruga, Clément de Faget, Jean-François Doulet, Georges Ducrocq, Jake Lamar, Fabio Lopes, Katherine and Charles McCracken, Diego Marguela, Deborah Mends, Molly and Ross Provance, Stewart Rayment, Sybil de la Renaudière, François Rhein, Scott Haine, Terin Smith, Almeta Speaks and other Parisians and longtime residents of the City of Light whose names escape us.

To David Shumway, who eschews artichokes and foreign travel, but is an inspiration to his friends just the same.

Special thanks are due to Anita and Albert Cesbron and Marie Louise and Bob Sigel for opening their homes to us and making their Paris ours.

Finally, we thank the bistro, brasserie, and restaurant chefs and other workers who have made this study so enjoyable. We've tried to emphasize bistros in areas popular with tourists, but a few special favorites happen to be in less visited areas, in hard-to-find places. They are well worth the trouble of seeking out.

You will not find the most famous and expensive bistros, like Chez Georges, L'Ami Louis, or Benoît in these pages—they are well beyond our cut-off point.

We have not solicited or accepted free meals from bistro chefs or proprietors, and we have not identified ourselves, so the food and service we describe should be the same that you, the reader, will receive. We think that our findings will delight you.

PREFACE TO THE
2ND EDITION

We began the first edition by musing on how a person can be intimidated by artichokes. We think now that most people are more intimidated by the strong euro.

So, how can today's traveler still eat well in Paris, avoiding fast food chains and boring *cuisine industrielle*? We have filled this book with ideas about how this can be done, mentioning everything from top-flight bistros offering gourmet fare to the simple sandwich shops with fresh made-to-order offerings.

You may decide to take your main meal at lunch. Many of our bistros are frequented by business people who expect high-quality food at reasonable prices, what they call the "rapport qualité-prix." They receive it at places we've found and listed here, even in districts like the chic Marais or touristy 6th arrondissement. Also, you could order just a *plat*, a main dish, which in most bistros comes with vegetables, accompanying it with a glass of wine or a *carafe d'eau*, the very drinkable Paris tap water. On the days when you're in a hurry to tour a museum or check the shops, you could try a simple bakery *formule* at noon—many *boulangeries* offer a lunch special of sandwich or quiche, dessert and drink. We have found this usually enough for the two of us. Then you can enjoy a more substantial meal at night.

Not all of the changes in Paris have been negative by any means: in fact some have been very good. The bistro of today is no longer a smoke-filled room. The French government has taken care of that. We spoke to French friends of our amazement at how quickly people have adapted—and were reminded that a heavy fine is levied on the smoker, and a much higher one on the bistro owner, if they flout the law.

As we have said before, bistro food can be impressive. The first really memorable meal we had in Paris was years ago at the bistro Allard in the 6th arrondissement. We recommended it to friends who were about to make their grand tour of Europe. In addition to Allard, they went to the famous Tour d'Argent, a *temple de gastronomie,* and compared the cuisine of the two restaurants favorably.

One summer evening years ago, my husband and I were passing the bistro and I saw an attractive brunette who turned out to be Fernande Allard herself standing outside. I stopped, greeted her, and briefly repeated the story I'd heard comparing her place with the Tour—and was rewarded when she asked me to come inside. "Tell my cooks what you just told me," she insisted, and I got the chance to repeat the story to two scrawny, perspiring young men in the kitchen. Smiles lit up their faces.

What is a Bistro?

> Until you have wasted time in a city, you cannot pretend to know it well. The soul of a big city is not to be grasped so easily; in order to make contact with it, you have to have been bored, you have to have suffered a bit in those places that contain it. Anyone can get hold of a guide and tick off all the monuments, but within the very confines of Paris there is another city as difficult of access as Timbuktu once was.

> Julien Green, Paris

What is a bistro anyway? Some have said that the word came to us from the Russians, who called out "bystra, bystra" to mean "quickly, quickly" when they wanted fast service. We would not always recommend this technique. Quite often it has the opposite result.

An American friend remembers an incident which occurred one evening in a Left Bank bistro. He and his wife were sitting at a side table, receiving impeccable service. During their meal they were embarrassed to observe a large group of their countrymen in full "ugly American" mode— waving their hands, snapping their fingers, and shouting "Garçon, garçon," at a dignified-looking man who was none other than the proprietor. The louder their shouts and more frantic their gestures, the less notice the proprietor paid to them. Instead, with a little smile on his face and effortlessly balancing a tray, he sauntered right past their table. He did this several times, completely ignoring the shouts and the glares. But he did make his way quite often to our friend's table, using a little French, a little English, and a lot of sign language to help them order something they would really enjoy, and, later, to make sure that everything was right.

In reading about the history of bistros, the word "café" keeps cropping up. In a French textbook, *Cours de Langue et de Civilisation Française*, G. Mauger described a bistro as "un petit café du quartier," a little neighborhood café. Books about bistros include establishments with the word "Café" blazoned on their exterior. Café or bistro? They are ultimately the same. Sometimes we think of a bistro as a café with a greater emphasis on food. But there are places called cafés with good food, and others called bistros with mediocre offerings.

In W. Scott Haine's scholarly research on cafés, he has noticed a looseness in the way the terms "bistro," "bar," "café," and "restaurant" have been used in the past. This extends to our own time. The Larousse *Histoire des Cafés et des Cafetiers* gives Humphrey Bogart's Casablanca nightclub and the Berlin cabaret where Liza Minelli performed as examples of cafés in the movies.

More recently, a bistro is thought of as a small, individually owned restaurant, often run by a family and patronized by regulars. There will almost always be a small bar and a number of small tables. The food will be simple country classics, *la cuisine grand-mère*, the sort of things grandmother used to serve. Prices are usually reasonable, although some famous bistros can be quite expensive. Most bistros have their own specialties, often regional dishes, which people ask for again and again.

Brasseries are larger, noisier, and less formal places, often with many square meters of brass and chrome, and a long bar dispensing a number of beers on tap. A brasserie was originally the retail outlet of a brewery; many in Paris were

founded by Alsatians who came to Paris in the 1870s, after the Franco-Prussian War.

Many brasseries still serve Germanic-influenced food and wine—sauerkraut, sausages, and the white wines of the southeast. You will also find typical French country bistro food in addition to the classic brasserie fare of seafood. Brasseries are usually open late at night. In Paris, many of the classic brasseries have been taken over by the Groupe Flo, sometimes to the consternation of the long-time regulars—see our discussion of the Balzar, in the 5th arrondissement.

The New Bistro

In recent years, there has been a trend toward something that is neither a café nor a traditional bistro, nor yet a classic restaurant. This new sort of eating place is not open for business all day like a café; you can't get a drink there at all hours, and the food is most definitely something grandmother would not even think of attempting—unless she were energetic and inspired, a Julia Child, perhaps. What has been happening is that young chefs, formerly *sous-chefs* in the most famous Parisian restaurants, have been leaving and starting up little restaurants of their own, places that they call "bistros." The absence of grand restaurant frills and fussiness, the minimalist decor, the limited wait staff—no maître d', just one or two friendly and helpful servers—make the place appealing, while keeping prices down to a level where these restaurants can compete with other bistros. Thus, you can dine for a reasonable price at a modest-looking restaurant where the chef has worked in the kitchens of Le Crillon, the Tour d'Argent, or even the Elysée Palace. And the cuisine reflects it: you taste outstanding food, you get a chance to sample the fare of someone who's on the cutting edge of the most recent developments in cuisine, and who has a chef's classical training lending substantial background to his or her ideas.

Why is this revolution in bistros happening now? Maybe it's a result of the natural urge that most of us feel to be independent and in charge, to use our skills for our own benefit and not just for the company. Maybe it is what one could call the Paul Bocuse phenomenon: the dream that a young chef could become a "name" and not have to keep on toiling anonymously for the glory of the establishment.

Another motive that nobody seems to mention is the atmosphere in the back room where the work gets done. If you've ever read George Orwell's *Down and Out in Paris and London*, you'll remember his horrifying description of working in the kitchen at the Hotel Lotti, where he toiled as a *plongeur* (dishwasher) in the 1930s.

By the time British designer and restaurateur Terence Conran made his own journey to the kitchen of a Paris restaurant to learn about food two decades later, conditions were not much better. He wrote: "La Méditerranée in Paris has changed little in its appearance since I worked there as a 'plongeur' in the early 1950s. But in those days, whilst the restaurant the customers saw was really quite grand, the kitchen was an eye-opening thieves' den of squalor and cruelty."

We would hope that restaurant conditions have substantially improved, that the helpers, whether they are *sous-chefs* or merely *plongeurs*, get decent treatment, but cooking is a high-pressure job anywhere. It must be particularly so in a culture as food-centered as the French, and one can imagine that in famous kitchens all over the city there must be *sous-chefs* who dream of the day when they may escape from the local tyrant and be the one in charge at their own small place.

Bistro Etiquette

Recently we picked up a French guide to travel, *Voyager aux Etats-Unis* (*Travel to the United States*) giving helpful—and unintentionally hilarious—hints to the French person planning a trip. The potential tourist is told how to manage in the country of "les Anglo-Saxons." Our puritanical streak, our strange foods, our disconcerting habit of addressing people by their first names, it's all in there. Warnings about the food *chez nous* focus on overcooked meat and undercooked vegetables, and the reader is cautioned against patronizing French restaurants abroad because they tend to be pretentious and overpriced.

With these cultural differences in mind, a few reminders on how to manage in the French capital. A nice surprise about bistros is that you often find great courtesy there. Even in a city the size of Paris, it's customary for people to greet and be greeted when they enter and leave a bistro; you'll hear "Bonjour, Monsieur, Madame, au revoir M'sieu, Madame" all the time. In return, you'll want to manage a polite "Bonjour"[bawnsjure] and "Au revoir" [oh-vwahr].

In many of the bistros we recommend, people dress informally: good jeans or slacks with an appropriate shirt or top would not be out of place. Women can wear slacks but usually wear skirts or dresses. Still, we were surprised to see a middle-aged man, a tourist, leave a restaurant in the 6th district speaking at the top of his voice and wearing, among other things, a baseball cap and shorts. At the time, we were sitting near some very well-dressed Parisians.

The French respect each other's privacy; conversation in a bistro will generally be in hushed tones. You normally do not hear loud talk or raucous laughter. On a few occasions during our research, we found that a restaurant could be completely dominated by one or two loud English-speaking tourists relating their stories. This is not typical, but it does change the ambiance in an unfavorable way. (There were many more savvy Anglophones who'd learned to adjust the volume of their conversation to Parisian levels).

Eating in Paris

Yes, it is possible to get a bad meal in Paris, and, unfortunately, it's getting easier and easier. Sad to say, many visitors to the French capital find themselves in fast-food restaurants, self-service cafeterias, and conveniently located chain restaurants, eating thin flavorless steaks and soggy fries while not knowing that a few blocks away there is a legendary bistro packed with local gourmands joyously wolfing down extraordinary food. Price is not always a good guide, although food of high quality can never be cheap.

Some observations:

⚜ The best-value restaurants are often on obscure side streets. For this reason we urge you to equip yourself with a detailed street-by-street map, available at any Paris newsstand.

⚜ Very simple-looking places can serve quite sophisticated food.

⚜ What we call a menu, the French call the *carte*. Most French restaurants have a fixed-price (*prix fixe*) meal with two or three courses called the *formule* or *menu*, offering a limited choice of what is listed on their *carte*. This is usually a good value, and many patrons will order from it.

⚜ By law every French restaurant must have the menu, or *carte*, posted outside along with the prices so you know what's available before you enter. Most waiters can speak at least a few words of English, although they may not know enough to discuss the fine details of ingredients or preparation of a specific dish with you.

⚜ French law requires each restaurant to provide ordinary tap water. If you don't see it on the table, ask for "Un carafe d'eau, s'il vous plaît," (ahn kah-raff dough, seel voo play). Most French people prefer to drink bottled water, and if you've never been to Paris before and are worried about the possibility of digestive disorders, you might want to stick to bottled water for the first few days. The tap water is perfectly safe and is purified by ozone, so has none of that unpleasant chlorinated taste.

⚜ Tipping is usually included in the price of the meal, indicated by the term *service compris* (service included) on the menu. You need not leave anything else, although if there are a few coins left over after you've paid your bill, you may want to show an unexpected generosity.

Words, Words Words— Avoiding Misunderstandings

French and English share a great vocabulary when it comes to food. Where did we get the words "hors d'oeuvres," "soup," "quiche," "beef," "carrots," "cream," "dessert," and a host of other terms for edibles if not from the French? But similarities can create confusion. It's important to remember:

* *entrée* means hors d'oeuvre, not main dish, in France.
* *plat* (think of "plate") is the word for the main course.
* after that, it's easy: dessert is the same word in both languages.

Ordering Wine

Even people who are familiar with California wines sometimes freeze when confronted with a wine list in France. Virtually all of the wines will be carrying names unknown to them. Few bistros have a wine specialist, and many waiters' level of English is minimal.

You don't actually have to order wine, of course. If you don't, you may wish to get bottled water with your meal. Coffee is always drunk only after the meal, and, of course, unless you're ten years old, don't ask for Coca-Cola.

Most wine in bistros is not as expensive as it would be in British or American restaurants. Wine lists are usually short, and there's often a "house wine," a decent and low-priced alternative to the bottled wine. This may arrive in a "carafe," "demi" (half liter), or a "quart." Sometimes it's included in the price of the *formule*, or fixed-price menu, but usually not. A few restaurants will have choices of half-bottles, but in general you'll have to order a full bottle or a glass.

Some observations:

⚜ In the United States and, to a lesser extent, Britain, the name of the grape used to make the wine is all-important. People will ask for a Chardonnay, or Merlot or whatever, but in France, the place where a wine is made is most significant. The French seem to have an almost mystical attachment to the soil, the *terroir*, and they think this is what's important to know. A wine specialist would know, of course, which wines were made with Chardonnay grapes and which were made primarily with Merlot, but the average waiter would consider that information trivia.

⚜ The old advice about red wine with meat and white wine with fish is generally useful, though any "foodie" can think of exceptions. Most French chefs make great use of sauces, and these can affect your choice of wine. It's very common for a couple to go into a bistro and find that one wants fish, the other, meat. When this happens it might be possible to order a *demi* of red and another of white, or to order the wines by the glass.

⚜ In most bistros there will be a minimum of wine-serving ceremony, but the waiter should show you the bottle before opening it and, after opening it, may give you the cork for your inspection. This is a bit of tradition—you don't have to sniff the cork or anything like that. Just look at it and put it down. He'll then pour a small amount in your glass and you'll taste it. Unless there's something terribly wrong—and that's unlikely—you'll nod and keep the wine. The only wines which are likely to have "turned" might be the oldest, most expensive vintages, and if you're in a position to order these, you'll know when they're not satisfactory.

⚜ If the wine list looks really unfamiliar and the waiter seems to have no English, don't panic. If you're ordering meat, find the *rouge* or red wines on the list. An inexpensive Côtes du Rhône should not be much over eighteen euros and you'll probably like it. Another possibility is Beaujolais. In most bistros, there's a strong correlation between the price of wines and the quality, but for most of us their less expensive offerings are perfectly adequate. If you order the dish that's one of the specialties of the restaurant, the waiter will usually be able to suggest the best wine to go with it.

An Embarrassment of Riches

There are many good bistros in Paris and a few great ones. The French traditions of producing first-rate ingredients for the cook; creating a demanding apprenticeship that will sometimes result in a top chef; more recently being willing to experiment and open to foreign cuisines, a combination yielding such inspired results—this is what you will experience as you try the bistros in this book.

The remembered pleasure of eating thoughtfully prepared meals in our own country or in France should influence us to try to keep our best traditions intact. Above all, what we should try to deter is the sort of brave new world of profit-driven food engineering so well described by Eric Schlosser in *Fast Food Nation*. Just one experience in a food laboratory changed his view of processed foods:

> *Grainger had brought a dozen small glass bottles from the lab. After he opened each bottle, I dipped a fragrance-testing filter into it... Before placing each strip of paper in front of my nose, I closed my eyes. Then I inhaled deeply, and one food after another was conjured from the glass bottles. I smelled fresh cherries, black olives, sautéed onions, and shrimp. Grainger's most remarkable creation took me by surprise. After closing my eyes, I suddenly smelled a grilled hamburger. The aroma was uncanny, almost miraculous—as if someone in the room were flipping burgers on a hot grill. But when I opened my eyes, I saw just a narrow strip of white paper and a flavorist with a grin.*

This is the science behind the *cuisine industrielle* that seems to be taking over the food preparation industry, in France as well as at home. When large conglomerates buy up restaurants and establish chains, what they market is an innocuous, standardized product that might not be far removed from airline food. You can be sure that there's no individual chef in these kitchens exercising his or her creativity.

We have reviewed a few eating places that happen to be owned by large companies: it's impossible to describe the brasseries, for example, without doing so. Some of these places are worth visiting, for the decor if not the food. But in none of them will you get food at the level attained by a good chef working with fresh ingredients. We urge you whenever possible to try some of the choice small bistros where the menu changes daily, to get an idea of what fresh food can taste like when prepared by a master chef.

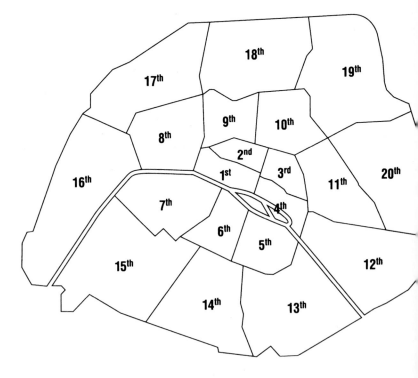

PARIS ARRONDISSEMENTS

UPTOWN: THE 1ˢᵀ & 2ᴺᴰ ARRONDISSEMENTS

Outside, the fire-red, gas-blue, ghost-green signs shone smokily through the tranquil rain. It was late afternoon and the streets were in movement, the bistros gleamed. At the corner of the Boulevard des Capucines, he took a taxi. The Place de la Concorde moved by in pink majesty, they crossed the logical Seine....

—F. Scott Fitzgerald

part from the Eiffel Tower and the Arc de Triomphe, what comes to mind when people think of Paris is usually something in the 1st arrondissement. Possibly you picture Paris with the Ritz Hotel and the great column of the Place Vendôme. You may remember the Louvre, once a royal palace itself, now an impossibly vast treasure house of art.

Marcel Proust dined often at the Ritz Hotel and liked to gossip with the waiters, who often provided him with ideas for his work. A dinner in July 1917 was interrupted by a German air raid. Proust watched it from a balcony and used the experience later in *Le Temps Retrouvé*.

We associate this part of Paris with luxury, although Janet Flanner, the *New Yorker's* famous Paris correspondent, once wrote to a friend: "I moved over here this afternoon into the room you occupied with me. The shabbiness of the Ritz is a great comfort after the garish modernism of the Inter-Continental."

The premier shopping district in the world starts in the 1st arrondissement on the ruc St.-Honoré, the longest street of first-rate shops in Paris. In the Place Vendôme, Cartier and Van Cleef and Arpels have watches and jewelry fit for the nobility. The rest of us enjoy them vicariously, in the way that Audrey Hepburn enjoyed breakfast at Tiffany's, peering into the window of the exclusive jewelry store as she sipped coffee and munched a pastry.

The 2nd arrondissement adjoins and continues the first. There is a strong financial flavor about this district—here are the Bank of France and the Bourse, the French version of Wall Street. Moneychangers line the streets, and little wine bars fill up at noon with men and women who whisper important information. It is no accident that Legrand, possibly the best winesellers in the city, have their shop here. So does the avant-garde designer Jean-Paul Gaultier. Agence France-Presse, the center of French journalism, is across the street from the Bourse. That, too, was probably not without design.

In his writing F. Scott Fitzgerald sketched a romantic Paris, the Paris of the Right Bank. But for Parisians, the 1st and 2nd arrondissements are not primarily places of romance, or of apartments and families. It's business, money, and work. It's strong coffee and high tension.

Some good addresses in central Paris:

L'Ardoise
28 rue du Mt. Thabor 75001 Paris (01.42.96.28.18)
Métro: Tuileries
Tue–Fri noon–2:15 P.M., Tue–Sat 7:00 P.M.–11:00 P.M.,
closed August

We had a curious experience. We recommended this restaurant and a few others to a young couple who were planning to spend their honeymoon in Paris. They came here on their first night in the city. They were so delighted with L'Ardoise that they returned night after night, ignoring the other recommendations on our list. We were not surprised.

There is nothing special about the decor: white tablecloths, cream walls with enlargements of old French postcards, and tiled floor. Your interest starts to peak when the waitress comes to your table bearing the 33-euro menu, scribbled in chalk on a section of old blackboard—they call it an *ardoise*—and you see a stunning variety of outstanding choices.

As appetizers, we chose shrimp set off with grapefruit, and *langoustines.* The shrimp arrived in a flower-like arrangement, the shrimp set off with scallions in a light vinaigrette in the center, sections of dark red grapefruit arranged like petals around it. The *langoustines* were large and aggressive-looking, in a light mustard-flavored mayonnaise. In between the hors d'oeuvres and main course, we could relish the ambiance, relaxed and friendly with everyone talking at once.

Our *plats* were not only good, they were memorable: a *porc rôti* (roast pork) done just right, with spinach in a sauce lightly flavored with citrus, and *barbue* or brill, a fish resembling turbot, in a rich sauce involving balsamic vinegar, with snow peas and *haricots verts* (green beans), and topped with tiny morsels of crisp fried onion.

To go with the meal we chose a rich Les Bastides, Côteaux d'Aix at 24 euros. Other wines were available by the bottle from about the same price.

Service was friendly: the two young women who waited on the tables were smiling and courteous. One even risked a trip to the kitchen to ask the chef about the ingredients of a sauce. A little later I heard the other cheerfully translating the dessert menu for a group of American diners.

We had ordered similar desserts: crisp little caramelized squares, one filled with a rich, dark chocolate mousse, the other with raspberries and a heavy crème, garnished with an impressionistic splatter of sauce.

The chef, Pierre Jay, originally from Savoie, finally appeared, slightly flushed from his exertions. A little heavier in recent years, he looks as you might expect Austin Powers's younger brother to look. Jay is a consummate professional who used to work at La Tour d'Argent.

❖ *L'Ardoise: memorable food you tell friends about, but hope there'll be a table available when you need it.*

Aux Bons Crus
7 rue des Petits Champs, 75001 Paris (01.42.60.06.45)
Métro: Palais-Royal
Open daily 9:00 A.M.–2:00 A.M.

Aux Bons Crus is a *bistro à vins* nearly a century old which might not attract one at first glance. There's nothing especially fetching about the long, narrow room, the new-style bar, and the deco-shaped cutouts on the ceiling for lighting.

But Aux Bons Crus deserves a second look. Besides some stunning historic gear—a formidable machine for bringing bottles up from the cave—and a good selection of wines, this wine bar offers attractive meals at reasonable prices in this high-priced arrondissement.

Here near the stock exchange since 1905, Aux Bons Crus has changed little over the years. Prewar wine barrels are stacked to the ceiling, although the original zinc bar may have been lost to the forces of the Occupation in the same war. The larger room at the back, must have one of the lowest ceilings in Paris. If you are tall, you will have to stoop.

Most of the wines are lower-cost regional varieties and recent vintages in the 18- to 31-euro range, but we chose the wine of the month, a *pichet* (pitcher) of young, chilled red Bergerac. It went beautifully with a *tartine saucisson de montagne*, an open-faced sandwich with spicy salami on a slab of *poilâne* bread, with a large dab of chutney. Salads run from 10 to 12 euros, plats from 15 to 18, but you may wish to sample the *tartines*—open-faced sandwiches—on the tasty and filling *pain poilâne*. They include *rillettes à l'oie* (minced spread of goose), *jambon cru* (smoked cured ham), *saucisson de montagne*, and Cantal or Camembert, served with vegetables.

If you like salami and sausages, you'll be delighted with Aux Bons Crus. There is a varied assortment of *saucisson,* a high-quality type of dry salami, the *tarte chaude du jour* (quiche of the day), and salad. Our *tartine,* of *saucisson* with *pain poilâne,* was appealing, with pickles, chutney, and the vegetables to add color and crunch.

Wines are available by the glass or bottle. There's always a *vin du mois*. It was a young red Bergerac when we were there, served in a 46-cl carafe.

Aux Bons Crus enjoys a clientele of unusual sophistication: journalists from Agence France-Presse and *Le Figaro*, shoppers from the chic Place des Victoires. Our neighbor, the magazine publisher, had to leave, and as he got up we noticed his magnificent briefcase. Priding myself on my knowledge of the latest French status symbols, I looked at it and said to him, "Louis Vuitton?" He smiled, and opening it discreetly, showed us the gold lettering: "Harry Winston, New York."

❖ *Aux Bons Crus: if you lunch there, you'll be in very good company.*

Café Marengo
2 Place du Palais Royal, 75001 Paris (01.42.97.09.96)
Métro: Palais Royal-Musée du Louvre
Tues–Sun 9:00 A.M.–7:00 P.M.

Are you looking for a crossbow? A piece of prewar Lalique? Then you'll surely find yourself in the Louvre des Antiquaires, and if hunger strikes, there's no place more convenient than the Café Marengo on the second floor. The *Pavé au saumon* at 12.50 euros is a speciality but there are other good things to whet your appetite, including the homemade desserts.

❖ *Café Marengo: a convenient and friendly spot. Lunch with antique dealers who know their trade.*

Café Noir
65 rue Montmartre, 75002 Paris (01.40.39.07.36)
Métro: Sentier
Mon–Fri 10:00 A.M.–2:00 A.M., Sat 4:00 P.M.–2:00 A.M.

Not a bistro, not even a conventional café, the Café Noir is a bar on the rue Montmartre in the banking district. With a highly individual decor—old chipped tiles in pastel colors

cover a black-lacquered wooden bar and a circle of orange and white neon edges a picturesque old mural high up on the walls—Café Noir draws a young and artistic crowd. Soft rock music thumps away and locals gather for after-work pick-me-ups and liquid sustenance at any time of the day or night. This café is a fun and welcoming place: an old bicycle is perched precariously above the door, an illuminated heart glows forth in red plastic, mirrors are plastered with stickers for unconventional causes. The young barman, head shaved in obedience to the fashion, barely glances up from his crossword puzzle when a new arrival comes by—but soon he glides over to offer good-natured service. Drinks are fairly priced, the coffee that's a euro at the bar will be 2 at a table and 3 on the terrace outside. A beer starts at 4 euros, with *plats* at lunch at around 11 euros.

❖ *Café Noir: fun and funky, a change from the serious-suited financial district.*

Les Cartes Postales
7 rue Gomboust, 75001 Paris (01.42.61.23.40)
Métro: Opéra
Mon–Fri lunch, Tue–Sat dinner, closed Mon eve,
Sat lunch, July 21–August 10

Bright walls and the white linen of the tablecloths lend a cheerfulness to this little hideaway tucked into an Asian-influenced street in the 1st arrondissement. Across the street are a Korean restaurant and an Asian caterer. Within, a welcome feeling of calmness and serenity—it is possible to have a quiet conversation here. Spot lighting focuses on the tables but is not harsh. The service is efficient and quietly polite. Except for one table of French people and ourselves, all of the customers were Asians.

The only thing not minimalist at Cartes Postales is the food, prepared by a Japanese chef trained in France. From the 25-euro menu—a tasting menu is available at 70 euros—two of us ordered crab cakes to start, the third a salmon hors d'oeuvre. The salmon was the largest plate of artfully arranged smoked salmon we have seen; it was marinated with dill and accompanied by tomatoes, chives, and greens. The crab cakes were warm rice-and-crab-filled spring rolls, lightly cooked and served with a rice vinegar-and-oil dressing, given piquancy by a sprinkling of grapefruit juice.

The 25-euro menu is simple: after the hors d'oeuvre, fish—depending on the catch of the day—or an *entrecôte*, for non-fish eaters. Anyway, it would be a shame to order anything but fish here, although we saw Japanese businessmen tucking into the steaks with enthusiasm. A large plate of various kinds of fish was served: *saumon, thon, dorade, barbue* (salmon, tuna, John Dory, brill) on a bed of tiny *haricots verts* (green beans) with little slices of leeks, and carrots, all in a subtly sweet sauce enriched with cream and chives. Never had we had such a variety of fish at one time, and never have we felt that it was so perfectly cooked.

A cheese plate of ripe Camembert and *chèvre* was artistically arranged on leaves of lettuce and watercress. A short dessert list: one *crème brûlée* was still available, but we settled for sorbet and *salade de fruits*, fruit poached but still crunchy.

❖ *Les Cartes Postales: Japanese precision and French attention to detail make it a special place.*

Le Dauphin
167 rue St.-Honoré, 75001 Paris (01.42.60.40.11)
Métro: Palais-Royal
Open daily

Le Dauphin is modern—even with the old zinc bar to your right as you enter—and has a great location looking out on the Place André Malraux. The decor is simple too, with reddish-brown banquettes, ochre walls, and small oak tables.

This is a place for a substantial, old-fashioned meal, with rich broths bubbling away in cast-iron pots, and intriguing blends of vegetables and meats. Le Dauphin has a fixed-price menu for 39 euros. Otherwise a *plat* goes for 21, and a dessert or cheese for 7 euros. Off the fixed-price menu, the specialty of the house is *parrilladas*, grilled meat or seafood, such as an assortment of grilled fish or a well-aged prime rib for two, from 22 to 55 euros.

Huge plates of hors d'oeuvres appeared: the *paella* was not the classic Spanish dish, but a base of fish *fumet* in aspic, with saffron rice and seafood, and bright touches of red pepper and zucchini. *Escargots* were served on a little plate, without shells, in the traditional garlic-and-butter sauce with artichoke hearts and olives. A *salade royale* was beautifully arranged slices of melon and grapefruit on a plate of zucchini, red pepper, tomatoes, and snow peas, with a pesto sauce and *frisée* lettuce.

The *cabillaud* (fresh cod) and *joues de porc* (pork cheeks) were served in little, black cast-iron casseroles. The cod came in a rich delicate sauce of butter and chives in a base of fish *fumet*. Described as "Louisiane," it was more complex than any Creole sauce we've tasted. The *joues de porc* were small pieces of tender pork flanked by carrots and little onions, in a rich garlicky broth that must have been simmered for hours before being flambéed with armagnac.

A good *vin du Pays d'Oc* was a satisfactory accompaniment to the hearty meals.

❖ *Le Dauphin: substantial and well-cooked fare. Worth a visit.*

> ### La Fresque
> 100 rue Rambuteau, 75001 Paris (01.42.33.17.56)
> Métro: Rambuteau
> Mon–Fri, Sat eves, Sun, closed 1 week in August.

Old white tiles are accented with a broad stripe of blue above the maroon banquettes, and naive paintings in the style of Henri Rousseau are here, there, and continue down the stairway. This is a narrow space with ochre in a glossy finish on the ceiling.

The 14-euro lunch menu started with cold gazpacho, its intense tomato flavors reviving us as we sat in this narrow little hallway of a main room, diverted by business people talking energetically on the banquettes against the wall.

When we arrived we saw mostly young women, business people enjoying this little bistro. We chose a refreshing rosé which arrived chilled in a *pichet*, just right to accompany the *filet de rascasse* (gunard or scorpion fish) in a white wine sauce and the *sauté de veau provençale* (sautéed veal with Provençal sauce). Both *plats* were generous, the fish garnished with puréed carrots, cooked endive, and overcooked peas—a detail, considering the value received here. The *sauté de veau*, in a hearty sauce of tomato, zucchini, and black olives, was well-flavored and filling.

We were entertained by the service; no stiff-looking waiters' uniforms here, the servers romp past in slacks and T-shirts. Their manner is friendly and informal: "Vous avez choisi, les gars?" (Made your choices, fellas?) one of them queried a table of businessmen.

❖ *La Fresque: A good little restaurant a few blocks away from the Pompidou Museum.*

Lescure
7 rue Mondovi, 75001 Paris (01.42.60.18.91)
Métro: Concorde
Mon–Fri lunch and dinner, closed in August

Lescure has an enviable location, just off the Place de la Concorde. And it must be doing something else right, because on a Wednesday night it was packed.

Lescure transports the diner to provincial France: you might forget you're in central Paris in this main room with its pastoral look of warmth and intimacy. The stone wall near us was covered with a large oil painting of a country scene; at the top of the painting was hung, improbably, straw hats. Wreaths of garlic were draped from the beamed ceiling. The tiled floor hinted at Provence. On the old zinc bar, a large bouquet of lilies and a lamp covered in burlap gave light and warmth.

A bargain 23.50-euro menu hasn't changed over the years. It offered a choice of *terrine de foie de volaille* (chicken liver terrine) or *saucisson de campagne ou saucisson sec* (dry salami) to be followed by haddock, *poulet au riz basquaise* (chicken Basque-style), or *boeuf bourguignon* (beef stew), and a choice of cheese or dessert. Also included, a half bottle of the house wine, very drinkable, probably from a small vineyard in the South.

The terrine was a large tasty slice served on a bed of red lettuce with pickles and generous enough for two. *Saucisson sec* came in a good portion on a large plate, to eat with butter and the *pain paysan* (dark country bread).

Tasty chicken croquettes followed, on a bed of saffron rice with a tomato sauce accentuated with basil. The well-flavored *boeuf bourguignon* came with carrots and boiled potatoes. Nothing subtle here, but hearty and good. And at Lescure in the 1st arrondissement, you're paying the same prices you'd pay in the country. Amazing.

We love French sorbets, so decided to try the *cassis* and mandarin orange. Both were refreshing, the *cassis* with intense black-currant flavor, the mandarin including orange pulp and deep citrus flavors.

❖ *Lescure: country charm and low prices in the center of town.*

Lina's Café, in Etam Building
67-73 rue de Rivoli, 75001 Paris
Métro: Pont Marie
Open Mon-Sat 10:00 A.M.–7:00 P.M.

Lina's is on the top floor of a high-styled Art Nouveau building overlooking the rue de Rivoli, the street running in front of the Hôtel de Ville and the Louvre. Elegant little armchairs surround circular tables in this eagle's nest high above the street. You choose your drink and freshly-made sandwich or salad and sit in a sorbet-colored fauteuil. If you're like us, you're instantly mesmerized by the views outside, views that are even more striking if you happen to arrive at dusk.

❖ *Lina's: decent food at fair prices and a dramatic view.*

Aux Lyonnais
32 rue St. Marc, 75002 Paris (01.42.96.65.04)
Métro: Bourse
Tues-Fri 7:30–11:00 P.M., Sat. eves. Closed August
Wheelchair access

A crowd of young people speaking several languages amongst them were seeking tables in this old bistro with its high ceilings, tall mirrors and vintage posters when we entered. Old fashioned charm is here, in the framed historic photos, the original tiles, the red-and–white linen on antique tables.

To start, an *amuse-gueule* of *fromage blanc* dressed with vinaigrette and served with toasted bread kept us pleasantly occupied while we studied the menu. One of us ordered the 30-euro three-course menu, while the others decided to take *plats*. A Samorens Côtes du Rhône was a good accompaniment for all of our choices, although we were surprised to see it brought to the table already uncorked.

The set menu started with an appetizing *salade de pissenlits* (dandelion salad), crunchy dandelion shoots accented with chicken liver and mackerel. Our *plats* arrived in hot Le Creuset dishes. One was a flavorful *St. Pierre rôti* with lima beans and *girolles*; another an intense veal stew with green vegetables. The *quenelles* were a poached fish filling, very delicately flavored, in puff pastry. Servings are generous and we all raved about the sauces that were part of each dish. Our friend's *St. Pierre*, a fish rarely available, had been roasted to perfection.

To finish we enjoyed strawberries at their peak in a Beaujolais sauce, with a scoop of intensely-flavored strawberry sorbet. We heard other diners commenting favorably on a spectacular *soufflé aux cerises*, a popular choice.

❖ *Aux Lyonnais: the cuisine of an area noted for its food does not disappoint. A first-rate bistro owned by 3-star chef Alain Ducasse.*

Pharamond
24 rue de la Grande-Truanderie, 75001 Paris
(01.40.28.03.00)
Métro: Les Halles
Open daily except Sun eves

In a city which still has many of its lovely and old-fashioned restaurants, Pharamond, in the old Halles section of Paris, deserves special notice. What astonishes is the decor— Belle Epoque at its most extravagant. Here are extraordinary century-old tiles in intricate patterns, some picturing yellow apple trees growing out of Delft-like vases, and some forming abstract patterns around the large mirrors. Immense old mirrors make this narrow restaurant with its high ceilings appear larger and more lively than it is. Most of the decor is original.

The specialty here is *cuisine Normande*. Dishes might contain a reduction of *pommereau*, and you could order a Calvados-spiked dessert. A good variety of main dishes are available, a vegetable plate of the day, and an assortment of cheeses. *Tripes à la mode de Caen* (tripe with vegetables and Calvados) is a specialty.

Office workers in the area come for the 15-euro lunch special, hors d'oeuvre and *plat* or *plat* and dessert, with the house wine a reasonable price for a half liter. One day the set lunch was *oeufs mimosa*, a Gallic variation on deviled eggs, served with salad greens, followed by *brandade de morue*, a tasty combination of salt cod and mashed potatoes, whipped with olive oil, chopped parsley, and a touch of horseradish. A generous serving came hot in a Le Creuset dish with a green salad on the side.

The set lunch included *fondant au chocolat*, a chocolate dessert resembling a rich chocolate truffle, complemented by *crème anglaise*. We couldn't resist a *moelleux au chocolat*, a partially-cooked cake, hot and intensely flavorful. Served with *crème anglaise*, this was garnished with raspberries, orange slices and mint.

❖ *Pharamond: good value in a setting of Belle Epoque charm.*

Le Rubis
10 rue du Marché St. Honoré, 75001 Paris
(01.42.61.03.34)
Métro: Tuileries
Mon-Fri 8:00 A.M.–10:00 P.M., Sat 9:00 A.M.–4:00 P.M.,
closed August

Before the glamour, before the high-priced houses of fashion had taken over this part of the city, there were retreats like the Rubis. An old-fashioned wine bar improbably located in a chic neighborhood not far from the Ritz Hotel, Le Rubis seems to belong to another era. There's something irrepressibly cozy about this little hangout, with its 1920s-era molding curving above a classic zinc-topped oak bar. Stripes of neon in pink and white zigzag above emphasize the Deco effect.

Permanently posted is an impressive list of wines available by the glass, at petite prices at the bar, a little more if you sit on a comfortable red banquette behind the formica tables. This is an informal place—a motorcyclist stops by for directions and everybody chimes in with advice, the couple behind the bar and an elegant, red-gowned lady with a dozing spaniel on the leash.

Hot food is available at lunch: try a *plat*, or you can make do very well with a plate of *charcuterie* or a sandwich, perhaps a *saucisson sec* on *pain poilâne*. In the afternoons peace reigns, and it's a perfect stop for a snack, a glass of wine, or a coffee, in a part of the city where most bars like this have long since ceased to exist.

❖ *Le Rubis: good* cuisine familiale *in an unspoiled wine bar from the past.*

Le Tambour
41 rue Montmartre, 75002 Paris (01.42.33.06.90)
Métro: Les Halles or Sentier
Open Tues-Sat 12:00–3 P.M., 6 P.M.–6:00 A.M.

If it's late or very early and everything else is closed, try Le Tambour, its emblem a sturdy little drummer in Napoleon's army. As the menu puts it: "André Camboulas et son équipe ont le plaisir de vous accueillir." (André and his team welcome you.) André, his uncombed hair and wild mustache giving him the look of an aging hippie, tends bar, occasionally calling out greetings in a resounding, gravelly voice.

Le Tambour gives you the possibility of a low-priced lunch in the center of the financial district, in a place with low ceilings in the usual faded café ochre, the walls decorated with real Paris street and métro bric-a-brac. There's an old métro map from the Stalingrad stop, plaques of instructions and warnings, and bar stools made from large red-and-yellow bus route signs.

Lunch at 18 and 25 euros offered good variety. There's a *plat du jour* at 12 euros. We started with artichokes, accompanied by a little pot of vinaigrette. Very good—a better hors d'oeuvre than expected at the price. The *tourte* resembled a hot quiche, with egg, spinach, bits of pork, and a savory cheese topping. An *assiette anglaise*, or cold meat plate, was sliced roast beef, a roasted chicken thigh, hot French fries, and lettuce and tomato—rather like a good picnic lunch with fries. To go with this, the *vin du mois*, a vin *du pays de l'Hérault*, was very drinkable.

Desserts were *tartes*—open-faced pies—and we chose the *poire-chocolat*, a creative and tasty if unlikely-sounding combination.

In the evenings, it's all à la carte. The mood at Le Tambour, when it's not lunchtime frantic, is pleasantly informal; our waiter sat down with some regulars to figure out their bill, there was jovial bantering at the bar, and occasionally the voice of André would thunder forth. Habitués are more likely to be readers of *Libération* than of the *Figaro*, which has offices just down the street, but thrifty stockbroker types stride in from the Bourse.

❖ *Le Tambour: loud and lively; bistro classics and excellent value.*

La Tour de Montlhéry (Chez Denise)
5 rue des Prouvaires 75001 Paris (01.42.36.21.82)
Métro: Châtelet
Mon 7:00 A.M.–Sat 5:00 A.M. closed weekends,
mid-July–mid August

When Les Halles was the great food market of Paris, there were dozens of all-night bistros like this one serving the locals. Most are gone now. The porters and meatcutters have gone to Rungis, and the workers crowding Chez Denise are now artists and young professionals.

You enter a typical bistro with a long bar and are ushered into a second room, a dining room with long tables on both sides. People squeeze in close to each other on the long banquettes. Your first impression is that this place is wild, raucous, exuberant beyond belief, that it recalls Paris student life as it has existed from the time of François Villon to our own.

Wedged in beside a Frenchman devouring a *steak tartare*, we have a few minutes to observe the old stone walls, huge beams above, dark sienna ceiling, framed art work, photographs, and unframed oils. There is joyous flirting and hand-holding on the dark red banquettes and across the narrow tables.

The waiter bangs down a metal basket with dark bread and a large plate of butter. There are *jambons d'Auvergne* and *saucissons* hanging down from the ceiling. An *ardoise* is chalked with the day's offerings—you struggle with the handwriting and the board is whisked away. But you succeed in bellowing out an order.

One of us goes for the haddock, large, orange-gold segments in a delicious sea of *beurre blanc*, with boiled potatoes lightly dusted with parsley. The fish has a slightly smoky, vaguely salty flavor and is wonderful with the white wine and butter sauce. The other orders beef, *onglet*, a large grilled flank steak served in its own juices with *frisée* lettuce and a side dish of fries. For wine we took the house Brouilly.

Students who come here have to be fairly well-off; *plats* are from 17 to 28 euros, but servings are large. After the filling *plats* we see some brave people nearby digging into great rectangles of *baba au rhum* with rosettes of whipped cream.

A smiling Chinese gentleman starts speaking to us just as we are paying our bill. "This is where people who don't know each other talk," he says, adding, "Artists, artistic people here. Singers from Opera."

Chez Denise is not for those who require refinement and elegance, white linen and obsequious waiters. So what! Chez Denise has old-fashioned charm, good-natured noise, well-cooked bistro food, and a chic and up-to-date clientele. Great fun.

❖ *Chez Denise: a Paris experience that should not be missed.*

THE MAGICAL MARAIS:
THE 3ʳᵈ & 4ᵗʰ
ARRONDISSEMENTS

...sometimes it seemed right to me that the capital should recall its history through the medium of the Marais, perform its intellectual tasks with the aid of the fifth district, and do its sums in the Stock Exchange quarter...

—*Julien Green, Paris*

If you miss the Marais, you miss the best part of Paris. The small streets near the Place des Vosges are vestiges of a human and personal city from before the time of the great boulevards. One of the oldest parts of the city, the Marais is now in some ways new and fashionable again. From the great squares close by comes the boom of rock music when there's a festival or a demonstration; in the Marais, canny street musicians practice their Bach.

For years the 3rd arrondissement was across the street from us when we lived in Paris. Cross the boulevard and you move from the 11th, which for years now has been the area to watch, to the more stable and prosperous 3rd district. In the 3rd can be found low buildings, still on a human scale, and, on some walls, intriguing old signs fading in blues and greens with the lettering partially worn away.

Here is a traditional trade, leatherworking. Skilled craftsmen still create fine garments for the couturiers; they still do impressive work in tiny ateliers, and in hot weather the doors propped open to give them a breath of air supply you with a glimpse of fingers flying over fabric and leather in crowded studios.

As you go toward the Bastille, you enter the 4th arrondissement. Today this is desirable property indeed. It

might be thought of as the Parisian version of New York's Greenwich Village or London's Chelsea. Many gay people live in the area. So did the bishop of the Episcopal Church. In recent years the 4th has become what the 6th, especially St. Germain-des-Prés, used to be: a place of such charm that it draws like a magnet the highly-placed and the intelligentsia who can afford to live here—Jack Lang, former minister of culture, has an apartment on the Place des Vosges. The district attracts tourists, chic Parisians, a large part of the gay community, and anyone else susceptible to the narrow streets winding between buildings that belong to Victor Hugo's Paris, pre-Haussmann and with a scattering of select small shops, art galleries, and bistros.

In the center is the Place des Vosges, a perfect square called the Place Royal when it was finished in 1612. Walk around this seventeenth-century wonder with the covered passage, admire the dark red brick façades and the vaulted ceilings above. Through an occasional half-open shutter you glimpse noble salons and dark beams.

Here in one corner at number six lived the author of *Les Misérables*. He was visited there once by Charles Dickens, who described Victor Hugo as a genius encumbered with a sinister-looking wife and daughter. He wrote: "Sitting among old armour, and old tapestry, and old coffers, and grim old chairs and tables, and old canopies of state from old palaces, and old golden lions going to play at skittles with ponderous old golden balls, they made a most romantic show, and looked like a chapter out of one of his own books."

Farther west from the Place des Vosges, the rue Pavée is in the historic and picturesque Jewish quarter, crossing the rue des Rosiers. This street has been the center of a small Jewish community since the 1770s, but became more populated in the late nineteenth century with immigrants arriving from Eastern Europe.

Nowadays the bistros, galleries, and artists' workshops in the Marais still draw visitors. Creative people live here— artists, and workers from the television and film-making world, young people of all colors and countries. Much of the nightlife of Paris spills out onto the streets, especially during the warm months.

Not many streets away, you ask yourself: "Is it a plumber's nightmare? A giant Erector-set construction in primary colors, a broken toy created and discarded by a deranged child?" Whatever it is, the Centre Georges Pompidou draws more visitors than any other attraction in Paris except, possibly, the Eiffel Tower. Here is street theater: jugglers, acrobats, fire-eaters, all manner of extemporaneous entertainment. And the crowds flock there to admire or scoff at their efforts.

Toward the west, going up the rue de Rivoli, you find yourself nearing two national institutions: on your right is the BHV (Bazar de l'Hôtel de Ville, or "bay-ash-vay" to Parisians), the department store for do-it-yourselfers,

including an amazing basement with incredible variety, a sort of super hardware store, fascinating even if you don't happen to need anything they're selling.

Continuing up the rue de Rivoli toward the Seine, on your left you see the soaring façade of the Hôtel de Ville, or Town Hall, a lofty and majestic nineteenth-century structure. Inside, in the reception rooms, are gilt, mirrors, and chandeliers in typical late nineteenth-century extravagance. Our favorite story about the Hôtel de Ville was told by the late president François Mitterrand in his memoirs. He related an experience that happened right after the liberation of Paris: General de Gaulle was giving a speech from the Hôtel de Ville. Since the building has no balconies, he had to lean far out of the window to deliver his speech. Mitterand and a friend were called on for support. Standing behind him, they had to clutch the General's legs as he leaned forward to keep him from toppling out onto his audience. After the experience was over, De Gaulle might have wondered if the effort had been worth it; the crowd, confused about who had been speaking, kept interrupting him with shouts of "Vive LeClerc!"

A profound loss to the city was Les Halles, the wholesale food market, which had existed for over 800 years. In 1969 it was relocated out to the suburb of Rungis. Many observers compared this to ripping out the city's center. In its place, a bland, American-style, covered shopping mall—le Forum des Halles—opened in 1978. It takes up some of the leftover space but will never have the liveliness of the old Halles.

Some bistros in the area:

Au Bascou
38 rue Réaumur, 75003 Paris (01.42.72.69.25)
Métro: République
Mon–Fri 12:00–2:00 P.M., 8:00–10:30 P.M.

This is one of those little, out-of-the-way restaurants people collect cards from to give to their friends. It's owned by a jovial, mustachioed man who looks as if he had just stepped off the train from his town in Southwest France. He rightly prides himself on the richness of the country food and regional wines here.

The interior is warmed with colors of the Southwest: terracotta, cinnamon, and sun-ripened pumpkin. The walls have the look of a picturesque ruin, with cracks and fissures painted over. Dried red peppers hang in bunches from the beams. In a second dining room is a wall of exposed stone

and another terra cotta-colored wall. The look is so inviting that one can almost forgive the naive paintings of a Basque farmer with his cows and another of a pair of starry-eyed young lovers.

Au Bascou gives you a chance to sample outstanding Basque cuisine at reasonable prices. There's a weekday two course 19-euro lunch. Otherwise hors d'oeuvres are 9, main dishes 17, and desserts 8 euros.

The *piperade* we sampled was a beautifully presented hors d'oeuvre, rounds of egg in layers with tomato and flat-leafed parsley, as attractive as in a multi-starred restaurant.

Plats were large and impressive: *tloro de Labourd*, a Basque fish soup resembling *bouillabaisse*, was a saffron-colored taste treat, with various kinds of fish, mussels, red bell peppers, tomatoes, onion, garlic, parsley, and potatoes. It was topped with two alarming-looking *langoustines*, which turned out to be delicious. The *magret de canard "Amatxi"*—the friendly waitress explained this as meaning "façon grand-mère" or in the old-fashioned style—was a generous serving of duck breast with crisp, slightly blackened potatoes in an intensely flavored sauce.

Desserts at Au Bascou do not disappoint: we shared a delicious *baba au Patxaran*, which a considerate cook had split elegantly in the kitchen; half a baba each on a base of *crème anglaise* over a *coulis* or sauce of red fruits, with a small *quenelle* of coffee ice cream and a spring of fresh mint. *Patxaran*, our waitress informed us, is a Basque liqueur made from *prunelles*, little wild plums. Whatever it was, it was good.

On a rainy Thursday night Au Bascou, which is not famous or in the center of town, was packed with happy diners.

❖ *Au Bascou: outstanding Basque cuisine at fair prices.*

Auberge de Jarente
7 rue de Jarente, 75004 Paris (01.45.51.78.08)
Métro: St. Paul
Tues–Sat noon–2:00 P.M., 7:30 P.M.–10:30 P.M.,
closed in August

Situated on little rue de Jarente in the Marais, this bistro is well named. The ambiance of an inn is conveyed in its dark wood, dark tablecloths, and small-paned windows overlooking a quiet corner. The Basque theme is carried out on the pale walls, with original posters of La Côte Basque, a Spanish wineskin, a copper bedwarmer, and *pelote* bats lending an intriguing informality.

Lunch here is still an amazing bargain: a 14-euro menu includes three courses and a quarter-liter of a French *vin du pays.*

At night, the three-course meal is 23 euros including a *pichet* of wine. Ours started with one of their own creations, a Kayola salad, fresh and delicious, a bright plateful of lean, smoked bacon, served warm, with diced yellow peppers, mushrooms, spinach, tomatoes, and parsley on a bed of lettuce. The *timbale de chiperons à l'estragon,* an intriguing cold hors d'oeuvre, was a concoction of tiny squid, served in a little clay pot with onions, lettuce, and pearl barley in a vinaigrette.

A couple in the corner on their way out praised the *cassoulet*: "Outstanding." So we ordered it and *marmiteko de thon,* fresh tuna cooked in a little clay pot of rich, mostly tomato flavors, with white wine, onions, and garlic to add further flavor. The *cassoulet,* which included a fair amount of duck, sausage, and lean pork, along with the white beans that form its base, was delicious, a memorable dish.

Following the *plat,* a choice of cheese or salad. Our waiter particularly recommended the Brie, which was ripe to perfection and just right with the pleasant *vin du pays.*

Desserts were more than adequate: the *pralinée,* an ice cream confection, layers of praline ice cream separated by toasted almonds, the whole on *crème anglaise.* A *fondant au chocolat* was moist and rich, and the fruit salad a winning combination of fresh nectarines, cantaloupe, and apple in their juices.

❖ *Auberge de Jarente: for flavorful Basque cuisine.*

> **Baracane-Bistro de l'Oulette**
> 33 rue des Tournelles, 75004 Paris (01.42.71.43.33)
> Métro: Bastille
> Mon–Sat noon–2:30 P.M., 7:00 P.M.–midnight

This bistro makes the most of a long, narrow room near the elegant Place des Vosges, by using pale yellow colors, black-and-white photos, and old brass fixtures.

Low-priced lunches here tempt business people: a *plat*, or main dish, with a glass of wine and cup of coffee goes for 12,

and a weekday *formule* with *plat* and hors d'oeuvre or dessert and glass of wine, 26 euros. You enjoy the friendly informality here almost as much as the good food.

Our hors d'oeuvre had more refinement and subtlety than many bistro offerings: it was smoked salmon topping a bed of lettuce and red onions garnished with dill in a pleasing mayonnaise with dill and chives.

Following was a fricassée of lamb with thyme, an attractive, generous serving in a tasty broth of tomatoes, carrots, and zucchini, accompanied by precisely-carved little potatoes. The *plats* were well-flavored and filling.

The wine list featured good selections from the South, available for 6 euros a glass. Some attractive wines are available by the half bottle. A Gaillac Château Lascours was a smooth red that went well with our *plats*.

Our friendly and efficient waitress was fluent in English.

❖ *Baracane de l'Oulette: good value.*

Bofinger
5-7 rue de la Bastille, 75004 Paris (01.42.72.87.82)
Metro: Bastille
Open daily noon–3:00 P.M., 6:30 P.M.–1:00 A.M.

When we're asked to recommend a place for a special celebration, we often suggest Bofinger, a legendary brasserie. Bofinger is at the Bastille, in a part of Paris that's lively and exciting, particularly after dark. It's on the edge of the Marais, near the 17th century Place des Vosges. Across the Place de la Bastille is the sleek and modern Opéra.

You enter Bofinger, are ushered into an elegant 19th century room and are dazzled by what you see: a great curving staircase, old stained glass, carved wood, antique bronze fixtures, a sea of white tablecloths. Divas from the Paris Opera across the Place sometimes sweep in after a performance, as did Maurice Chevalier and almost every French president and prime minister.

If you're here in the afternoon, a lunch *formule* at 24 euros offers *entrée* and *plat* or *plat* and dessert. It's available weekdays except on holidays, and attracts businesss people from the area. If you dine at night, a 32-euro *prix fixe* menu includes hors d'oeuvre, *plat*, and dessert.

We started with gazpacho: colorful, with deep, intense tomato flavor, it was dotted with tiny croutons and little bits of cucumber and parsley. A tangy delight, cool and refreshing, almost a meal in itself.

Plats are well presented: a *navarin* of lamb was served on a background of dark sauce, the plate ornamented with small tomatoes, potatoes, and sprigs of parsley. It was a tender lamb stew in a rich gravy. A delicate fish, the *merou* was on a tasty bed of carrots and zucchini in butter. The sauce had just the right touch of mustard for piquancy.

The little attention we could spare from lunch was irresistibly drawn to Bofinger's stunning decor.

❖ *Bofinger: good if sometimes predictable food in a setting of Art Nouveau splendor.*

Brasserie de l'Ile Saint-Louis
55 quai de Bourbon, 75004 Paris (01.43.54.02.59)
Métro: Pont Marie
Mon, Tues, Fri–Sun noon–1:00 A.M., Thurs 5:00 P.M –
12 A.M. closed August

Nothing is subtle about the Brasserie de l'Ile: everything speaks of Old Germany on a night of celebration, the noisy, cheerful, roof-lifting din. Above and around you are turn-of-the-century original posters, some featuring brasseries, mounted heads of small animals and others not so small, and the enormous head of a *sanglier*, or wild boar, complete with tusks, glares aggressively down. Colors are strong and vibrant: huge, burnished copper pots gleam against dark beams. In some ways the Brasserie may remind you of the legendary old taverns frequented by generations of Ivy League students. The waiters, though, are defiantly Parisian, and, like the traditional Parisian waiter, they manage to seem both servile and superior at the same time.

The Brasserie is on the top of the Ile Saint Louis, a tiny island in the heart of Paris with some of the most expensive real estate in the city. Though the tables in front overlook the river and Right Bank, most patrons head back to a room which takes you to an old-fashioned restaurant in pre-war Germany, or, in this case, Alsace. Everything about this place, from the casual greeting of the maître d' as he waves you to a table, to the food and ambiance, has a Teutonic flavor.

You choose from hot and cold German specialties, *plats* priced from 18 to 22 euros, to be washed down with Alsatian wines, or, if you prefer, beer. This is hearty, rib-sticking fare—even the starters lend one ballast.

The wine list includes mainly wines of Alsace and some French standards, including Rothschild's Mouton Cadet and a number from Georges Duboeuf. Most are priced from 4.80 euros by the glass and 22 euros by the bottle.

Our three orders, *choucroute garnie, onglet de boeuf,* and *omelette mixte* were good if not subtle. The *choucroute*—sauerkraut—is not as sour as we're used to, the cabbage crisper and with less of a vinegary flavor, but the portions are huge and the accompanying crisp juicy sausage, pork slices, and smoked bacon were tasty and filling. An *onglet de boeuf,* or flank steak, was flavorful, and the *omelette mixte,* a fluffy, golden ham-and-cheese omelet, was well-made and delicious.

You don't come to the Brasserie de l'Ile Saint-Louis for sophisticated French cuisine or a quiet tête-à-tête, but if you want a time-warp experience, a "Sound of Music" pre-war *bierstube,* 55 quai de Bourbon is the place to go.

❖ *Brasserie de l'Ile Saint-Louis: a taste of Alsace.*

Camille
24 rue des Francs-Bourgeois, 75003 Paris (01.42.72.20.50)
Métro: Bastille
Open daily noon–midnight
Wheelchair access

A cheerful little bistro on the corner of rue des Francs-Bourgeois and rue Elzevir, Camille is open when you need it. The decor is simple: sponged ochre walls, a few posters, including an impressive original of a circus. But it's a cosy place to go when you want decent food at a price that won't break your budget: a lunch *formule* offers *entrée* and *plat* or *plat* and dessert.

Our meal started with *salade de chèvre,* rounds of warm goat cheese on toast topping a salad of mixed greens in a tasty vinaigrette.

We proceeded to the *plats.* The *bar* (European sea bass) was three subtly-flavored filets over a mixture of tomatoes with a savory blend of red peppers, lemon juice, and chopped parsley. With this, boiled potatoes. The *rouille d'agneau* was a large center cutlet of grilled lamb, the herbs contributing a Provençal flavor, on a bed of ratatouille—again, the good flavors of the South. With the *plats* we chose a Pays d'Oc Sauvignon. At Camille, the servings are such that a *plat* can be a meal. But if you want to indulge yourself a little further, desserts are 10 euros à la carte. We found the bittersweet chocolate tart an excellent finish.

At night prices are à la carte, with hors d'oeuvres for 9 to 13 and *plats* from 19 to 23 euros. And the choices are tempting: hors d'oeuvres sometimes include escargots and foie gras; *plats* are generous and fairly-priced—*magret de canard* (duck breast) or a steak with pepper or Béarnaise sauce is 23 euros.

There's a pleasant informality about this bistro, and we soon found ourselves chatting with the Breton on our left and a couple from Hong Kong.

❖ *Camille: a useful address in the Marais.*

Chez Janou
2 rue Roger-Verlomme, 75003 Paris (01.42.72.28.41)
Métro: Chemin Vert
Daily lunch and dinner

You know you're approaching something special when you pass under shiny-leafed magnolia trees on your way to Chez Janou. This old-fashioned, self-consciously romantic bistro, a favorite of actress Kate Hudson, is tucked away on a side street just behind the Place des Vosges. Although you're in one of the most glamorous parts of a large city, you feel as if you could be in a small village inn near the coast. Chez Janou stays open in the afternoons, and the people who pop in for a drink here are workers and residents of this exclusive area. You hear traditional French folk songs with the strains of an accordeon backing up the singer.

Inside we relaxed in the warm interior dating from 1911, with its old café chairs and authentic Art Nouveau tiles.

Vintage posters of long-forgotten French cabaret stars line the back room. This day was warm and the *terrasse* was crowded.

Lunch in this setting was a bargain at 14.50 euros for two courses: we started with large plates of salad heaped with cured country ham, flakes of parmesan cheese, and tomatoes in a light vinaigrette. It was substantial and good, the peppery *roquette* a foil for the milder-flavored tomatoes and cheese. Then came huge servings of *faux filet* with crisp snow peas and cubes of sautéed potatoes, the beef set off by a green peppercorn sauce. The bread basket tempted us with *pain de campagne au levain,* a crusty sourdough that we couldn't resist. We decided to skip dessert, but noticed several people ordering the attractive *tarte de fruits.*

In keeping with the modestly-priced cuisine are the affordable wines: there's a *vin de maison,* currently a Côtes de Luberon, 3.50 euros by the glass, 9.50 the half bottle *pichet* or 14 euros for the bottle. Other wines include a Côteaux d'Aix.

❖ *Chez Janou: everyone's little secret: a country-style bistro with a very urban clientele.*

La Fontaine Gourmande
11 rue Charlot, 75003 Paris (01.42.78.72.40)
Métro: Filles du Calvaire
Tues–Fri noon–2:15 P.M., 7:00 P.M.–10:15 P.M., Sat dinner only, closed August

La Fontaine Gourmande is a little bistro that draws from the sophisticated set in the 3rd arrondissement. It's a neighborhood hangout, in a neighborhood that's gay and artsy with a touch of Greenwich Village about it. The Denise René Gallery, home of puzzling paintings and sculpture, is just down the street, as are the offices of the Socialist Party. Small workshops abound..

La Fontaine offers low-priced lunches: a *plat* is 12 euros, a two-course lunch menu 15 or 20 euros. You might enjoy a *tartine,* an open-faced sandwich flanked by green salad. We tried the *vosgienne*, a delicious concoction with three types of cheese—Emmenthal, Conté, and Reblochon—melted on new potatoes with *lardons* (bacon), all on *pain poilâne*. A very successful *plat* was *cabillaud* (fresh cod) in a good cream sauce, with crisp green beans, broccoli, and small boiled potatoes. A small carafe of a fruity white Georges Duboeuf wine made a nice accompaniment.

❖ *La Fontaine Gourmande: very competent cooking and friendly ambiance.*

Les Fous d'en Face (The Crazy People Across from Us)
3 rue du Bourg-Tibourg, 75004 Paris (01.48.87.03.75)
Métro: Hôtel de Ville
Tues–Sat lunch and dinner, closed August

Les Fous is liked by just about everybody and it's no wonder. Here you can have a sophisticated lunch at a reasonable price in the heart of the Marais.

The noon menu one day offered interesting possibilities. Typical offerings might start with *charcuterie Corse, terrine de lapin* or *foie gras*, from 9 to 18 euros, followed by *magret de canard* (duck breast), *filet de boeuf,* or *pot-au feu* (beef stew) from 17 to 25 euros.

A short wine list offered wines mostly from the Loire. We settled on a very satisfactory rosé from Touraine.

While waiting for our *plats* we glanced around at the clientele—business and professional people, with some government workers from the nearby Hôtel de Ville. We were diverted to hear two well-dressed men grumbling about the investigations for corruption that had been going on. One of them was complaining about lawyers:

"Les avocats, ils sont tous nuls," (Lawyers are all zeros) pronounced a mustachioed gent. "La justice est pourrie." (The courts are rotten). Later we were to hear the same man discussing the situation further and using words that do not belong in a family guidebook.

The *gigot* (leg of lamb) was a hearty meal, generous slices of flavorful lamb in sauce, with crisp, scalloped potatoes, and *haricots verts*—green beans. The *julienne,* or burbot fish, dotted with flecks of red pepper and basil, was served with a delicious cream sauce, rice and cooked zucchini. Both *plats* were good and substantial meals.

The desserts brought to mind tropical climes and exotic fruit. A colorful mango sherbet, as delicious as it looked, was garnished with tiny slices of peach and strawberry; the *flan de noix de coco,* a delectable creation, half cake, half Bavarian cream, was served on *crème anglaise* with slices of strawberry and mint leaves.

❖ *Les Fous d'en Face: the location is superb, and lunch a gourmet treat.*

Le Grizzli
7 rue Saint-Martin (01.48.87.77.56) 75004 Paris
Métro: Hôtel de Ville
Open daily 9:00 A.M. – 2:00 A.M.

At the Grizzli, you'll find yourself in a charming small bistro, with classic dark ochre walls, turn-of-the-century type molding—and bears! Within, in addition to the small tables and unusual marble bar, are large framed drawings of bears. The bear motif is appropriate because in the early 1900s bear trainers would bring their animals to perform outside this old bistro. Inside, well-placed soft lights are reflected in the mirrors, and the lacy café curtains allow a look at street life. The black banquettes along the sides of the room have aluminum rails, probably original, in a Deco design.

Most hors d'oeuvres are 7 to 12 and *plats* 17 to 23 euros. We started with *brochette de moules,* sticks of breaded mussels, sautéed until golden, with a pot of Béarnaise sauce to accompany them. Delicious, with touches of garlic and butter. Other possibilities included crab with avocado and *millefeuille* with *foie gras.*

The *plat* we chose was a large salmon steak topped with a sprinkling of sea salt which heightened the flavor. Pesto sauce and a bed of well-flavored ratatouille made this a variation from the usual. A carafe of the good house rosé was a refreshing accompaniment.

Desserts, between 6.50 and 9 euros, include the classics as well as a daily special. The ice creams come in intriguing flavors, like *pruneaux armagnac,* the plum-flavored ice cream and the armagnac complementing each other nicely.

❖ *Le Grizzli: an old-fashioned Parisian favorite.*

Le Hangar
12 Impasse Berthaud, 75003 Paris (01.42.74.55.44)
Métro: Rambuteau
Mon eves only, Tues–Sat noon–3:00 P.M., 6:30
P.M.–midnight, closed in August
Wheelchair access No credit cards

Le Hangar is one of those trendy, contemporary bistros that have been attracting a young crowd. The owners have brought a minimalist elegance as well as serious cooking to this backlot commercial area. Le Hangar is attractive, with exposed stone walls, pleasant terrace, and Provençal tablecloths. It's well located, only a few steps from the Pompidou Museum.

An interesting and inventive cuisine here: hors d'oeuvres were all between 6 and 10 euros. *Plats* including f*ettucine au citron et crevettes roses* (fettucini with shrimp) and *escalope de foie gras de canard* (slice of fattened duck liver) varied between 12 and 20 euros.

We chose the *filet de boeuf aux morilles* and *dos de saumon* from the menu. The steak came in a delicious sauce of morel mushrooms and cream, with a small plate of scalloped potatoes. The *dos de saumon avec courgettes* was less impressive: a small portion of salmon with rolled-up zucchini made for a skimpy, uninteresting *plat*.

The real strength of Le Hangar may be its desserts. The *petit gâteau mi-cuit au chocolat* was a partially cooked—*mi cuit*—cake that arrived still warm, the interior of dark chocolate oozing out at a touch, melting onto your spoon. If you don't care for chocolate, Le Hangar typically has possibilities like *clafoutis à la rhubarbe* (rhubarb cake) and *crêpes à l'orange*. Thoughtful touches were the *amuse-gueules* at the beginning, *tapenade* with toasted bread, and mini-desserts at the end.

❖ *Le Hangar: results uneven, but if you're in the neighborhood, it's worth a stop.*

Au Petit Fer à Cheval
30 rue Vieille du Temple, 75004 Paris (01.42.72.47.47)
Métro: St. Paul
Open daily to 2:00 A.M.

Nothing much has changed here since Au Petit Fer à Cheval opened in 1903. Then as now it was dominated by the remarkable horseshoe-shaped bar, crowded with regulars jostling for space as they downed their drinks. If you want a meal you'll try for a seat in the back room where the seats are old Métro benches, and appetizing plates like *jambon cru*, or *salade auvergnate* are served up from noon to 1:15 a.m. A hot *plat du jour*, a *filet de veau* or *onglet de boeuf*, will run from 14 to 16 euros. If you're not that hungry, sandwiches are a reasonable 3.50 to 6 euros.

Here is a smoky tan room dominated by a vintage poster, an immense mirror and historic mosaic tiles curving and swirling underfoot—it's an ambience where you settle in and feel at ease. Au Petit Fer à Cheval caters to students, artists, writers, people from the neighborhood; many of the clientele know one another.

❖ *Au Petit Fer à Cheval: a friendly bar for a quick snack or even a meal.*

Le Louis Philippe
66 quai de l'Hôtel de Ville, 75004 Paris (01.42.72.29.42)
Métro: Hôtel de Ville
Open daily noon–3:00 P.M., 7:00–11:00 P.M.

The Louis Philippe looks like a place where time has stood still. Leaving the picturesque bar to go to the restaurant side, we chose a table with a view of the tiny kitchen. We had a good look at an antique sign in wonderful Art Nouveau lettering on glass: *Café 20c la tasse*. The sign is right over an antique green coal stove, on a cracked-tile floor with "Louis Philippe" in mosaic.

Service was swift: the 14-euro lunch offered traditional starters, including *charcuterie* (cold sliced meats), *salade d'endives*, and *oeuf dur à la mayonnaise* (hard-boiled egg). (A la carte, hors d'oeuvres are from 7.50 to 12, and *plats* from 10 to 16 euros).

To follow the *plat du jour:* it might be *agneau* (lamb), *escalope de volaille poêlée citronelle* (sautéed chicken with lemon), or *onglet à l'echalotte* (flank steak with shallots).

Our hors d'oeuvres were acceptable: if the *quenelles au brochette* (fish dumplings on a skewer) didn't have much flavor in themselves, the hot cheese sauce surrounding them did. A good *salade aux endives* involved chunks of Bleu d'Auvergne and walnuts in a vinaigrette on endives.

The trout that followed was accompanied by a tasty tomato and eggplant sauté; the *onglet à l'échalotte* was rich and filling, the meat in a well-made sauce. Classic bistro desserts followed and were just right. To go with the meal, we chose a pleasant rosé, Côtes de Ventoux.

An upstairs dining room offers spectacular views of St. Gervais and Notre Dame, and the experience of climbing the antique staircase, a marvel in wrought iron.

❖ *Le Louis Philippe: terrace and cuisine attractive to Parisians and tourists alike.*

Les Philosophes
28 rue Vieille-du-Temple, 75004 Paris (01.48.87.49.64)
Métro: Hôtel de Ville
Open daily to 2:00 A.M.

There are cafés in Paris in which weighty matters are discussed, and there are even some where these conversations are regularly scheduled. This is not the case with Les Philosophes. The only serious matter we heard under discussion was about that lightest of all ideas, the frivolous subject of fashion.

Although it is in the Marais, with all of the strange and exotic flora and fauna swirling by in these narrow streets, Les Philosophes keeps the look of a standard Paris bistro, with an old-fashioned circular staircase near the exposed stone on the far wall. Art Deco light fixtures brighten the interior, and you notice that bistro trademark, the *ardoise* with the day's specials noted in chalk.

The 23-euro lunch menu offers soup, a *plat* and dessert; the higher-priced menus involve 3 courses and a greater choice. Wine is about 4 euros a glass, but some nice wines from the South are available in carafes. The *rillettes* of haddock was a nice little fish salad with toast points, along with a classic tomato-and-lettuce salad in a light vinaigrette. The next course varied in quality: one serving of *osso bucco* was tasty and well-flavored, the other disappointingly full of gristle. (At that point we noticed that the regulars were ordering fish). A glass of the pleasant Languedoc reconciled us to the failings of the *plat*, and we finished up with a *tarte Tatin*, not the classic but made with *mangue*, or mango.

A scattering of tourists have also discovered this pleasant bistro, and we heard the earnest young Frenchman beside us charming a long-haired New Yorker with talk about the fashion industry in both countries.

❖ *Les Philosophes: a reasonable choice for the area.*

Le Réconfort
37 rue de Poitou, 75003 Paris (01.49.96.09.60.)
Métro: St.Sébastien-Froissart
Mon–Fri lunch and dinner, Sat–Sun dinner,
Closed 1 week in August

Attractions at Le Reconfort are the warm welcome and opulent decor. In a pleasant ambiance that recalls Provence, the colors are soft orange and muted reds, with ochre walls and ceiling—even the beams. You might be in a tale from the Arabian Nights, with *faux* Oriental rugs continuing the reds, oil paintings on the walls, fresh flowers in yellows and oranges on the tables. Upstairs a chest of drawers is covered with old newsprint—probably from *Libération,* a left-wing newspaper. The unisex WC is considered, according to one of the black-costumed workers, to be one of the most artistic of such facilities in Paris

Lunch here is easy on the wallet: noon menus or *formules* go for 13 or 18 euros, depending on whether you choose just two of the daily hors d'oeuvres, *plat,* and dessert, or take all three. At Le Réconfort, most wines are available only by the glass or full bottle; we chose a half bottle, a St. Nicholas de Bourgueuil.

A cold cucumber salad was attractively presented, with tomatoes and flat-leafed parsley setting off the cucumbers in a cream sauce with fresh dill. The cucumber, sliced to look like pasta, was cool and refreshing in a portion large enough to share.

An enormous, tender and tasty *entrecôte* steak with *gratin dauphinoise* (scalloped potatoes) kept one of us occupied for some time. The *salade du jour* was, like antipasto, made up of a selection of good hors d'oeuvres, with pleasing contrasts—sardines on toast, a blend of chopped olives and anchovies, mozzarrella on tomatoes, *jambon cru,* smoked raw ham on ripe, sweet cantalope, grated carrot and zucchini with a *fromage blanc* and dill dressing.

A la carte, typically hors d'oeuvres and desserts run about 7 to 10, and *plats* from 16 to 21 euros. Our desserts were pleasing: rich slices of cold *fondant au chocolat,* sprinkled with toasted almonds on a swirl of *crème anglaise,* and a *bavarois au fromage blanc,* a light jellied custard, much lighter than cheesecake, served on a base of *coulis aux fruits rouges,* an intensely flavored sauce, raspberry and blackberry the dominant flavors.

❖ *Le Reconfort: "Good, and they're nice there," as a local from the area remarked.*

Le Rouge-Gorge
2 rue St. Paul, 75004 Paris (01.48.04.75.89)
Métro: Bastille or St. Paul
Mon–Sat noon–4:00 P.M., 6:00–2:00 A.M.
Wheelchair access

A jovial trio in the corner warmed this little wine bar on the rue St. Paul with their laughter, but the Rouge-Gorge is cosy and inviting in its own right, the old exposed stone set off by glossy walls done up in a sophisticated celery green.

Smart people show up here for lunch, which at 12 euros is an outstanding buy in the pricey Marais. Dinner at night is more romantic and more expensive, with hors d'oeuvres from 6 to 10 and *plats* at 18 euros.

Here the service is warm and attentive, the food delicious. A delicate entrée, a circle of *chèvre* enclosed in leeks with a mayonnaise-and-chive garnish was followed by a hearty *plat* of seared pork cutlets with perfect, crunchy green beans. They were brought by a smiling *serveuse* in the shirt and jeans that are a uniform among the young. We're close to the Village St. Paul, an historic enclave with bookstores and jewelry shops behind the handsome façades.

At Le Rouge-Gorge, the food and wines follow a theme. This time it was Corsica, and a hearty Domaine d'Alzipratu went just right with the tasty pork.

❖ *Le Rouge-Gorge: good value at the end of a lively street in the Marais.*

Le Temps des Cerises
31 rue de la Cerisaie, 75004 Paris (01.42.72.08.63)
Métro: Bastille
Mon–Fri noon–3:00 P.M., 7.30 P.M.–11 P.M., closed August

At the corner of the rue de la Cerisaie and the rue du Petit Musc, this Temps des Cerises is not at all like its rowdy cousin with the same name in the 13th arrondissement. This is a romantic little hideaway, a picture-perfect version of a neighborhood bistro, with a real zinc bar, attentive and friendly proprietors, walls with historic photos, highly-polished oak tables, and a variety of wines at fair prices.

Yves and Michèle Boukobsa run it now: Yves usually serious, attending to the bar and Michèle, her hair a flame-colored aureole about her head, enchanting the clientele with her warm smile and attentive service.

There's a 13.50-euro three-course lunch menu on the *ardoise.* At any weekday lunch you'll find Le Temps crammed with locals who include musicians and journalists enjoying the day's specials. They might start with classics like *oeuf mayonnaise* (egg with mayonnaise), or *poisson pommes à l'huile* (fish with cold potato salad), and go on to *tendron de veau* (veal rib roast), *agneau à la crème d'ail flageolets* (lamb with garlic cream and kidney beans), finishing with *tarte aux abricots* (apricot tart), *crème caramel,* or cheese. With lunch we'd recommend the Réserve Maison.

Having enjoyed this Temps des Cerises for years, when we met old friends who were in the city on a brief visit, we decided to take them here. They were enchanted by the ambiance, looking about them in wonder that something so authentic is still alive and well and existing in Paris.

❖ *Le Temps des Cerises: a very special bistro with unforgettable ambiance and good* cuisine familiale.

La Tartine
24 rue de Rivoli, 75004 Paris (01.42.72.76.85)
Métro: Hôtel de Ville
Open daily 8:00 A.M.–10:00 P.M.
Closed 2 weeks in August

Although La Tartine is actually much older, dating from somewhere in the nineteenth century, your immediate image of it is from one of those famous Brassai photographs of Paris in the 1920s and '30s. That is, your image would be if La Tartine hadn't been bought up and brutally modernized several years ago. What follows is our tribute to the original Tartine:

"The dark, somewhat ominous interior, the stone-faced women well past the first bloom of youth, the moody reflections in old mirrors, the half empty glasses left on wooden tables—it was all here, unchanged in the twentieth century at La Tartine.

Trotsky came here during his time in Paris. Even in his day it would have been thought of as an old wine bar. Here is a triumph of unimproved decor: nothing has been renovated, updated, or desecrated in the name of progress; here is aged molding, the walls and ceilings a smoky dark ochre and burnt sienna so old it looks like cracked leather.

A marble-topped bar is black with Second-Empire details in gold. Dour waitresses preside, wearing put-upon expressions and looking as if they could have emerged from the canvases of Toulouse-Lautrec.

Here is an extraordinary list of wines near the bar, wines available for small prices because they come in small glasses (8 centiliters). If you feel like a normal-sized glass, double the listed price. So the lovely Côteaux de Layon we ordered on a late afternoon was 4 euros, not 2. There's a *plat du jour* at mealtime, or a plate of *charcuterie* or *fromage* available anytime.

Over the wine, the buzz of animated conversation— intellectuals from the Marais. A note above the bar announces: Beaujolais Médaille d'Or Concours Générale de Paris. We'll have to go back and try the Beaujolais another day. Young people from the area show up, attracted by the special appeal of this historic wine bar. Some are there for coffee on the *terrasse*, where cane chairs—no garden store plastic, thank you, for the Tartine—are arranged behind the traditional pedestal tables.

The sour-faced maîtresse d' limps out to the terrace to take an order. A young bearded would-be hippie, a living ana-chronism, sips his Coca-Cola at the bar. What a travesty!

The elegant-looking French-Canadian woman on my left announces to her companion: "Je vais aller pisser avant de diner" (I'm going to pee before dinner). One doesn't envy her sweeping toward the downstairs in her long black dress, knowing that La Tartine has what are called Turkish facilities, clean but primitive, probably the same ones used by James Joyce, Trotsky, and others who made this place part of their Paris experiences."

❖ *La Tartine: What was once an extraordinary wine bar has been Disneyfied by new owners. Proof that even in Paris historic preservation laws protect only the buildings, not their interiors.*

> ### *Trumilou*
> 84 quai Hôtel-de-Ville, 75004 Paris (01.42.77.63.98)
> Métro: Hôtel de Ville
> Open daily noon–3:00 P.M., 7:00 P.M.–10:30 P.M.
> Closed 2 weeks in August
> **Wheelchair access**

Although Trumilou is on the banks of the Seine, when you're inside you feel as if you could be out in the French countryside. Yet this bistro is centrally located. Even on Sundays, Trumilou keeps its prices low: only 16.50 and 19.50 euros for the *formulas* or *prix fixe* menus, including the *plat* (main dish) with hors d'oeuvre or dessert, or all three.

At Trumilou we see an intriguing hodgepodge of objects relating to farming: a handmade pitchfork, a rake, wooden clogs probably worn by some farm worker, a small model of an oxcart, burnished copper pots, pewter measures, collector's plates as if from a country kitchen, dried sunflower bouquets, a stuffed Mallard duck. In contradiction to these are the elaborate crystal chandeliers lighting up the room.

Our hors d'oeuvres were pleasing, the eggplant caviar smooth and tasty with the thin toasted rounds of baguette, on a bed of *frisée* lettuce with chunks of tomato. Marinated salmon was a very successful *entrée*, good-sized pieces of salmon arranged on greens including spinach and tomatoes. A light, lemony vinaigrette set off the flavor of the salmon. Bread—the ever-present baguette—was fresh.

Our main dishes were found acceptable by everyone in the group. *Carrelet*, or plaice, an unusual flat saltwater fish, was presented in boneless filets on a large platter with peeled, boiled potatoes and a white sauce delicately flavored with sorrel.

The spareribs were in a sauce with a light barbecue flavor, satisfactory and not overly sweet, despite being cooked *au miel*. A thick beefsteak was well-flavored and chewy in a red wine sauce with a quantity of fries on the side.

❖ *Trumilou: substantial if not gourmet fare at a reasonable price.*

Les Vins des Pyrénées
25 rue Beautreillis, 75004 Paris (01.42.72.64.94)
Métro: Bastille
Open daily noon–3:00 P.M., 8:00 P.M.–11:00 P.M., closed 2 weeks in August

An eye-catching red façade on quiet rue Beautreillis, just off the rue Saint-Antoine attracted us to the Vin des Pyrénées.

Inside, the number of *ardoises* devoted to wines convinced us that here is a place where the grape is taken seriously.

In this old-fashioned bistro, a 19th-century cast-iron chandelier still hangs near the door. The original tile floor has not been replaced. Some sur-prising touches will appeal: a spiral staircase, antique hall trees, and old advertising signs.

But on this afternoon, the customers—mostly local business sorts, the men in suits and the women in casual dresses—were there not for the decor but for lunch à la carte, with *entrées* 8.50 to 13 euros and *plats* from 13 to 18 euros. The *entrée* claimed our attention: we started with a copious salad of *jambon du pays* (cured country ham), with green beans, corn, black olives, and tomato on a bed of lettuce. It was crunchy and delicious, with a welcome contrast of flavors and textures.

Described on the *ardoise* as a *suprême de pintade aux pleurottes*, the *plat* was a large serving of well-flavored guinea hen, with puréed potatoes and pleurotus mushrooms in a rich sauce of cooking juices fortified with red wine. Half a carafe of the house rosé was a suitable accompaniment.

Satisfied with the good hors d'oeuvres and *plats*, we finished with small cups of strong espresso. Although it was getting on past 3:00 in the afternoon, the black-clad young waitress did not rush us; she spoke fervently of her upcoming vacation, enough to convince us that she does, indeed, speak English.

❖ *Les Vins des Pyrenées: good food, fair prices, and friendly service.*

WRITERS' WATERING HOLES: THE 5TH & 6TH ARRONDISSEMENTS

Physically Montparnasse was little more than a gray and dull street holding a broken double row of cafés, but in spirit it was stronger than home or religion...

—*Jimmie Charters, This Must Be the Place*

This is the Paris of our collective memory, of our youthful imagination. This is Henry Miller, James Joyce, Richard Wright, Hemingway and Scott Fitzgerald, Sartre and De Beauvoir. This is the Paris of the famed literary cafés—Le Sélect, Le Café de Flore, La Rotonde, Les Deux Magots. This is the Latin Quarter and the Sorbonne, the puppet shows in the Luxembourg Gardens and the boulevards of St. Germain and St. Michel.

This is still the Paris of the tiny little streets, the basement jazz clubs, the steamy Greek restaurants with their windows stacked with slabs of cooked meat and tomatoes. Young couples clutch in a half embrace and wander down these streets, looking first at one side and then at another.

This is the Latin Quarter, a Paris for night people. During the daylight hours you can see the aged and dirty buildings, the poor and foreign workers, the garbage overflowing the green plastic containers, but at night, this all disappears and the magic of Paris descends.

Montparnasse nights! This was the Paris that crowds of pleasure-seekers chose for their revelry. The sense of escape and abandon that we associate with the Moulin Rouge and the Folies Bergère was once sought in a string of bistros on the Left Bank. Bistros of the 5th, 6th, and 14th arrondissements provided perfect places for the Lost

Generation and for the sophisticates who knew what they were looking for, to lose themselves in hours of pleasure-seeking. Some sought a refuge from Prohibition. Others just wanted a liberating foreign experience. Still others desired an escape from the responsibilities of home, a place to while away the time in the company of friendly compatriots.

The café scene appears in Hemingway's *The Sun Also Rises:*

> *Those who work have the greatest contempt for those who don't. The loafers are leading their own lives and it is bad form to mention work. Young painters have contempt for old painters, and that works both ways too. There are contemptuous critics and contemptuous writers. Everybody seems to dislike everybody else. The only happy people are the drunks, and they, after flaming for a period of days or weeks, eventually become depressed.*

In a certain stretch of the dreary boulevard de Montparnasse runs a series of bistros with names that resonate in history, associated as they are with the great names in literature and the arts.

The two most popular bistros for Americans were singled out for comment by American writer Robert McAlmon. He observed American life in Paris during the 1920s: "The influx of expatriates had begun before this, but now they hung out in Montparnasse at the Dôme and the Rotonde," he wrote.

The Dôme won out over the Rotonde because of a cigarette. Jimmie Charters, former boxer and barman at the Dingo, told how this happened. In the early 1920s, the manager of the Rotonde saw a young American girl smoking on the terrace of his bistro. Shocked at this brazen behavior, he asked her to move inside. She refused. He insisted. Finally she rose and left. She marched across the street, over to the Rotonde's main competition, the Dôme, taking much of the English and American clientele with her.

From then on, the Dôme was a focal point for expatriates abroad. As Jimmie Charters remembered:

> *In the normal course of events you went there in the morning, or whenever you got up, for a breakfast of croissants and coffee, to read the morning paper, and to rehash with your friends the events of the night before.... But by afternoon you would be back again*

on the terrace of the Dôme drinking your apéritif,
that stimulating forerunner of the night to come.

Many expatriates, while not creative geniuses themselves, were still unforgettable characters. Florence Martin, or Flossie as she was known, a *zaftig* former chorus girl from New York, tended to dominate her favorite bistro, the Dôme. She was popular for her jolly disposition. "Flossie was a dashing bit of color, of the Rubens type. Her orange hair was piled neatly above her clear, baby-smooth skin," noted writer Robert McAlmon. Flossie was not obviously affected by drink, and was rumored to start her day with a breakfast of potatoes and gin. James Joyce found her totally beyond his understanding: "He had difficulty in believing that such a person actually existed," McAlmon observed.

Competition between the bistros could go too far. Hilaire Hiler, a painter who took over the Jockey Bar, found Finnety, a lawyer, about to succumb to a fatal dose of poison in the bar's washroom. With a stomach pump, he managed to save the man's life. Then he learned that Finnety, suffering from a bone disease, still wanted to do away with himself. "Next time go somewhere else," suggested Hiler, adding "The Dôme is my rival, you know." The following night Finnety's dead body was found in the washroom of—of all places—the Dôme.

Farther down the boulevard du Montparnasse, set back today behind a hedge not of lilacs but arborvitae, is the Closerie des Lilas, which Hemingway described as "the nearest good café when we lived over the sawmill." Converted into an "American" bar in the 1920s, the Closerie became a favorite of many writers. There, F. Scott Fitzgerald gave Hemingway the manuscript of his new novel, *The Great Gatsby*. Hemingway wrote much of his own novel, *The Sun Also Rises,* at the Closerie's bar. He also wrote the short story "Big, Two-Hearted River" there. Some say that the famous writer actually preferred to work standing at the bar, kept on his feet by painful hemorrhoids.

The crash of 1929 and an abrupt change in many people's fortunes caused a sudden exodus of foreign pleasure-seekers from Paris. One who stayed on was perhaps the most poverty-stricken of all, Henry Miller. At first completely destitute, he was rescued by the kindness of acquaintances who would pass on a few francs, an item of clothing, a part-time job. He shared little other than nationality with most of the Americans the French had become used to seeing in their bistros.

In a letter written to Anaïs Nin in 1932, Miller reported that morning for him had taken on a pattern: "Oranges first, and then porridge at the Coupole." Poor as he was, he had to resort to the bistros: "Am writing from a café because the cold drives me out of the room. Am going over the *Tropic of Cancer* with a fine comb. A little dull, here and there, but on the whole good. If anybody had written a preface for it, they might have explained that the book was written on the wing, as it were, between my 25 addresses." Many of those addresses were Left Bank bistros.

Later, during the war, Simone de Beauvoir, the French writer associated with the Existentialist movement, was to give the same reason, the coldness of the hotels, for her own regular patronage of the cafés. She recalled a moment from her first years of acquaintance with philosopher Jean-Paul Sartre:

> As soon as our favorite café, the Closerie des Lilas, opened for the day, we sat down on the terrasse with cups of hot chocolate and piles of croissants lined up in front of us. There was still the problem of paying for them though. Sartre left me there as a kind of hostage, got into a taxi, and did not reappear for an hour.

No one was more at ease in the bistros of Montparnasse and St. Germain-des-Prés than de Beauvoir. She told about how she and Sartre set up their "general headquarters" at the Dôme, with German refugees all around. Their conversations didn't distract her, for as she felt, "facing a blank sheet of paper all alone is an austere experience." A few weeks later in the winter of 1938 to 1939, she became seriously ill with an infected lung. During her period of recuperation, Sartre brought her helpings of the *plat du jour* from the Coupole. At night she made do with ham and fruit in her hotel room.

Another friend took her for the first time to the Flore, the café which later came to be most closely identified with de Beauvoir and Sartre. The Deux Magots, when it was mentioned in her journal, was only a second choice: "The

Flore is shut, so I sit on the *terrasse* of the Deux Magots," she noted.

But work in her cold little hotel room was impossible, so she would go to the Flore whenever she could. Mornings were very special, and she has left us with an unforgettable picture of Paul Boubal, the proprietor:

> ... *I loved the moment when Boubal, a blue apron tied around him, came bustling into the still empty café and began to bring his little world to life again... A pair of bloodshot eyes would blink at one from that tough, solid Auvergne face; for the first hour or two he would remain in a perfectly filthy temper. He would shout out orders, irritably, to the kitchen hand... he would also discuss the previous night's goings-on with the waiters, Jean and Pascal, and send back a cup of ersatz coffee, the same stuff the customers drank without raising an eyebrow, with... the contemptuous comment: "Give them shit, they'd still eat it." He received and got rid of salesmen in the same cantankerous fashion.*

Later Boubal was often questioned about his famous clients. Of Sartre, he used to say: "He was my worst customer. He stayed there scribbling for hours from morning to night, in front of him just one drink, never a second one." But Boubal never considered putting the philosopher out or suggesting that he order another drink. Once he confided to a journalist: "Ah! If I had only kept Sartre's scribblings, his rough drafts. They would be worth millions...."

This part of Paris is changing. James Joyce would no longer be able to afford it. A major drugstore has been bulldozed and now Armani has a shop there. A beloved record store has been replaced by Cartier. Well-regarded bookshops are gone and trendy boutiques have taken their place. The historic cafés are still there, most of them, but even these have capitulated to fame. Schoolteachers like Sartre no longer take their morning coffee at Les Deux Magots. Le Dôme serves admittedly good food, but few struggling American writers would feel comfortable there now.

❖ *The area where Sartre scribbled and Miller mooched drinks still has worthwhile bistros and brasseries:*

Allard
41 rue St. André-des-Arts, 75006 Paris (01.43.26.48.23)
Métro: St. Michel
Mon-Sat noon-3:00 P.M., 7-10:30 P.M. Closed August

Allard has the old-fashioned yet undeniable appeal of a great historic bistro. We had our first taste of memorable cooking here: Allard's signature dish, the *canard aux olives*, was what we experienced, and it was something of a revelation. The duck with olives is on the menu again, and the service is attentive. We remember this place with its warm wood façade from the days when the Allards ran it.

There followed a low period, but now, we're glad to say, Allard is back up to standard. A way to experience this historic bistro is to try the set two-course lunch, featuring a different *plat* each weekday. You can decide according to your food preferences what day you'd like to come and take in the ambience of this elegant dining room, with its warm cream walls, framed photos and frosted glass windows.

❖ *Allard: a famous bistro is back.*

Au Beaujolais
9 rue Grégoire de Tours, 75006 Paris (01.43.29.84.05)
Métro: Odéon
Open daily 11 A.M.–1:00 A.M.

Au Beaujolais fulfills most people's romantic image of a French bistro. In an ancient building on the Left Bank, Au Beaujolis is small and intimate, with red tablecloths, lace curtains, low ceilings, exposed stone walls and massive beams overhead: the lot.

A savvy friend put us on to this amazing value in the overpriced, touristy 6th district, among the chic boutiques and the narrow winding streets. At Au Beaujolais, you get three courses of competent *cuisine familiale* for less than the price of a *plat* elsewhere in the area.

The 13-euro menu offers the classics. One of us chose *cassoulet*, which was not on the set menu but turned out to be rich and delicious. So was the *poulet à la Normande*, roasted chicken in a cream and mushroom sauce. A house wine was available, but we chose a Chardonnay, perfect with the main dishes. The desserts that followed were bistro standards. We sampled the *mousse au chocolat* and found it very acceptable.

❖ *Au Beaujolais: warm, friendly, and a very good value on the Left Bank.*

Le Balzar
49 rue des Ecoles, 75005 Paris (01.43.54.13.67)
Métro: Odéon
Open daily noon to midnight
Wheelchair access

Le Balzar, a well-known brasserie at the edge of the university quarter, gathered attention when it was the subject of an Adam Gopnik article in the *New Yorker*. An old-fashioned and well-loved local hangout, it was being sold to the Flo Group. Some feisty and articulate supporters—the neighborhood was, after all, the Sorbonne—organized a group called "Friends of the Balzar" and unsuccessfully attempted to stop the sale. They felt that the brasserie's original character would be destroyed.

When we went there, we found the decor of the Balzar undistinguished but pleasing: a large, attractive room with mirrored sides, the typical banquettes and rails above them. Posters of current art shows could be seen against the brown paneling, but there was no serious attempt at a studied decor.

The service was friendly, but the headwaiter seemed uptight. At first he tried to steer us to a tiny table near the kitchen. When we protested, we were wedged into a similar-sized one opposite the door. Noticing our scribblings, the headwaiter came back to our table to remark "C'est de l'espionage industrielle?" (Industrial spying?) We cheerfully admitted it, and he backed off.

Hors d'oeuvres, from egg with mayonnaise to smoked salmon and foie gras are from 7.50 to 17 and most *plats* from

19 to 25 euros. Wines are priced from 5 euros a glass, 14 for a half bottle. Around the room, people tended to order the same wine, a red Chateau de Brague, smooth and rich. A well-flavored *oeuf en gelée* was a a partially cooked egg, ham and a black olive in a little ramekin-shaped aspic.

When the *plats* arrived, the fish, *raie* (skate or ray), was floating in butter, covered with capers, and edged with small boiled potatoes. The fish was well-flavored, but the quantity of butter really excessive. A *rumsteak* was a good value, flavorful and tender, served with French fries that were first-rate by any standard.

For dessert, the Parisians next to us recommended the *millefeuille*. It was light and flakey, with a good *crème pâtissier* and a topping of powdered sugar. Another successful dessert was *tarte au citron*, with a pure and intense lemon flavor and not overly sweet. Both are made on the premises.

The headwaiter showed up again to question one of the regulars on our left about his veal cutlet. The young Frenchman assumed a dreamy expression: "Jadis, il y avait du croustillant..." (Formerly, there was a crunchiness about it). We had the impression that he might have been one of the "Friends of Balzar" organized to keep the Groupe Flo at bay.

The Hotel St. Jacques, the setting for the old Cary Grant–Audrey Hepburn movie *Charade,* is just down the street. Probably the movie people took their meals here.

❖ *Le Balzar: standard fare in a brasserie favored by the intelligentsia.*

Les Bookinistes
53 quai des Grands-Augustins, 75006 Paris
(01.43.25.45.94)
Métro: St. Michel
Mon–Sat noon–2:30 P.M., 7:00 P.M.–11:00 P.M.
Wheelchair access

One of the recent trends in the French food world has been the opening of "baby bistros" by famous chefs. Les

Bookinistes, a Left Bank bistro opened by Guy Savoy, a Michelin 3-star chef, is one of the better-known among them.

The look here is international elegance: soft pastel walls and ceiling, tall mirrors with intriguing lines of Gustav Klimt-type colors around them, and modern black designer chairs. Serious money was spent here.

At noon, the *menu* offers *entrée, plat,* dessert, a glass of wine and a cup of coffee for 29 euros, or 2 courses for 26 euros. A la carte, *entrées* run from 12 to 18, *plats* from 19 to 33, and desserts from 10 to 11 euros.

We were first treated to a dish of small red olives. The *menu du marché* gave two choices for each course. Taking both possibilities, we chose the *vin du mois*, Saint Chinian Domaine Navarre, an excellent value.

An endive hors d'oeuvre was endive stuffed with tuna salad with sprouts and cream. The hors d'oeuvre involving duck was unusual: slices of duck rolled with tapenade. An accompanying snow pea salad provided a contrast in texture, adding that needed bit of crunch.

Plats came to the table on hot dishes: a small serving of *dorade* resting alone in the center of the too-hot-to-touch plate was complemented by tomatoes, chopped yellow bell peppers, and onions in a separate cast-iron dish. The chicken, served on a hot cast-iron platter, was flavorful and moist. In midsummer, however, it might be well to reconsider the policy of having dishes reach the table sizzling hot, radiating heat up at the diners. This is also not the best way to treat fish.

Desserts chosen from the regular menu were good: the *fruits rouges au jus de cerises* (red fruit with cherry juice) was pleasantly piquant and without excessive sugar. *Cappucino aux framboises et griottes, glace pistache* (blackberry and raspberry soup with pistachio ice cream) was even more successful—intense flavors with pistachio ice cream adding smoothness and sweetness.

❖ *Les Bookinistes: Disappointing considering the hype, but with satisfactory if not particularly special food. Just across from the real bouquinistes (booksellers) by the Seine.*

Bouillon Racine
3 rue Racine, 75006 Paris (01.44.32.15.60)
Métro: Cluny-La Sorbonne
Open daily noon–3:00 P.M., 7:00–midnight
Wheelchair access

The original Parisian *bouillons* were late nineteenth-century restaurants serving inexpensive food to the working poor. Yet some of these restaurants were quite elaborate if not elegant. Probably the best-known is Chartier near the Bourse.

The Bouillon Racine is an Art Nouveau dream with its curves, swirls, and fanciful shapes around mirrors that send back even more fanciful reflections. Here it is not Mucha-type women such as the ones that embellish Chez Julien, but sensuous flowers around which the swirling green woodwork curves. The backs of the wrought-iron chairs and bar stools curl about like tendrils of twigs and branches.

Set lunch was a simple 15.50-euro menu offering an entrée and *plat*, or *plat* and dessert. Drinks are extra.

Belgian cooking is not known for its delicacy and finesse and the Racine is no exception. Even the hors d'oeuvres can be substantial: the *prix fixe* lunch began with a plateful of smoked salmon, garnished with wisps of fresh dill.

We had no sooner tasted a few forkfuls of that than our waiter whisked away our plates and brought the main dish, a *carbonnade de boeuf Flamande*, or Flemish beef stew cooked in beer, served in a deep soup plate with tomatoes, carrots, and parsley, and surrounded by potatoes. As we said before—filling. We were back in *cuisine familiale* territory, but the *carbonnade* could have used more garlic and a better quality of dark beer in its background. It would be a sustaining meal for a cold day.

Service was brisk and efficient, although not particularly friendly. Jean, our waiter, was efficient to the point of being intrusive. He seemed to be always hovering about, the better to keep things moving and get them over with. No sooner had we ordered than the hors d'oeuvres were slapped down in front of us. A lunch which should have taken at least an hour here lasted around 30 minutes.

Jean may be the old régime's answer to McDonald's and

the fast food industry. It would have been pleasant to be allowed to relax for a few moments in such a setting.

❖ *Bouillon Racine: great if you have never quite believed in calories and would enjoy a glorious decor.*

Brasserie Lipp
151 blvd St.-Germain, 75006 Paris (01.45.48.53.91)
Métro: St. Germain
Open daily noon–1:00 A.M.
Wheelchair access

We were ready to dislike the Lipp—over the years it's developed a reputation for being snobbish, expensive, and mediocre. At the top of the menu in red letters and in English is the brusque statement, "No salad as a meal." Some assert that the waiters are cool to foreigners, and Lipp food was said to be overpriced.

It's not just that the Brasserie Lipp doesn't permit its customers to indulge in a salad as a meal. A tendency toward the use of the imperative is continued in other signs. Still, all reservations aside, this is an entertaining experience for people who are in love with literary history or who wish to glimpse a famous face. This is the place that Hemingway remembered: "The beer was very cold and wonderful to drink. The *pommes à l'huile* were firm and marinated and the olive oil delicious."

You enter and are guided past the dazzling main room where people scrutinize you to find out if you're worth a second look, to a smaller, less ostentatious one in the back, with Art Nouveau features but not so many of them. Only the famous, celebrities from show business and the media and VIPs from politics make it into the first *salle*. (The late French president François Mitterrand was a regular). In the second one, where the Lipp tends to place French people of less consequence and foreigners, we heard French, Italian, and English spoken around us.

Heavy white linen, immense linen napkins, Art Nouveau tiles in a floral theme, an elaborate light fixture above that is mirrored to look like a dozen busy waiters in the traditional black and white, large fresh bouquets of flowers, a ceiling painted to resemble old leather... this is a heady experience.

Once there, we had time to study the menu: hors d'oeuvres à la carte run between 9 and 24 euros, *plats* from 21 to 32 euros. Looking at the wine list, you could choose the Réserve Lipp. Most wines come by the full and half bottle, and range from a simple Bordeaux to a vintage cuvée of Dom Perignon.

One of us took *pavé de rumsteak au poivre* the other *filet de thon*. The tuna was well flavored and highly satisfactory. *Rumsteak*, a large broiled steak topped with a pat of butter, simple with nothing but its own juices and a touch of pepper was one of the best we've tasted in Paris. The French fries on a large separate plate were moist and slightly crisp. Bread was ordinary Paris baguette.

Cheeses included Crottin de Chavignol, Roquefort, and Brie de Meaux, all around 8 euros. We found the Roquefort excellent, served with butter and the good baguette.

Like most brasseries, the Lipp doesn't offer complex French cuisine, but satisfying, simple basics. Service is good-natured. Our waiter suggested a finale: "Café? Cognac?" Our response: "On va aller aux Deux Magots" (threatening to go to their even-more-famous competition accross the street). He made a face and turned away in mock disgust.

❖ *Brasserie Lipp: worth a trip to the 6th arrondissement.*

Le Buisson Ardent
25 rue Jussieu, 75005 Paris (01.43.54.93.02)
Métro Jussieu
Mon–Fri lunch and dinner, closed August

Even if this bistro is right across from one of the ugliest buildings in France—the Jussieu campus of the University of Paris, a modern design that combines the charm of a cattle stockyard with that of an old-fashioned American prison—when the Buisson's wonderfully crunchy, homebaked bread reaches your table, you stop caring about the view.

Just across from the Jussieu campus of the Sorbonne, Le Buisson Ardent has to cope with a setting one has to describe as unpromising. Or, as the English writer John Russell put it in his book *Paris,* "The Sorbonne is ugly beyond belief."

But a special effort has been made with this interior: There's an elegance about the slender-stemmed table crystal, the linen tablecloths, and apricot-colored café curtains.

A three-course lunch menu is available at 17 and a *prix fixe* dinner at 32 euros. Hors d'oeuvres and *plats* show an engaging inventiveness with a tendency to favor the cuisine of the South and Southwest. The chef trained with greats Alain Senderens and Jacques Cagna.

We glanced at the wine list. Most wines were sensibly-priced reds from the South or Southwest, with a sprinkling of others. We chose the *vin du jour,* a low-priced but perfectly adequate *vin du pays* from the Tarn in the Massif Central region of southern France.

For starters we selected the *moules* and *roulé de jambon,* and were pleased: the mussels were cold, in a spicy sauce of tomato, red peppers, onions, and even pickles. The *roulé de*

jambon—tasty slices of ham rolled around avocado—were arranged around a bright summer salad, with the orange, purple, and green tones of slivers of carrot and red cabbage on a bed of green lettuce.

Along with the hors d'oeuvres came the house wine, a well-flavored red, slightly chilled as a concession to the hot weather, and the best bread we've tasted in Paris this year, possibly because the cook bakes his own.

Plats were simple and appealing: a large steak with chives came on a plate with yellow beans and slivers of tomato; a *pintade* or roast guinea hen was served with slivers of zucchini and tomato. No sauces, just the *jus* they came with, but flavorful just the same, and for lunch on a hot day, cream sauces would have been too heavy.

Of the dessert choices, the apple crumble was deliciously tart, apples with a touch of peach. A *mousse au chocolat* had a deep, not-too-sweet flavor of chocolate.

Service was friendly, and we left the Buisson Ardent feeling we'd spent time in a place with people who really care about pleasing their clientele.

❖ *Le Buisson Ardent: worth a trip, even if you have to go to Jussieu.*

Aux Charpentiers
10 rue Mabillon, 75006 Paris (01.43.26.30.05)
Open daily until 11:00 P.M.
Wheelchair access
Métro: Odéon

If you want to impress friends with your knowledge of the "real" Paris, take them to Aux Charpentiers. You'll lead them into an attractive, old-fashioned bistro, with special touches of its own, appropriate to its past as a gathering-place for a guild of carpenters. Passing a lovely old zinc bar from pre-war days, you tread the planks of an old oak floor on your way to the typical café table. (Perhaps you'll be directed to the table where, years ago, Jacques Chirac celebrated his 60th birthday.)

Aux Charpentiers has warm wood featured in its decor. Small dark wooden structures like parts of cages are mounted on the walls. Our waiter explained that they represented individual projects done by workmen who were trying to be received as full master carpenters. An impressive wood structure in the window won a bronze medal at the 1889 exposition.

The better-than-average menu has *plats du jour* according to the day of the week: Monday, veal Marengo, Tuesday, *boeuf à la mode* (beef stew), etc., all the way to Sunday, with the traditional lunch of that day, *gigot d'agneau de lait d'Aquitaine* (leg of lamb from Aquitaine). Prices run from 16 euros to a high of 20 euros for the lamb. So you might choose your day according to your favorites.

Arriving late for lunch this day, we chose *plats*: he was attracted to the *faux-filet poêlé sauce Roquefort* (sautéed steak with Roquefort sauce), and I the *caneton rôti sauce olives* (duck with olives). A house wine, Rouge Charpentiers, was fairly priced.

We dug into our *plats* with relish when they arrived: the *canard aux olives*, large portions of well-cooked duck with many olives in a savory sauce, was served with white boiled potatoes, and was filling and well-flavored. The steak was huge and succulent, as rare as requested, accompanied by rounds of crisp fried potatoes. It was set off by a good Roquefort sauce, the cheese enhancing the flavor of the beef.

At one point during the meal we saw a departing tourist giving the *bise* (kisses) to her waiter. (You and I do not need to go this far in expressing our appreciation, by the way.) But we were quietly appreciative, and look forward to returning.

Note: George and Barbara Bush have been seen here. Bush's successor, Bill Clinton, likes L'Ami Louis in the 3rd district—a place too rich for our budgets.

❖ *Aux Charpentiers: Good value in an attractive setting.*

La Closerie des Lilas
171 blvd du Montparnasse, 75006 Paris (01.44.27.00.30)
Métro: Port Royal
Open daily 11:00 A.M.–1:00 A.M.
Wheelchair access

La Closerie was described by Hemingway in *A Moveable Feast* as "the nearest good café when we lived in the flat over the sawmill at 113, rue Notre-Dame-des-Champs, and it was one of the best cafés in Paris. It was warm inside in the winter, and in the spring and fall it was very warm outside..."

The regulars at this bistro, a remarkable group, included the Russian revolutionary Lenin. La Closerie has a warm, intimate-looking bar in dark wood. If you want to try the food, stick to the Brasserie side, where you can eat at a more reasonable price with *plats* of fish and chicken from about 22 euros.

❖ *La Closerie des Lilas: literary history in a cozy setting.*

Le Comptoir du Relais
9 carrefour de l'Odéon, 75006 Paris (01.44.27.07.50)
Métro: Odéon
Open daily noon–10:30 P.M.

Yves Camdeborde was one of the first classically trained young men to open a new kind of bistro, one offering affordable but high-quality meals in simple surroundings. His first restaurant, La Régalade, became one of the most talked-about bistros in the city. People called from Tokyo trying for the coveted reservations.

When La Régalade was sold, there was much discussion about what he would do next. His answer was a small hotel in a very popular part of the Left Bank, with a tiny bistro. It's currently one of the hottest choices around.

"Une cuisine qui a du caractère–pas quelque chose qu'on trouve partout," (Cuisine with character, not what you find everywhere), confided the diner to our left, a retired Parisian who lives on the rue Jacob and often stops in for lunch at Le Comptoir. He went on to tell us that this is also a "cuisine de charcutier," and that the family owning Le Comptoir are from Les Landes, a region of southwest France celebrated in the novels of Mauriac.

With this in mind we selected hearty and substantial *plats*—most go for between 14 and 19 euros—and attacked them with gusto. One was *saucisse* with puréed potatoes garnished with thin slices of black truffle, and the other a *joues de boeuf,* beef cheeks tasting like a good beef bourguignon, with beans, carrots and macaroni in a rich sauce, presented in an sizzling hot earthenware dish.

With these, a half liter of the house wine, a Saumur Champigny 2005, was modestly priced and went perfectly with the midwinter fare. Baskets of crusty *pain de campagne* were refilled as often as we liked.

Our new acquaintance savored a flavorful *pied de porc*. He noted that he likes to drop in here because of the flexibility of the schedule. From noon to 6 p.m. Le Comptoir is a brasserie, and you can eat whenever you like. After that, in the evenings, it becomes a sought-after restaurant, reserved months in advance.

❖ *Le Comptoir: where sophisticated clientele crowd into a small room that's wildly popular, noisy, friendly, and fun. Cooking on a high level. If you can't get in at night, try an afternoon. A must.*

> ### L'Epi Dupin
> 11 rue Dupin, 75006 Paris (01.42.22.64.56)
> Métro: Sèvres-Babylone
> Mon–Fri lunch and dinner, Closed weekends 3 weeks in August
> **Wheelchair access**

The offerings at L'Epi Dupin show a lightness and originality that you do not find elsewhere at twice the price.

Usually when you're surrounded by tourists in a Paris bistro, you're right to be suspicious. In this case it means that there are some very savvy people who've heard of L'Epi Dupin and have booked well in advance to taste extraordinary cuisine at the price: a 25-euro lunch menu, and a 34-euro *prix fixe* menu at dinner.

Hors d'oeuvres one day included *carpaccio de saumon, millefeuilles de queue de boeuf* (oxtail in puff pastry), and *aubergines à la bordelaise* (eggplant in red wine sauce). Around us, opinions were unanimous: "Very good indeed," remarked the Englishwoman to my right about her *millefeuille de queue de boeuf.* "Exquisite," was the judgment pronounced by a visiting American about his *carpaccio.*

Main dishes promised and delivered originality. *Caille*—quail—was roasted deliciously crisp in a well-seasoned sauce, with whole roasted garlic and tiny mushrooms. My husband could not be induced to part with any of his *filets de rouget grondin au pistou* (red gurnard filets in Provençal sauce), which he pronounced: "Delicious—best fish I've ever tasted." The San Francisco lawyers on our left, who had requested our help to keep them from ordering lambs' brains, had finished by choosing the *onglet de boeuf* (flank steak). They were calling it exquisite.

Servings are generous and each dessert involves several flavors: one consisted of the nougat-flavored ice cream served on a *coulis*, or fruit sauce, with large *tuiles*—thin, almond-flavored cookies studded with almonds—the whole garnished with mint leaves delicately frosted with powdered sugar. The *poêlée de cerises* looked like an exotic flower, with quantities of red cherries lightly cooked in a sauce surrounded by the leafy garnish.

At lunch, our end of L'Epi was crowded with tourists, most of them congratulating themselves on having succeeded in getting a reservation.

Note: We have always had a wonderful experience here but have heard of some dissatisfied clients; L'Epi's cuisine draws a crowd and the service can be affected as a result.

❖ *L'Epi Dupin: sophisticated food at close to cuisine familiale prices, an outstanding value.*

Café de Flore
172 blvd St. Germain, 75006 Paris (01.45.48.55.26)
Métro: St. Germain
Open daily to 1:30 A.M.
Wheelchair access

Sartre's remark about the ways of liberty passing through the portals of the Flore is repeated on the front of the menu, but what you note here is their liberty with your money. Drinks in this bistro are expensive: a glass of wine is 7 to 11 euros, a beer 8, and coffee almost 5 euros—well above the going rate. Still, when you're not obsessing about your slimming wallet, you can look around and appreciate the understated elegance of the Flore: the Deco lighting, the spare clean lines, the tall potted palms, the red banquettes. Large mirrors are edged with brass, and the waiters, efficient but not especially friendly, are in their usual black and white. On this sunny day, the clientele inside looked like old regulars, while tourists preferred the terrace.

There are economical ways of experiencing the Flore. Drinks are high-priced but a few foods are not too far above the usual range. We chose a ham and cheese omelet. Presented on a white Café de Flore plate, the omelet was good if a trifle greasy. Salads or sandwiches are also a reasonable choice.

Unusual fan-shaped mosaic tiles are on the floor, framed posters of art shows lead up the stairs to the fabled first floor, still the most "in" part of the Flore, a place where today's intellectuals meet and talk. But the main floor is better to look at, and it's where young Simone de Beauvoir spent hours writing her books and helping Sartre revise his. It's where they met Albert Camus and where Simone first saw Truman Capote, whom she dismissed as "tiny... smaller even than Sartre... looking like a giant mushroom."

Lalique crystal or something that looks very much like it conceals the lighting in the wonderful Art Deco wall sconces. An enormous bouquet fills much of the window ledge, right in front of the lacy café curtains.

❖ *Café de Flore: if you go, go for the ambiance, which is still special, the legend which is still part of this place, not for the so-so food and the over-priced drinks.*

Chez Marcel
7 rue Stanislas, 75006 Paris (01.45.48.29.94)
Métro: Notre Dame-des Champs
Mon–Fri noon–2:00 A.M., 7:30 P.M.–10:00 P.M.,
closed August

On a little street off the boulevard Raspail and close to the Alliance Française, Chez Marcel strikes one as a place where everything is done right. The narrow room is warm and welcoming, with wallpaper in subdued tones to set off the rich, gleaming copper pots, posters, and oil paintings that give this the warmth of an old-fashioned dining room in a friend's home.

Prices are a pleasant surprise for the 6th arrondissement: an 18-euro lunch menu provides better than the usual bistro fare. A variety of wines are available by the *pichet*. We shared a *pichet* of rosé from the Pays d'Oc for 12 euros.

We were seated at a little table, one of a line leading to the door. Near us were French businessmen in intense conversation. A nice touch was a large bouquet of pink hydrangeas separating us from their table, like a floral hedge.

But it wasn't so effective that it separated us from their witticisms. One must have spilled a little red wine on the table (covered with paper over white linen), and he quipped: "Oh, now I suppose I'll be charged extra for a stain on the *dentelle de Sèvres* (Sèvres lace)."

To start, the *oeuf mayonnaise* was nicely prepared, homemade mayonnaise piped on eggs, with tomatoes and parsley adding color. A tasty terrine was served on greens, with pickles to pique the appetite.

Brochette d'agneau (grilled lamb on a skewer) was a large, generous *plat*, the flavor of the lamb enhanced withs sautéed onions, red peppers, and zucchini and accompanied by sautéed potatoes. *Quenelles* came in a small cast-iron casserole with little white potatoes. The *sauce à la nantua*, a cheese sauce, provided just the right balance for the light and subtle flavor of the fish *quenelles*.

On the way out, after finishing the good espresso accompanied by a small bittersweet chocolate, we asked the owner-managers who had given us attentive service the eternal question: is Chez Marcel a restaurant or a bistro? "Plutôt bistro," said the gray-haired proprietor. "La service, les plats, la décor—bistro lyonnais" (The service, the food, the decor—Lyon-style bistro). His blond wife interjected, "Non, c'est un restaurant traditionnel." "Non, pour moi c'est bistro," (No, for me it's a bistro) insisted her husband.

You'll have to decide for yourself.

❖ *Chez Marcel: you'd love to have it in your own neighborhood.*

> ### Le Petit Saint-Benoit
> 4 rue St. Benoit, 75006 Paris (01.42.60.27.92)
> Métro: St. Germain
> Mon–Sat noon–2:30 P.M., 7:00–10:30 P.M.,
> closed in August
> **No credit cards**

Nothing could be simpler than finding the Petit St. Benoit. You walk up rue Saint-Benoit, the little street that runs between the most famous cafés in Paris, the Deux Magots, and the Flore. Soon you reach Le Petit Saint Benoît. Inside it's standard bistro: an old zinc bar, red tablecloths covered with paper, dark banquettes, historic tile on the floor, brass hat rails, a venerable clock, obscure mirrors, and even the numbered drawers for regulars who kept their own cloth napkins there.

Intellectuals from the neighborhood stop by for a before-dinner drink. We noticed a gray-haired individual with piercing eyes who might have stepped out of a Cartier-Bresson photograph of the district.

The Petit St-Benoît is easy on the budget: hors d'oeuvres are from 2.50 to 8, *plats* from 11.50 to 17.50, and desserts 4 to 5 euros.

Our *plats* arrived quickly—one had visions of dishes lined up in the kitchen, ready to be whipped out for customers. One of them, the salmon, was an acceptable filet served on puréed potatoes, a cream sauce with sorrel supplying extra flavor. *Blanquette de veau* (veal stew), a bistro standard, came with rice and was tasty and filling.

Pichets of pleasant house wines are available at 7 or 12 euros depending on the size selected. Our *demi* of chilled rosé was perfect for a warm summer night.

❖ *Le Petit St.-Benoît: low-priced cuisine familiale, old-fashioned charm, unbeatable location.*

> ### Au Pied de Fouet du 6ième
> 3 rue St. Benoît, 75006 Paris (01.42.96.59.10)
> Métro: St. Germain-des-Prés
> Mon-Sat noon-2:30, 7-9:30 Closed Sunday

Someday, you think, I'll find a warm and inviting restaurant nearby, a place redolent of savory stews and well-done cuisine, with friendly people serving comfort food at low prices. This is such a place. We were guided by the novelist Diane Johnson, who in *Into a Paris Quartier: Reine Margot's Chapel and Other Haunts of St. Germain,* mentions a favorite restaurant, La Brocherie. Now it has become Au Pied de Fouet, similar to its sister restaurant in the 7th district.

A handful of young professionals were finishing lunch as we were shoehorned in next to them on the balcony. Later one of them gave us her evaluation: "C'est la cuisine normande: très bon rapport qualité-prix ici." (It's Norman cuisine, and a very good value for this area."

At Au Pied, everything is à la carte. We started with *salade marinère,* one of the starters available from 3 to 5 euros. It was a chewy mixture, basically potato salad with seafood; we tasted bits of crab, shrimp, olives and shallots, combined with a good mayonnaise.

For *plats,* one of us chose the *filet de lieu,* slightly overdone but well-flavored pollock, served with puréed potatoes and turnips. The other *plat* was *lapin à la moutarde,* rabbit in a well-made sauce involving mustard, accompanied by canned peas and pearl onions. Wine is available by the *pichet* for 10 euros. A Touraine Sauvignon "Les Roches" went well with both *plats*.

❖ *Au Pied du Fouet du 6ième: a tiny restaurant with remarkable values. Go early or late for a better chance at a table.*

> ### *Le Reminet*
> 3 rue des Grands-Degrés, 75005 Paris (01.44.07.04.24)
> Métro: St. Michel
> Thurs–Mon lunch and dinner, closed Tues and Wed.

With a choice location in the 5th arrondissement, just off Quai Montobello near the edge of the Seine, you would expect Le Reminet to be in the "big splurge" category. After all, Notre Dame is virtually across the way. Yet it's one of the few bistros in this high-priced area to offer ambitious cuisine at reasonable prices.

On entering the small dining room we noticed the 14-euro lunch menu scrawled on the typical *ardoise*, giving hors d'oeuvre, main course, and dessert. A la carte, starters are 12 to 15 and *plats* 21 to 24 euros. That day you could choose between *harengs pommes à l'huile* (herring with potato salad) and *tomate avec mozzarella* to start, then a *plat: sauté de porc* (pork chop) or *sardines aux xeres* (sardines in sherry sauce). For dessert, there was *poire marinée au vin rouge* (pear marinated in red wine) or *mousse de châtaigne, crème fouettée* (chestnut mousse with cream).

Lunch was outstanding, starting with a small plate of *amuse-gueules* or appetizers including olives and slices of *saucisson*. Soon the herring was served, prettily presented with lettuce, carrots, and other vegetables in a flower-like arrangement. The flavorful tomato was a particular treat, garnished as it was with slices of mozzarella.

Main dishes were equally successful: the *porc sauté* came in a sauce lightly flavored with orange, and the sardines were crisp and tasty on a bed of slivers of carrot and zucchini. A light and pleasant finish to lunch was the chestnut mousse with whipped cream and the marinated pears.

With the food we enjoyed an Alsatian wine, Gewurtztraminer, a white with a touch of sweetness that set off the pork to perfection.

The chef is Eric Ponchet, who has worked under Guy Savoy and Alain Ducasse. He has kept the tradition here of using fresh market produce.

❖ *Le Reminet: outstanding food at reasonable prices.*

Le Sélect
99 blvd du Montparnasse, 75006 Paris (01.42.22.65.27)
Métro: Vavin
Open daily to 3:00 A.M.

Of the American literary cafés of the 1920s, only the Sélect would today look much the same to Hemingway and Fitzgerald. The Dôme has become a horrid example of

Atlantic City glitz combined with Las Vegas flash, though it does have good, if expensive, food. The Coupole might seem somewhat familiar to expatriates from the twenties, although they would shudder at the prices people pay for brasserie offerings. The Rotonde has location but little else: it has acquired all of the romance of a New Jersey diner. The Closerie des Lilas, long lacking the lilacs, has become an expensive French restaurant. Others such as the Jockey have totally vanished.

Like many other such places, Le Sélect is enjoyable for the banter you hear between waiters and customers: when we heard the distant sound of glasses crashing to the floor for the second time, we asked our waiter about it. "Ils boivent trop" (they drink too much), he said seriously, miming someone pulling on a bottle.

We love the Sélect for its ambiance: ochre-colored walls, the original moldings from 1923, fine Lalique-influenced lighting fixtures, wrought iron, the sense that here is a place where time has stood still. Before, we'd always considered it a place for a drink or light snack. The thing to realize is that they also offer real food.

We ordered a *pavé grillé sauce roquefort* (steak with Roquefort sauce) and a *salade niçoise*. Both *plats* were large and generous: the steak, accompanied by sautéed potatoes and tiny *haricots verts*, compared favorably with some we'd been served at much more expensive bistros, and we were really surprised at the attractiveness of the plate with all the ingredients of a classic *salade niçoise*.

If we hadn't made those choices, the Sélect offers other salads and café classics such as *croque monsieur* and onion soup, as well as the sort of thing that would please a committed "foodie:" smoked salmon salad, foie gras, *côte de veau*, *magret de canard*, and various cheeses.

A good half bottle of Beaujolais, a Brouilly, was a smooth and suitable accompaniment for our meals.

A lively discussion with our waiter made for an interesting finale. We asked if he knew when the infamously tough proprietress of the café who was generally known as Madame Sélect had died. "Il n'y avait pas de Madame Sélect" (There was no Madame Sélect), he maintained. He was adamant about it, not backing down even when we pointed to a framed sketch from the old days with the words "Madame Sélect" beneath the caricature of a lady with strong jaw and upswept hair.

❖ *Le Sélect: a time-warp experience from the Jazz Age.*

AFRICAN-AMERICANS IN PARIS: THE 6TH ARRONDISSEMENT AND BEYOND

> ...I love this café life, this quiet existence mixed with noise and quick motion which is attached to every large city... In Paris I find everything that appeals to me: lights, noises in the night, places where one has fun according to one's liking, a sympathetic and tolerant world, in sum, a true civilization.
>
> —Countee Cullen

For African-Americans, particularly writers, bistros were fundamental to survival in the strange city. They were meeting-places, outdoor living rooms for people who would otherwise be whiling away solitary hours in cold hotel rooms. The bistros gave writers a chance to observe street life and get to know the city even if they had only rudimentary French. Here was the possibility of meeting people and making friends. Ever since World War I, African-Americans had discovered that the racism which blighted their lives and threatened their safety in the United States did not seem to be such an issue in France. Even now, the social barriers between the races that exist elsewhere seem less important in Paris.

For writer Chester Himes, who left the United States in search of a better life in Paris, this acceptance was to be a crucial part of the city's appeal. Already published in the US, Himes came to be well known as a writer of the *Serie Noire* books, featuring Grave Digger Jones and Coffin Ed. (The best-known book in the series, *Cotton Comes to Harlem*, was later made into a movie). His sometimes raunchy, frequently misognyistic and often rambling autobiography, *The Quality of Hurt* and *My Life of Absurdity* is one of the most entertaining accounts of life abroad written by any expatriate.

For years Himes was frustrated in his efforts to survive as a writer in the United States. France seemed a better alternative; he was attracted by accounts of the City of Light sent by his old friend Richard Wright, already well known for his novels *Black Boy* and *Native Son*. Wright had made a home for himself in Paris and urged his compatriot to follow.

Himes's entry into Paris on April 11, 1953, didn't go as planned. He arrived at the train station and missed the people who were supposed to meet him. After waiting for a time, he finally took a taxi and, with difficulty, managed to communicate to the driver Richard Wright's address in the 7th arrondissement. Once deposited in front of the building, Himes dragged his luggage up several flights of stairs. Suddenly the lights gave out and another light appeared from behind curtains. Then, as he told it:

> ... *a monster charged forth, the likes of which I had never seen. She looked like some prehistoric species of the human race; obviously female, judging from the huge drooping breasts topping a squarish big-hipped body beneath a flagging purple robe and the things in her hair, and she seemed in a rage....* *'Allez!'* she screamed. *'Allez! Allez! Vite! Vite!'*

This was his introduction to Paris and its people.

Not able to communicate with any assurance in French, knowing few people in Paris, and having very little money, he nevertheless quickly became a part of the group that gathered in the café-bistro Le Tournon, on the rue de Tournon in the 6th district. As Himes tells it—and one must allow a little latitude for the male penchant for exaggeration—he had no trouble attracting female companionship for the evenings. He and his friend, cartoonist Ollie Harrington, would get a repartee going of jokes and not-too-serious put-downs, almost a comic routine, and people would crowd near to witness the fun.

Of course, African-Americans who decided to emigrate to France had a variety of reasons for doing so. Not all imagined that life in Paris would be easy. Some might have said with James Baldwin, "I have never, thank God—and certainly not

once I found myself living there—been even remotely
romantic about Paris.... My journey, or my flight, had not
been to Paris, but simply away from America."

As Baldwin also discovered, "the moment I began living in
French hotels I understood the necessity of French cafés."
The Deux Magots was part of his first experience of Paris. He
went there when he arrived in November, 1948, and was
sitting at the Deux Magots when he recognized Richard
Wright, who helped him to find a hotel.

The Deux Magots was also where Baldwin and Himes first
met. Himes had been visiting Richard Wright when there
was a telephone call from Baldwin, who needed a loan.
According to Himes, Wright had been annoyed by Baldwin's
attacks on him in several articles. Their conversation at the
famous bistro led to a heated argument over Baldwin's

denunciation of Wright for creating a stereotype in Bigger Thomas, the main character in *Native Son*. Himes saw the situation—Baldwin's needing money—as an occasion for Wright to get his own back:

> *Dick accused Baldwin of showing his ingratitude for all he had done for him by his scurrilous attacks. Baldwin defended himself by saying that Dick had written his story and hadn't left him, or any other American black writer, anything to write about. I confess at this point they lost me... All of the women and the majority of the men... took Baldwin's side—chiefly, I think, because he looked so small and intense and vulnerable....*

Sometimes a café experience could turn wrong. One turned out very badly for Baldwin. One night in a St. Germain-des-Prés café, Baldwin was, as he said, "discovered" by a tourist he'd met before in New York, adding "only because we found ourselves in Paris we immediately established the illusion that we had been fast friends back in the good old U.S.A." Before the evening was over, Baldwin had promised to find a room in his hotel for his new friend.

The tourist came to Baldwin's hotel, bringing a sheet belonging to the place he'd just left. Baldwin borrowed the sheet, putting his own dirty ones in the hall for the chambermaid. He didn't think any more about it until his new friend was visited by the police. Then the gendarmes went to Baldwin's room and spotted the sheet with, as he described it, "Lettered in the most brilliant scarlet I have ever seen, the name of the hotel from which it had been stolen." Baldwin found himself under arrest.

Days of misery followed. As he remembered: "For once, locked in, divested of shoelaces, belt, watch, money, papers, nail file, in a freezing cell in which both the window and the toilet were broken, with six other adventurers, the story I told of *l'affaire du drap de lit* (the case of the sheet) elicited only the wildest amusement or the most suspicious disbelief."

Added to the physical discomfort was the mental agony of not knowing what was going to happen. A French boy who'd stolen a sweater from Monoprix would, everyone agreed, receive a six-month sentence. And, Baldwin added:

> *... my cellmates had been amusing themselves with me by telling terrible stories about the inefficiency of French prisons, an inefficiency so extreme that it had often happened that someone who was supposed to be taken out and tried found himself on the wrong line and was guillotined instead... though I knew they were teasing me, it was simply not possible for me to totally disbelieve them.*

What did happen was that a kindly prisoner who was due to be released offered to take out messages for anyone in the cell. At first Baldwin refused; then he thought of someone who might be able to help, a former employer. This man came to see him and found him a lawyer. When Baldwin came to trial, the case against him was dismissed with general laughter at the absurd situation that had caused the arrest in the first place.

> *Blues in the rue Pigalle. Black and laughing, heartbreaking blues in the Paris dawn, pounding like a pulse-beat, moving like the Mississippi!*
>
> *—Langston Hughes*

Some African-American writers, members of the Harlem Renaissance movement, had tried life in Paris years before Wright, Himes, and Baldwin. Langston Hughes reached Paris in February 1924 with only seven dollars in his pocket. He lived in a garret near the Place de Clichy and survived by working at odd jobs—doorman at a small nightclub on the rue Fontaine, dishwasher at the Grand Duc Cabaret at 48 rue Nollet in the 17th district—and wrote poetry when he could. About his life in Paris, he wrote:

> *The room was right out of a book . . . I guess dreams do come true and sometimes life makes its own books. Because here I am, living in a Paris garret, writing poems and having champagne for breakfast (because champagne is what we had with our breakfast at the Grand Duc from the half-empty bottles left by unsuspecting guests).*

Despite this romantic picture of the poet's life abroad, Hughes found reality tough enough that he would warn friends: "Stay home!.... Jobs in Paris are like needles in haystacks for everybody and especially for English-speaking foreigners."

Sometimes the available jobs became too challenging even for a starving poet. His first job as a *chasseur* (doorman) at a nightclub on the rue Fontaine ended when he discovered he was also supposed to be the *videur* (bouncer) and stop fights. "I didn't like the task of fight-stopping, because the first fight I saw there was between ladies, who shattered champagne glasses on the edge of the table, then slashed at each other with the jagged stems," he wrote. After that incident, a job as dishwasher at the Grand Duc looked good. But the experience of life in Montmartre was not lost on Hughes, who incorporated the rhythms of the jazz all around him into poems like "Jazz Band in a Parisian Cabaret."

When he got back to the United States, Hughes had to adjust to the segregation in the nation's capital. He wrote: "I felt very bad in Washington last winter, so I wrote a great many poems. (I wrote only a few poems in Paris, because I had had such a good time there)."

An African-American who founded an important cabaret in Montmartre was Ada Smith du Conge, commonly known as "Bricktop." Her club, on the rue Fontaine, became a hangout for the famous and the socially prominent.

She had left New York because she was offered a job at the Grand Duc. Her start in Paris was not promising, however. Seasick on the way over, she reached the city and found the Grand Duc not an impressive nightclub, but a tiny bar. As she recalled, she was tempted to say something inappropriate, but "a handsome young Negro" came out of the kitchen and offered her something to eat, getting her away from the club owner. Later she remembered that the young man had been Langston Hughes.

Countee Cullen spent a few days in Paris in 1926 as part of a trip with his stepfather. Cullen travelled to France with many more advantages than Hughes had had, including an M.A. from Harvard. Returning later with a Guggenheim grant to study, he evaluated Paris as "a peerless city. Liberty, equality, fraternity are not only words. They express the spirit of which Paris is made." While he lived there, however, most of his contacts were not French but American. Cullen's relative prosperity contrasted with Hughes's poverty and gave opposing impressions to Americans in the United States of the ease of life in Paris.

Poet Claude McKay had no illusions about the French, but could perceive advantages to the cafés: "Paris, away from Montmartre and Montparnasse, seemed to me to be the perfect city of modern civilization. It was the only city I knew which provided quiet and comfortable clubs in the form of cafés for all its citizens of every class."

"I sat at my first sidewalk café last night and fell in love with Paris on the corner of Place de l'Opéra and Boulevard des Capucines," wrote Arna Bontemps. Also part of the Harlem Renaissance, Bontemps was not able to visit Paris until 1960, almost 40 years after his friends became acquainted with the city. During this visit Bontemps was guided around the city by Richard Wright and Ollie Harrington.

When Josephine Baker first went to Paris in 1925 as a dancer in the Revue Nègre troup, she expected to be just another member of the chorus. That was not how it worked out. French artist Paul Colin had something to do with Josephine's startling debut. Colin had been commissioned to design a poster to publicize the Revue Nègre, which was to appear at the Théâtre des Champs-Elysées. He needed a striking model for his poster, and, looking at the leading lady, felt discouraged: "Maude de Forest looked like a washerwoman." Spotting a beautiful girl in the chorus, he thought: "What a pity she's not the star."

The show was reworked, the beautiful chorus girl whom Colin featured in his poster became the focus of attention, and Josephine Baker was on her way. At first, Baker's shyness was a problem. "In spite of her magnificent body, she was extremely modest," commented Colin. "I couldn't seem to make her understand that I wanted her to pose *nude*."

Janet Flanner, who reported on Paris for the *New Yorker*, remembered Baker on her opening night:

> She made her entry entirely nude except for a pink flamingo feather between her limbs; she was being carried upside down and doing the split on the shoulder of a black giant.... She was an unforgettable black ebony statue. A scream of salutation spread through the theater.... Within half an hour of the

> *final curtain on opening night, the news and meaning of her arrival had spread by the grapevine up to the cafés on the Champs-Elysées, where the witnesses of her triumph sat over their drinks excitedly repeating their report of what they had just seen.... She was the established new American star for Europe.*

Suddenly the toast of Paris, Josephine went on to make her life in France.

> *The French adopted me immediately. They all went to the beaches to get dark like Josephine Baker... I felt liberated in Paris. People didn't stare at me. [But] I was afraid to go into prominent restaurants in Paris. Once, I dined in a certain restaurant with friends. An American lady looked at our table and called the waiter. "Tell her to get out," the lady said. "In my country she is belonging only in the kitchen." The French management asked the American lady to leave.*

> —*Josephine Baker*

Baker would courageously work for the French Resistance during World War II, eventually receiving the Légion d'Honneur in recognition. She continued to work as a dancer long after most dancers abandon such a grueling profession. When the costs of supporting her adopted children at her chateau in the Dordogne became too great, she made a final comeback. Benny Luke, former dancer and manager at Haynes, remembers her triumph at the Bobino Music Hall in 1975. Baker had been unwell, but managed to glide about an enormous stage, putting on a performance that gave no sign of what the effort must have cost. At the end, "She held up her arms and we all cheered." It was her last show. Days later, she died and was given a great state funeral at the Madeleine.

Duke Ellington recalled later how touched he felt about something that happened during his first engagement in Paris. During an intermission at the Salle Pleyel there was a reception backstage. It turned out that a duchess lost a valuable diamond ring. Everybody, including musicians and guests, started looking for it, but the duchess soon called off the search, saying,"I can always get diamonds, but how often can I get a Duke Ellington?"

Years later, novelist Maya Angelou had her chance to experience Paris as part of a tour of Europe. She was hired to sing and dance with a touring company presenting *Porgy and Bess*. In Paris they appeared at the Théâtre Wagram. Opening night went well, and soon an African-American who lived in the city took her around. She recalled:

> *We went to the Left Bank, and he showed me where F. Scott Fitzgerald and Hemingway did some flamboyant talking and serious drinking. The bareness of the bar surprised me. I expected a more luxurious room with swatches of velvet.... High up over the facade hung a canvas awning on which was stenciled the romantic name DEUX MAGOTS.*

Later she saw L'Abbaye, a bar owned by Gordon Heath, a black American, and the Rose Rouge, which, she wrote, was "closer to my idea of a Parisian night club. It had velour drapes and a uniformed doorman; the waiters were haughty and the customers well-dressed." After appearing in *Porgy and Bess*, she would sing a midnight show at the Mars Club, then take a cab to the Rose Rouge to finish the evening with another appearance there.

Friends urged her to leave the company and take up residence in Paris, and for a while Angelou seriously considered it. Then a telling incident occurred that made her question how tolerant the French really were. Hired to sing at a fund-raising event, Angelou arrived with two Senegalese friends. When the Parisian hostess found out that the men were from Africa, not America, her smile disappeared. Angelou never saw her again.

Similar stories are told by African-Americans who live in Paris today. Singer and professor Almeta Speaks, originally from North Carolina, has made her life in Paris. She says that the French have a mythology about themselves as rescuers of blacks. But, she says, "If I go down the street, I'll be treated as an African. When I open my mouth and they find out that I'm American, it's all different." The African-American community in Paris, she says, is not as cohesive or as small as it once was. People are more transient these days." Still, she concludes, "There is a freedom here, and writers have written about that freedom."

The late Janet McDonald, dynamic author of *Project Girl* and *Spellbound*, discussed life in Paris for African-Americans:

> *It's infinitely easier than in the U.S. There's all the difference in the world.... I felt like I could actually live there.... I don't know what it is about the French—they seem to like us. There's a different kind of racial dynamic—there is racism in France, but we are not the recipients of it. For an African-American [life] feels pretty comfortable, and it feels different in the U.S.*

The expatriate novelist, Jake Lamar, author of *Rendezvous Eighteenth* and *Ghosts of Saint-Michel*, has spoken of what led him to make Paris, and specifically Montmartre, his home:

> *. . . it's a smaller community here . . . . I have friendships with people I might not have been able to develop in the States, because there are all sorts of unwritten social barriers in the States. We're all Americans, black, white or whatever. We've all chosen to live in this town. I find a great feeling of warmth and camaraderie in the American community here . . . [Montmartre] is really the Greenwich Village of Paris . . . . there is this eccentricity, this crusty but friendly aspect among the people. And I felt very much at home here from the start.*

There are no present-day equivalents to the Café Tournon in its heyday as a bistro for expatriate African-Americans. But the question of how to choose a good bistro was addressed by Richard Wright in 1953. Wright outlined some of the inadequacies of many Parisian hangouts. He emphasized that one shouldn't give up too easily, that the perfect place might be just around the corner:

> *In my search for a café I strayed into the Deux Magots, the Flore, the Montana, the Reine Blanche, Lipps, the Royal St. Germain.... It was no go—too many tourists, too many tense characters on the make.... One could not sit a quarter of an hour without somebody violating that most sacred rule of café life: leave your neighbor alone.... I finally found my favorite bistro by straying one day into the Monaco, just off the Carrefour de l'Odéon.*

Restaurants of historical African-American importance in Paris include:

Brasserie Lipp
151 blvd St.-Germain 75006 Paris (01.45.48.53.91)
Métro: St. Germain
Open daily noon to 1:00 A.M.

Frequented by James Baldwin, who mentions the Lipp in his last novel, *Just Above My Head*. Richard Wright also patronized this brasserie. Described in detail on pages 58–59.

Café de Flore
172 blvd St. Germain, 75006 Paris (01.45.48.55.26)
Métro: St. Germain
Open daily 7:00 A.M.–1:00 A.M.

James Baldwin often went to the Flore, where he wrote *Crying Holy* and worked on *Go Tell It on the Mountain*. At the time, the upstairs room was a hangout for gay men. Incidentally, *Go Tell It on the Mountain* saved him from trouble with the French police. One evening when they were checking papers, Baldwin had forgotten his *carte de séjour*, but was carrying a copy of the novel. It had a large photograph of the author on the dust jacket. When he showed his book as a makeshift proof of identity to the policeman, he was surprised at the respectful reaction he received: "Vous êtes écrivain, Monsieur!" (You're a writer, Sir!)

Much of his writing was done in the rather plain upstairs room, now a favorite of French journalists.

❖ *Café de Flore: over-priced, but an important literary café.*

Haynes
3 rue Clauzel, 75009 Paris (01.48.78.40.63)
Métro: St-Georges
Tue–Sat 7:00 P.M.–12.30 A.M., closed in August

The Haynes of today is sadly diminished from what it used to be. In the past, Haynes was the historic landmark bistro and gathering spot of the African-American community since 1949, serving food reminiscent of the American South.

Haynes was started by Leroy Haynes, a G.I. who settled in Paris after World War II. It quickly became a favorite stop for almost every African-American writer and jazz musician who visited or resided in Paris during the postwar years. Richard Wright used to come here. So did James Baldwin.

These days, Haynes is more likely to feature in fiction than to be a vital presence in the French bistro scene or in the lives of African-Americans in Paris. In Jake Lamar's novel *Ghosts of*

Saint-Michel, the main character, Marva, has her own restaurant, Marva's Soul Food Kitchen. It is easily recognizable as Haynes:

> *Naima [Marva's daughter] stared straight ahead at Marva's Wall of Fame. . . . The pictures were all in black and white, most of them taken before Naima was born. Marva was in every one of them, smiling victoriously as she stood beside the likes of Ray Charles, Aretha Franklin, Jean-Paul Belmondo, Toni Morrison, Jeanne Moreau, James Baldwin and a couple dozen other prominent personages of the era. It was a stunning display of star power . . .*

Service at Haynes was part of the fun: for years the bar was presided over by Benny Luke, well known as a dancer and actor (he was Jakob in the original *Cage Aux Folles*). Benny ran Haynes with cheerfulness and charm.

Food at Haynes has the flavors of Creole cooking and the American South. We've sampled New Orleans-style shrimp gumbo and fried chicken, red beans, and rice platter there. The food was tasty and savory, and the wine drinkable and fairly priced. If you go there, you'll have time to admire the stuccoed wall with photographs of great stars who have stopped by. Taylor and Burton, in their youthful and beauteous stage, are the ones that stand out.

We remember one visit when we chatted with Benny Luke about the two leading actors in *Cage aux Folles.* "What were they like to work with?"

"I didn't know Ugo—he was an Italian I'd never met before, but the actor who played Zaza was a friend; we'd been playing the roles on stage for years before they made the movie," he said.

We hope that Haynes will resurrect itself.

❖ *Haynes: a significant part of African-American history in Paris.*

Polidor
41 rue Monsieur le Prince 75006 Paris (01.43.26.95.34)
Métro: Odéon
Mon–Sat noon–2:00 P.M., 7:00 P.M.–midnight

Richard Wright liked the Polidor, which is not far from the five-room apartment at 14 rue Monsieur-le-Prince where he lived from 1948 to 1959. The Polidor is an historic bistro from the late 19th century, with traditional French paneling in dark cream, a venerable tiled floor, oilcloth- and paper-covered tables which you'll be sharing if you go there for one of their low-priced, crowded lunches. The convivial atmosphere is

greatly enhanced by the motherly waitresses who whisk about. Featured are the old standards of bistro cuisine, with a main dish depending on the day of the week. On Tuesdays it's *hachis parmentier,* similar to meat loaf with mashed potatoes.

There's dark wainscotting, elegant old plate glass mirrors, some with the *vin du mois* (wine of the month) and other available vintages handwritten on them. A cheerful bistro feeling pervades this place. Mostly business people lunch here, but a few longhaired Left Bank intellectuals can be seen. The maîtresse d', a hefty, buxom blonde, bounds about the restaurant, greeting, shifting a placemat here and there, showing people where to go.

We started with fresh *crudités* and *oeuf mayonnaise* along with good bread. The main dish was an old reliable, puffy and golden *hachis parmentier,* meat loaf crowned with mashed potatoes. It's good, stick-to-the-ribs *cuisine de grand-mère.*

The service, although cheerful, was rather negligent; one of us received our *plat* several minutes earlier than the other, so we nibbled from one plate.

For dessert, we enjoyed the *baba au rhum,* the characteristic doughnut-shaped cake in a *crème anglaise* heavily fortified with rum, a delicious if intoxicating finish. The ice cream, two intense-flavored scoops of chocolate and coffee, may well be *fait maison* (made on the premises) as the menu claims.

❖ *Polidor: good value in an expensive area.*

Le Sélect
99 blvd du Montparnasse, 75006 Paris (01.42.22.65.27)
Metro: Vavin
Open daily 8:00 A.M.–3:00 A.M.

Le Sélect is the best preserved of any of the historic cafés. Here in 1957 Chester Himes worked on *A Jealous Man Can't Win,* part of his *Série Noire* novels for Marcel Duhamel, a director at Gallimard.

❖ *Le Sélect: worth a visit. Described in detail on pages 73–75.*

> ### *Le Tournon*
> 17 rue de Tournon 75006 Paris (01.43.26.16.16)
> RER: Luxembourg
> Mon–Fri 7:00 A.M.–8:00 P.M., closed August

Near the Senate behind the Jardin du Luxembourg, Le Tournon is an unremarkable little bistro, with nothing about it to indicate its importance in African-American life in the 1950s and '60s, or its status as virtual headquaters for George Plimpton's *Paris Review*. Even so, we've heard French people praise this café for its welcoming ambiance. A circular, copper bar has rounds of white neon above, but the café tables in this simple place are not marble, but formica. Tan banquettes line the walls, and the floor tiles are in a crazy-quilt pattern. A large pinball machine—possibly the same one Richard Wright used to play—blocks a view of handsome buildings across the way. An amiable-looking, middle-aged French couple tend bar.

Outside regular lunch and dinner hours you can choose large salads, sandwiches with *pain Poilâne*, or tasty cold plates of *jambon de Paris* (ham) or *rosbif* (cold roast beef) with salad. Prices are reasonable: sandwiches are from 3.50 euros and if made from *pain Poilâne*, from 5 euros; omelets and salads are from 6 to 8 euros. A hot *spécialité du jour* is available at mealtimes. Wines by the glass or a quarter, half or whole carafe, range from 4 to 12 euros. A Côtes du Rhône went well with our light lunches.

Our friend enjoyed her *rôti de porc* (roast pork) with *salade verte*. "It's a wonderful salad: the dressing is very mustardy and the pork is good," was her comment.

Regulars include a few retired people, businessmen from the area, an occasional politican from the Senate.

❖ *Le Tournon: an historic bistro that's worth a stop.*

MOVERS AND SHAKERS: THE 7TH & 8TH ARRONDISSEMENTS

People come to Paris, to the capital, to give their lives a sense of belonging, of an almost mythical participation in society.

—Marguerite Duras

The imposing seventh, the glamorous eighth: their importance is declared in the monuments around you, monuments like the Eiffel Tower, the Arc de Triomphe and the golden-domed Invalides. Like a ribbon through the center is the Champs-Elysées, splendid boulevard of trees and shopfronts dedicated to luxury or power, where citizens of the world come to promenade and take in an extraordinary vista stretching from the Arc to the Place de la Concorde.

What has not happened here? What could not happen in here? The air is alive with possibilities.

This was F. Scott Fitzgerald's Paris. When he got to France, with the best seller *The Side of Paradise* behind him, he had already "made it." No putting up in a squalid writer's garret on the Left Bank for him. To a friend he wrote, "We have taken an appartment [*sic*] in the Rue de Tillsit near the Etoile for 8 months and I have taken a studio near by to write in. We're glad to leave Italy and Paris in the Spring is no easy place to settle down to work. In fact most of our time is taken up in dodging our friends, most of whom seem to be over here."

For James Joyce, however, going out to see his friends was essential: "After I have worked all day, the thought of eating at home becomes unbearable. I want to see people,

I want to get away from the work.... One is free. It is wonderful to let go, to chat without reservations," he explained to a friend. To escape the monotony of home, Joyce frequented Fouquet's, on the Champs-Elysées. There he ordered oysters, chicken, mushrooms or asparagus, usually leaving them untasted. Instead he would concentrate his attention on the white wine that he consumed nightly. Once he told about meeting Proust. In their conversation the great French writer spoke about nothing but duchesses. "I was far more interested in their maids," Joyce recalled.

Here in the 7th arrondissement are concentrated the centers of power: the National Assembly and the ministries of Defense, Education, Industry, and Commerce. The 7th is the seat of the French government, an all-encompassing entity. The Eiffel Tower is here; so is the Musée d'Orsay, a favorite for most tourists. Much of the aristocratic "old money" lives here. Cole Porter had a large apartment in the 7th during the 1930s; his elaborate gilt Steinway is now tucked away in a corner of the American Cathedral parish hall. Celebrities like Alain Delon, the French counterpart of Marlon Brando, have apartments overlooking the river.

The 8th, lying directly north across the river from the 7th, houses much of the opulence and flamboyance of Paris. Many of the great fashion houses are here. Givenchy is on the avenue George-V, as is the luxury hotel of that name. Across the street is the Crazy Horse, the world's most famous—and expensive— strip club. Fouquet's, the legendary café that's a favorite of Arab princes and movie starlets, is on the corner of the Champs-Elysées. Avenue Montaigne, lined with the shops of fashion houses, used to be the home of Marlene Dietrich. If you see a red Ferrari or a yellow Lamborghini parked outside a building, it will almost certainly be here.

For real, old-fashioned glamor, what our generation (which advertising has taught the use of superlatives) refers to as "superstars," look above you. What could be loftier than the Jules Verne, on the second level of the Eiffel Tower, with a view over the most beautiful city in the world? Here, if you're going to spot them, come celebrities, people like Sylvester Stallone, Arnold Schwartznegger, and Madonna.

In the 8th arrondissement are the *temples de gastronomie*: Lucas Carton on the Place de la Madeleine, Taillevent on the rue Lamennais, and, on the vast sweep of the Place de la Concord, Les Ambassadeurs..

But the 8th arrondissement has been known as much for its stars and brilliant débuts as for any refinements of cuisine. At the Théâtre des Champs-Elyées, 13 to 15 avenue Montaigne, Josephine Baker and La Revue Nègre opened in 1925 and stunned the audience, many of whom were artists themselves, like Fernand Léger and Robert Desnos.

Near the Théâtre des Champs-Elysées is a bistro open to all: the Bar des Théâtres at 6 avenue Montaigne in the 8th district does not require that you belong to the world of fashion or the arts to sip coffee or wine at its bar or partake of substantial food in the restaurant section. There you can rub shoulders with a glamorous set: fashion models, actors, actresses, and others from the theater and film world including the theater across the street.

The Place de la Madeleine is not a bad beginning for a gourmet, with Fauchon on the northeast corner. The splendid interior is the closest French equivalent to Fortnum and Mason in London, a lavish, extravagant display of good things. Whether or not you have needs or desires, it is good to stop here for the visual delight of it all. Across the way, on the opposite side of the Place is Fauchon's rival, Hédiard. Different colors, of course—Hédiard packages in dramatic scarlet and black.

Although we started out with Fauchon, where we first learned the sublime possibilities of a French *sorbet*, in recent years we've come to spend more time at Hédiard. Somewhat smaller than its rival, less crowded, Hédiard seems less of a tourist attraction and more of a serious source.

Leave Hédiard and the Place de la Madeleine, and walk toward the Concorde. You are on the rue Royale, and one of the most impressive delights is still ahead. Forget monuments for a moment. A block to the right, on the rue du faubourg St.-Honoré is Hermès, with windows that are extraordinary in their color and originality. Inside, the sales assistants are courteous and expertly snap open glowing squares of silk for browsing shoppers.

Some dining possibilities in these exclusive districts:

L'Affriolé
17 rue Malar, 75007 Paris (01.44.18.31.33)
Métro: Alma-Marceau
Tues-Sat noon–2:30 P.M., 7:30–9:30, closed August
Wheelchair Access

"On est vraiment gâté ici" (we're very spoiled here) murmured a French businessman on our left as we sat down at L'Affriolé. By the look of the food he and his friend were contemplating, we'd agree that he had a point.

While waiting we looked about us, at the long, narrow room with a dozen tables, topped in bright mosaic tile, and at the rounded bar in deep red mahogany.

We took the 19-euro set lunch which promised 3 courses and a glass of wine. It's a sampler menu: a teaser of small portions of hors d'oeuvre, *plat,* and dessert, all served at the same time in little white dishes, a presentation reminiscent of Oriental restaurants. The starter was a *mousse de foie de volailles,* a chicken liver pâté with cream. Rich yet light. The

plat, a *sauté de boeuf et betteraves*, was tepid and lacked flavor. Dessert, *riz au lait à la vanille* (rice pudding) was more successful, a sophisticated version of the classic. With lunch we enjoyed a glass of Côtes de Luberon. A pleasant lunch, just enough to make us want to try the regular menu.

❖ *L'Affriolé: worthwhile if you're in the area, as is L'Ami Jean on the same street.*

Altitude 95
Eiffel Tower, 75007 Paris (01.45.55.20.04)
Métro: Champ de Mars or Trocadero
Open daily noon–3:00 P.M., 7:00 P.M.–11 P.M.
Elevator ticket: 4 euros
Wheelchair access

By the time we managed to ascend 300 feet to Altitude 95 in the Eiffel, we felt we'd helped to construct the famous tower—it was that challenging. You have to get a "lift" ticket, and you have to find the ticket window, or *guichet*, near the north *pilier* to get one. After that, it was just a matter of hiking briskly around the hundreds of grim-faced tourists who'd been waiting for the lift in the ordinary queues, getting to the north *pilier*, and waiting briefly for the elevator that would take us to the restaurant.

Altitude 95 has a fabulous view, and it is one of the few places in Paris where you'll see lots of children munching *frites* and sipping Coca-Cola from the 8-euro children's menu. Their parents, some in T-shirts and baseball caps, will be tackling substantial fare, possibly the 23-euro menu, like asparagus vichyssoise, followed by *rascasse* or chicken with green curry sauce, and after that Camembert or *île flottante*. The *menu du chef* not available, we chose *plats* à la carte: salmon with tomatoes and red bell peppers and chicken in a garlic and cream sauce for 23 euros. The *plats* were better than expected, the chicken well-flavored in a cream sauce with a subdued flavor of garlic, and the salmon hot, with the flavors of the South—tomato, bell pepper, and zucchini.

We were impressed by the house wine. It was very drinkable, better than many house wines we've tasted closer to the ground.

Desserts à la carte are 9 euros. We chose the *palet*, a multi-layered chocolate confection, with a base of vanilla-flavored *génoise*, topped with bittersweet chocolate and a layer of coffee bavarian. All in a *coulis de framboise*—raspberry sauce. A special conclusion to a palatable meal.

❖ *Altitude 95: a way to avoid the long lines for the Eiffel Tower. Reserve 5-6 weeks ahead for a window table, and don't be late.*

L'Atelier Renault
53 avenue des Champs-Elysées, 75008 Paris
(01.76.84.19.19)
Métro: George V
Open daily to 2:00 A.M.

This is an elegant designer café where people come to eat, drink, and watch the action on the Champs-Elysées. We have fond memories of a day when there was more action than usual, as we watched Lance Armstrong finish the Tour

de France bicycle race from a privileged lookout here.

L'Atelier Renault is a showplace for the car manufacturer, although no cars are sold here. No expense has been spared. In a sleek gray-and-silver interior you sit on Harry Bertoia designer chairs and admire the Champs-Elysées below. Like more ordinary cafés, Atelier Renault allows you to order just a drink. And since it was a warm day, we, and most of the people around us, also requested a *carafe d'eau* (ordinary Paris tap water) which came chilled.

There's usually a lunch special: this time it was pasta, ice cream or tiramisù and a glass of wine for 21 euros. We were content with club sandwiches with salad and mustardy mayonnaise on the side. Larger *plats*, including cod, slices of beef with tagliatelli, and Moroccan-style glazed lamb were from 18 to 20 euros.

And we remember the thrill years ago of watching the cyclists, as well as the company nearby of a quintet of United Airlines stewardesses, some of whom couldn't resist shouting encouragements to their favorite—"Go Lance!"—to the consternation of the serious-looking French people nearby.

❖ *Atelier Renault: a well-located designer café. A must-see.*

Au Babylone
13 rue de Babylone 75007 Paris (01.45.48.72.13)
Métro: Sèvres-Babylone
Mon–Sat lunch, closed August
No credit cards

There's no doubt about it—Au Babylone is the real thing. It's a buzzing, smoky, alive little bistro crowded with people, even toward the end of the regular lunch period. This is a no-nonsense, old-fashioned place, right next to the Bon Marché department store.

A good regular 20-euro bistro menu includes wine and hors d'oeuvres like *mousse de canard au porto* (duck mousse with port). A *plat* might be free-range chicken with potatoes, roast beef, leg of lamb, or *sole meunière*. After that you can have salad, cheese, and desserts like *clafoutis aux cerises* (cherry cake) and *glaces* (ice cream). Two or three wines are available with the noon menu.

One day we arrived late to find a dearth of choices left from the *prix fixe* menu at lunch. "Rosbif ou poisson?" (Beef or fish) asked the waitress. The *plat* pleased us both. A generous portion of *julienne*, a firm-fleshed white fish in *beurre blanc* (white wine and butter sauce) was well-flavored, accompanied by new potatoes.

The house pastry long gone, we chose *glaces* (ice cream) and were delighted with the French versions, in bitter chocolate, intense coffee, and pistachio.

The owner-chef, a dark-haired young man, emerged from the hot kitchen after all the clients were served. He told us about the beginnings of Au Babylone: His father came from Italy years ago, and discovering that the French weren't receptive to any cuisine but their own, he had started this as a French restaurant.

❖ *Au Babylone: authentic, completely unlike the slick, anonymous establishments we noticed on our way.*

Bistro de Paris
33 rue de Lille, 75007 Paris (01.42.61.16.83)
Métro: rue du Bac
Open daily noon–2:30 P.M., 7:00 P.M.–10:30 P.M.

This bistro is convenient to the Musée d'Orsay, a former train station and now a museum, once used by Orson Welles as a movie set. If you're in the 7th district, you may want to try this shiny, mirrored bistro. A small room is transformed with mirrors which give the illusion of an infinite number of tables extending out into the distance. The design suggests elegance and formality.

There's no set lunch but starters à la carte from 6 to 20 euros are varied and interesting, including items like red pepper with avocado and smoked ham, artichokes with goat cheese and thyme, and *carpaccio* of red tuna and small salad.

Plats range from 12 to 31 euros. For main dishes we chose fish and braised veal. Portions were ample, the *rascasse* (a Mediterranean fish used in bouillabaisse) hot and attractive on a bed of penne, with tomatoes and parsley giving color. The *fricassée de veau* (braised veal in wine sauce) was similarly garnished. The flavor of the veal was enhanced by a rich tomato base which included chunks of cooked artichoke. Le Bistro de Paris shows a strong Provençal influence, using a lot of tomato, olive oil, olives, eggplant, and zucchini.

Desserts, priced between 6 and 10 euros, are creative: soup of summer fruits, green apple sherbet with calvados, bittersweet chocolate dessert with raspberries, as well as traditionals like *crème brûlée*.

❖ *Le Bistro de Paris: a convenient choice in an expensive area.*

Boulangerie-Caféteria de la Tour Eiffel
21 ave. de la Bourdonnais, 75007 Paris (01.47.05.59.81)
Métro: Alma-Marceau
Tues–Sun 7:00 A.M.–7:00 P.M.

Not glamorous in itself, this *boulangerie-salon de thé*, but it's warm, bright, and provides better-than-average sandwiches and pastries. Above all, la Boulangerie has a terrace where you can sip your coffee and have a good look at the Eiffel Tower. Now that's worth something.

❖ *Boulangerie-Cafétéria de la Tour Eiffel: for the view.*

Le Café du Musée Jacquemart-André
158 blvd Haussmann, 75008 Paris (01.45.62.04.44)
Métro: Miromesnil
Open daily, 11:00 A.M.–6 P.M.
(Museum admission not necessary to visit café)

Would lunch in a fabulous mansion appeal to you? Then we would suggest the Musée Jacquemart-André, a museum on the boulevard Haussmann. The museum café used to be the dining room of the millionaire who built this extraordinary home in 1875. Before Madame Jacquemart-André died in 1912, she willed the mansion to become a private museum, open to the public.

When we go to the café we find ourselves in a palatial room. The walls are soft yellow, the ceilings high, the molding elaborate. Bas-reliefs around the edge of the ceiling recalling stories from mythology border a fresco which was brought from a villa near Venice. Tapestries soften the whole effect, and elaborate red-shaded lamps, lights emerging from leafy shapes in gold, give warmth and intimacy.

Too late for lunch one day, we ordered tea and pastry. Choosing was difficult, but we settled on a *framboisier*, an elaborate confection of *génoise*, pastry cream, and fresh raspberries, and a *truffée au chocolat*, like a rich and dense

chocolate mousse. With this there's a pot of the tea of one's choice.

On a Sunday, we heard a Parisienne mutter "Formidable!" as she stood on the magnificent stone terrace viewing the formal French garden with its colorful beds of wax begonias. Lunch or brunch is available on Sundays. Brunch, at 25 euros, starts with a basket of *viennoiserie* (pastries)—a croissant, *pain au chocolat*, sesame-seed rolls and bread with butter and jam, and a large glass of freshly squeezed juices. With the breads you have all of the strong coffee you can drink, and a plate of smoked salmon, a green salad, potato salad, and a warm poached egg topped with *fromage blanc* and chives. After all this there's fresh fruit salad or pastry.

❖ *Le Café du Musée Jacquemart-André: reasonable prices in palatial elegance.*

Le Café du Marché
38 rue Cler, 75007 Paris (01.47.05.51.27)
Métro: Ecole Militaire
Mon–Sat 7:00 A.M.–midnight, Sun to 4:00 P.M.
Wheelchair access

In the chic 7th arrondissement, would you expect to find a restaurant with an attractive terrace and cheerful service, offering enormous helpings of family-style food? If such a place existed it would be mobbed—and so it is. Rain was sprinkling a glossy finish on the paved street as we walked up from the Ecole Militaire métro.

At Le Café du Marché, we found ourselves waiting in line, glad to finally get a table wedged in between others on the plastic awning-covered terrace. The café was wild and noisy, full of energetic young twenty-somethings and their older compatriots. Most of the patrons were dressed-down yuppies from the area, what the French call "branché," but their avant-garde eyeglass frames gave them away. The elegant young men had short sculptured haircuts; their girls were more Calvin Klein than Gucci. We saw a Woody Allen lookalike in one corner, discussing, most likely, post-structural film theory with

his animated white-haired friend.

The salads served at Café du Marché are large and attractive—but it being chilly, we chose hot *plats*, the duck and the steak. They came on huge plates with more than enough rounds of rather greasy fried potatoes. Both were good, and served in portions that would satisfy a hungry Arkansas truck driver. A demi-carafe of St. Pourçain red was fairly priced. Around us *steak tartare* was popular, the young Frenchmen who'd ordered it dousing the raw ground beef with Heinz ketchup and Tabasco sauce. Others were munching club sandwiches.

We could (and should) have done without dessert, but the curvacious young waitress particularly recommended the *moelleux au chocolat*, the partially-cooked cake. One serving with *crème fraîche* was ample for the two of us. Other tempting desserts included *profiteroles*, *crème brûlée*, and *tarte tatin*.

❖ *Le Café du Marché: a high-density, high-energy place with noise levels to match. Simple meat-and-potatoes cooking at reasonable prices. Great fun.*

Le Clos des Gourmets
16 avenue Rapp, 75007 Paris
Métro: Alma-Marceau
Tues–Sat lunch and dinner, closed in August

Le Clos des Gourmets has a creative menu and an elegant setting near the Eiffel Tower. Upon entering, we found ourselves in a bright room, the interior attractive in yellow tones, with scumbled blue on the molding. The Irish artist in our party remarked on the beautifully finished decor.

Starters and *plats* were well prepared: the *carpaccio* of duck from the 33-euro menu looked like a flower, with lamb's lettuce and thin wafers of parmesan cheese for contrast and flavor. Duck *pâté* was presented in two slices of aspic, very flavorful with the good baguette and butter. Goat cheese-filled ravioli was a subtle and unusual starter with the warm olive oil and balsamic vinegar dressing. However our party of four found the portions skimpy, and we relied heavily on the Guigal red Côtes du Rhône and the bread to fill the gaps.

The *thon*, or tuna, was delicious with a crisp coating of sesame seeds and a warm vinaigrette on the greens and cooked tomatoes. The *foie de veau* (calf's liver) in a rich beef sauce, had with just a hint of balsamic vinegar to add a slight sweetness.

Desserts also showed ingenuity, and we were impressed by the *millefeuille,* crisp puff pastry of outstanding lightness with a delicious filling of lemon cream.

❖ *Le Clos des Gourmets: for an evening out with well-to-do Parisians. Recently we've been hearing mixed reviews.*

Le Village
25 rue Royale, Cité Berryer, 75008 Paris (01.40.17.02.19)
Métro: Madeleine
Mon–Sat 8:30 A.M.–7:00 P.M.

You can unpack your Jean-Paul Gaultiers and your Issey Miyakes—here you can wear them and feel right at home. Le Village is part of the expanding empire of the Costes Brothers. Their places are known for extravagant high styling, the kind seen in expensive decorating magazines. You see it here too. There are two ends to this little street where Le Village is: a graceful arch at one end opens on to rue Royale, and at the other near a wine shop is the rue du faubourg St-Honoré. One doesn't get much more exclusive than that. The flagship store of Hermès is around the corner. If you sit on the terrace you can see shoppers entering Chanel.

Many of the elegant *BCBGs* (yuppies) who come here sip from flutes of champagne and toy with plates of *saumon fumé.*

In a setting of unusual sophistication you can lunch on light *plats*, and salads, with wines by the glass. The food and drink are not inexpensive: *plats* go for from 20 to 28 euros, and wine by the glass from 7 euros. Lavish pastries are available for 11 euros.

Colors, soft and intense by turns, warm this little passageway. Across the street is the light periwinkle blue of a boutique that specializes in crystal. Beside it is the *vert wagon*—hunter green—of Barbour, competing with the deep red façade next door.

❖ *Le Village: great people watching. Style, not food, is the main attraction.*

La Fontaine de Mars
129 rue St-Dominique, Paris 75007 (01.47.05.46.44)
Métro: Ecole Militaire
Open daily noon–2:30 P.M., 7:30 P.M.–11:00 P.M.

Here even the table linens give one the feeling of being in a special place. They top the tables in red and white, with the words "La Fontaine de Mars" worked into the jacquard pattern. Framed posters and old photographs decorate the dark cream walls, along with old crockery jars, gleaming

copper pots, and antique Victrolas. A sense of intimacy is enhanced by the warm color and the red-and-cream gingham curtains at the windows. Outside is the real fountain of Mars. A basket of rough-textured, tasty *pain de campagne* was the right accompaniment for a terrine of lettuce with pickles, part of the 23-euro set lunch. An extra crock of pickles was put on the table. Our friend enjoyed a *salade de lapin* (rabbit salad) with preserved lemon, romaine lettuce, tomatoes, and red bell peppers, in a lemon and olive oil dressing.

Most wines are 19 euros and up—a half-bottle carafe is 11 euros. We chose the house red, a Brouilly, lighter than the Cahors which was the *vin du jour*.

The salmon was a large, perfectly-cooked portion with a small portion of white rice, on sizzlingly hot plates. Sauce Béarnaise, passed in a separate dish, was a simple and effective accompaniment.

We decided to forgo dessert, and walked outside to see the fountain and stone arches of the Place St. Dominique.

❖ *La Fontaine de Mars: an old-fashioned bistro in a lovely setting.*

La Petite Chaise
36-38 rue de Grenelle, 75007 Paris (01.42.22.13.35)
Métro: Rue du Bac
Open daily noon–2:00 P.M., 7:00 P.M.–11:00 P.M.

When does a monument become a tourist trap? At least that's what has happened to La Petite Chaise. Impressed by the location, we decided to try it.

First, its background: founded in 1680, la Petite Chaise is said to be the oldest restaurant in Paris. George Sand and Toulouse-Lautrec went there, and later Colette, Gide, and Giraudoux. The late president François Mitterrand was a regular in his student days. (We can understand why he later moved on to the Brasserie Lipp.)

The *formule* or set menu at 29.50 euros, available at lunch and dinner, allows an hors d'oeuvre, main dish and dessert.

The best part of our meal was the hors d'oeuvre: six little snails, served with garlicky butter, were hot and tasty. From there it was all downhill: the *parmentier de poisson* tasted as if there was little fish involved. The *cuisse de canard à l'orange* came with scalloped potatoes, both barely warm, served on cold plates. And there was no waiter in sight to listen to our comments. We had the distinct impression that duck and sauce had been cooked earlier in the day and inadequately reheated.

Accompanying the meal was a quite drinkable wine from the Touraine. Around us were tourists delving into the old standards with gusto—favorites were the onion soup and the *escargots*.

For dessert we chose the *entremet fruit de la passion*, a slice of jellied passion fruit nectar in a *coulis* of red fruits. Fair enough, but it was cloyingly sweet, completely contrary to the trend in desserts described by Chef Yannick Alleno of the Hotel Meurice. Speaking at the Cordon Bleu, he stated that people are requesting less sugar in desserts, not wanting to feel uncomfortably full.

That's unlikely to happen here, but the servers were friendly—when they're around—and the setting attractive if you happen to like gold brocade.

❖ *La Petite Chaise: cuisine fair-to-middling, with nothing very special.*

Le Petit Troquet
4 rue de l'Exposition 75007 Paris (01.47.05.80.39)
Métro: Ecole Militaire
Mon dinner, Tues- Fri noon–2:00 P.M., 7:00–10:30 P.M.,
Sat eves only
Closed Sunday and in August

Deeply romantic, Le Petit Troquet looks as if it could have been lifted from the pages of a prewar magazine. We went there after hearing about it from a knowledgeable Parisian. The dining area is small, with another little room in the back. Nothing here is minimalist or modern. Sitting at one of the snugly-fitted square marble tables, you get the feeling that you're in a welcoming place. A majestic brass coffee machine sits atop an old-fashioned marble-and-zinc bar. Everything shows attention and care here, all is clean and polished.

Soon after we entered the proprietess, slender and elegant, came to take our order. We noted that for 19.50 euros we could start with mixed salad with parmesan cheese, pumpkin soup, or risotto. The wine menu offered several possibilities: a red from the Touraine was ideal with lunch.

A good risotto, flavored with mushrooms, the tang of escargots, and plenty of butter, came in a black jasperware bowl: a warming *entrée* for a winter day. The pork that followed was a fragrant rich-bodied stew in a small cast-iron casserole with carrots and small potatoes, the meat so tender that it could be eaten with a fork. *Steak au poivre de sechwan* featured an unusually successful sauce. Both *plats* were generous, an encouragement to share.

The desserts were enticing, but we finished with cheese, Fourme d'Ambert, Pont l'Evêque, and Livarot, served with the good country-style bread.

After lunch, we talked with the proprietress, who explained what they're attempting to accomplish at Le Petit Troquet: to serve the *cuisine du terroir*, with "beaucoup de goût, bistrot mais raffinée." We'd say they have succeeded.

❖ *Le Petit Troquet: a small family-run gem in the chic 7th. Deservedly popular.*

Au Pied de Fouet
45 rue Babylone, 75007 Paris (01.47.05.12.27)
Métro: Sèvres-Babylone
Mon–Fri noon–2:30 P.M., 7:00 P.M.–9:45 P.M., Sat
noon–2:30 P.M. closed August
No credit cards

Alain Passard, the legendary chef at L'Arpège, one of Paris' great restaurants, was asked, "Where do you like to eat when you're not at work?" One place he mentioned was Au Pied de Fouet. Years ago Jean Cocteau, the artist and film director, was also a regular.

Au Pied de Fouet is one of the smallest, most old-fashioned bistros we've ever seen—and certainly the most popular. This combination led to the situation that a friend recalls: "It used to be mobbed. I remember Andrée yelling to everybody to take their coffee at the bar, so somebody else could have their place."

It's still mobbed. Over the years, this tiny hole-in-the-wall on the rue Babylone has maintained its popularity. Au Pied is highly original, and at lunch is crowded with "suits" and with people who know food.

The emphasis here is clearly on the cuisine, but the decor is memorable too: the zinc bar, the red-and-white checked tablecloths and curtains, postcards from all over thumbtacked to the rafters, colorful bric-a-brac above the bar including a cartwheel, a horse's harness, and other bits of farm memorabilia.

As you enter, if you know the elegant, gray-haired maîtresse d' (and most people do), you're greeted as if you were an old friend.

Au Pied de Fouet gives many hors d'oeuvre choices, at around 4 euros each, and several *plats*, most from 8 to 11 euros. It's typical bistro fare: *oeuf dur mayonnaise, crudités, assiette de charcuterie*, and so on. There's a *vin de la semaine*— in this case, a very drinkable Gamay Marionnet.

The food here is surprisingly well-flavored: the fish (*grenadier*, a delicate-flavored sea fish) in a delicious cream sauce was accompanied by white rice, the *faux-filet* (steak) good-sized with an accompanying purée of potatoes. There's not a major effort at presentation, but nobody cares when a meal tastes this good.

Afterwards, we shared one of the trademark desserts, *tarte aux amandes sauce chocolat*, the bittersweet chocolate sauce setting off the sweet almond tart.

The clientele are French, mostly regulars, including a number of longhaired, intellectual-looking types.

❖ *Au Pied de Fouet: a delightfully old-fashioned little retreat, not to be missed. Check out its equivalent in the 6th district, described on page 71.*

Chez Savy
23 rue Bayard, 75008 Paris (01.47.23.46.98)
Métro: Franklin D. Roosevelt
Mon–Fri noon–3:00 P.M., 7:30 P.M.–11:00 P.M.

Chez Savy has an immediate charm for lovers of Art Deco. There's a wonderful old train car feeling about this place—a train car preserved from the Jazz Age. This is true Deco. The mirrors that line the place are dimmed by age. Under them are bars and rails of aluminum at Deco right angles, and there are Deco fan shapes in the molding around the ceiling. Little lamps on Deco mounts shed a warm light. At odds with the stylish interior is the huge mounted head of a wild boar, glaring down from over the door leading into the back dining room.

Little booths and little tables cramp the back of the first *salle*; still, French businessmen and women, lawyers and journalists crowd in here for lunch and the air is punctuated by their staccato speech and animated gestures.

For 28.50 euros noon and night there's the starter, *plat* and dessert. On the regular menu, Chez Savy provides hors d'oeuvres like *oeufs pochés à la crème de ciboulette* (poached eggs with chives) or salads for about 8 euros all the way up to *foie gras* for substantially more. *Charcuterie* is a house speciality, as is beef from the Auvergne. Wine is available by the glass for 5 or 6 euros, and a 50 cl. (two-thirds of a bottle) carafe is from 12 to 19 euros.

We started with a raw mushroom salad with an olive oil and chive dressing. It was crisp and different. The bread was darker and more flavorful than the usual baguette. A *carpaccio de boeuf* was paper-thin slices of cured raw beef arranged over a plate with lemon and a sprinkling of mint. A salad complemented the flavor of the beef.

The *steak-frites*, better than we'd tasted at the Lipp, was topped by fried shallots and with *pommes allumettes*, tiny fried potatoes, light and not greasy.

Dessert, a scrumptious *tarte aux pêches*, was made on the premises.

❖ *Chez Savy: decent value in a high-priced area.*

Le Square
31 rue St-Dominique, 75007 Paris (01.45.51.09.03)
Métro: Latour-Maubourg
Mon–Sat to 10:45 P.M., closed Sat in August

The lesson everyone learns when traveling is to be flexible. We learned this again the other night when we were going to another well-known bistro. A look at the menu displayed outside was sufficient to discourage us. Imagine a fixed-price menu featuring *boudin* (blood sausage)! We felt we could do better than that. So we walked further along the rue St. Dominique and discovered Le Square.

Le Square is full of "squares"—conservatively-dressed people who expect value for their money. And they're getting it here. The printed menu lists an entrée and *plat* or *plat* and dessert for 19.50 euros at lunch or for 26 at night. Hors d'oeuvres might include *croustillant de crevettes* (crisp shrimp cake), *filets de rouget* (red mullet) and *six escargots* (snails).

In a hurry, we took two *plats*, duck with figs and rumpsteak, and were very satisfied. The duck was served in generous quantity and with delicious ripe figs in a dark, well-seasoned sauce, tasting of the sweetness of the fig and the rich meatiness of the duck. The beef was a good amount of sliced steak, arranged around the plate in an effective peppery sauce. A few vegetables would have been welcome, but we couldn't complain about the size of our portions or the quality of the meat.

Desserts included apple tart, *moelleux au chocolat* (half-cooked chocolate cake) and *vacherin fraise, coulis de fraises rouges*. We chose the latter, a meringue in a rich strawberry sauce with whipped cream. Delicious!

❖ *Le Square: outstanding value in a coveted location near the National Assembly and Les Invalides. You may need to reserve ahead.*

PARIS WITH A PAST: THE 9TH & 10TH ARRONDISSEMENTS

In Paris one should have everything or nothing. We often had nothing, and that had a special charm, because Paris more than any other city has pleasures available to the poor.

—Eleanor Perényi, *More Was Lost*

While the 7th and 8th arrondissements exude a feeling of privilege, the 9th and 10th bring us back to earth with a bump. They suggest life's realities—hard work and the struggle to get by, sometimes by dubious means.

Even the old Opera came into being because somebody tried to kill Napoleon III. On his way to the opera in 1858, he narrowly missed death in an explosion. One hundred and fifty Parisians and the horses pulling the emperor's carriage were killed. Napoleon was determined not to let anything like that happen again. He had the whole area redone, taking out some of the little narrow streets that could shelter future attackers, and replacing them with l'Avenue de l'Opéra.

He also commissioned a new opera building. Charles Garnier won the competition and designed what is now the old Opera, splendid in the ruffles and flourishes of its mid-19th-century decor.

Just north on the boulevard Haussmann are the department stores. Galeries Lafayette and Au Printemps bring in the crowds and make the 9th a major shopping district. The most striking part of each grand *magasin* is its oldest store, which you will find here. In the middle of the

115

original Galeries Lafayette on the ground floor is a center from which you can see all around you the different levels or galleries, each edged by elaborate railing, circling around and up toward a brilliant, multicolored dome at the top. Au Printemps has an even larger dome of fabulous stained glass.

The seedy side of the 9th runs along its edges, particularly the western side bordering the Gare St. Lazare. Garish and pathetic-looking streetwalkers strut in front of shopfronts dominating a short stretch near the rue d'Amsterdam. Farther north, where the 9th arrondissement meets the 18th, the boulevard de Clichy and the Places Blanche and Pigalle are infested with sexshops and associated activity.

This is Henry Miller's Paris. He worked briefly for the *Chicago Tribune* at 5 rue Lamartine in the 9th. His friend Alfred Perlès, who was working as a proofreader, got Miller a job doing the same thing. They would work at night, stopping after work to eat at a nearby bistro. Other customers at the bistro included pimps, prostitutes, and newspapermen. Miller relished the café atmosphere, which he described in a letter to Anaïs Nin:

> It's like the monkey house... And such a noise! Laughter from the bar, like shrieks from the madhouse. I don't know of any café in Paris where there is such a diversity of types. It's foul—but exhilarating. And you can get a casse-croûte at all hours.

The street of Notre-Dame de Lorette, running through the center of the 9th, was named after the church. "Lorettes" was the name given to young girls who came up to Paris from the countryside intending to make a living in the capital, and who were often lured into the oldest profession. Emile Zola gives us a view of that life in his novel *Nana*:

> There, until two o'clock in the morning, the lights of the restaurants, the brasseries and the pork butchers, blazed away, whilst a swarm of women hung about the doors of the cafés.

The poverty of this area, the cheap rents, and the notoriety kept out the bourgeoisie, but it did not deter writers from making the Notre-Dame de Lorette district their home. Thackeray, De Maupassant, and Dumas all lived around here.

The rue Pigalle, now scruffy and disreputable, was home to artists and writers: Edouard Vuillard and Pierre Bonnard lived at number 28, George Sand and Frédéric Chopin at number 16. Victor Hugo was home at number 55 and at number 60 you could have found Charles Baudelaire.

If you continue north on the rue du faubourg Montmartre, going up the street and to the right when you get to the rue Richer, you will see the Folies Bergère. A surprising sight, the Folies doesn't seem to belong. The façade is an Art Deco masterpiece, out of place among the dark little streets, kosher delis, and small shops, an island of illusion in an otherwise dilapidated district. Here Josephine Baker made a famous appearance in 1926. Clad in little more than a string of bananas, she was a triumph. Charlie Chaplin and the novelist Colette are among the other legendary names who appeared here.

Nowadays, the show at the Folies Bergère is still entertaining and tame enough that tourists who are not offended by bare-breasted dancers sometimes take their children along to enjoy the show. A former dancer at the Folies told us about the reality behind the glamorous show. His memories of the place are not particularly positive: "They expected us to do an incredible amount of work for little money. Two shows a day. We finally had to go on strike."

It is hard to believe now that the Grands Boulevards running on the southern edge of the 9th and 10th arrondissements were ever anything more than they seem today, noisy, polluted, and dominated by the traffic. John Russell has written that the boulevards today have lost the "wayward, improvisatory quality" that we most value in Paris. Yet soon after their creation by Haussmann in the mid-nineteenth century, they were the place to be, the Paris equivalent of Fifth Avenue in New York or Oxford Street in London. Fashionable people met their friends in the cafés on the boulevard des Italiens, particularly at the Café de Paris, Tortoni's, the Café Riche, and the Café Anglais. You would need an introduction to be accepted by the well-to-do habitués of what would seem to us like private clubs.

Not every visitor, however, is an enthusiast of the Railway Quarter. The clifflike tenements, the Alsatian restaurants, the disquieting glass-roofed passages, and the submarine smells that drift from the shellfish stalls along the Rue Saint-Lazare—these are not for every taste....

—John Russell, Paris

Farther east in the 10th arrondissement are the two railway stations, the Gare du Nord and the Gare de l'Est, their great fan-shaped roofs beloved of Impressionist painters and filmmakers.

But the neighborhoods around the great railway stations tend to be drab and dilapidated. Not exactly prime territory for bistros. No one expects to sit out on a terrace with the soot and grime that go along with railway stations, and half the fun of a Parisian café or bistro is the chance to sit on a terrace and observe street life. Yet striking exceptions to the dreary conventional bistros are scattered here and there in the 9th and 10th districts. One of them is the Brasserie Terminus Nord, across the street, now owned by the Groupe Flo, splendid with its mirrors and long curving bar.

When we think of the 10th arrondissement, the name Strasbourg-St. Denis comes to mind. Strasbourg-St. Denis is one of the major *ponts de change*, or métro changing stations in Paris. From there are a multitude of possibilities. The neighborhood above the métro has brightened up, become somewhat safer than it used to be, but one should still be cautious about walking there late at night.

Is there anything romantic about the 10th arrondissement? Yes there is if you go to the Canal Saint-Martin, angling down from the north. This canal is the site of the French movie named after the Hôtel du Nord on its bank. Arletty, the celebrated and controversial French actress, star of Marcel Carné's great films *Les Enfants du Paradis* and *Hotel du Nord,* lived in an apartment overlooking the canal. Romantic little bistros and wine bars are dotted here and there along the quays, and in the evenings, intense young couples wander hand-in-hand beside the water.

An anomaly in the 9th district, the Café de la Paix is something you'll see just as surely as you will view the Eiffel Tower and Notre Dame. Situated at 5 Place de l'Opéra, this

has been one of the watering-places of the great and famous. The menu boasts of habitués that included King Edward VIII, Enrico Caruso, Oscar Wilde, Maurice Chevalier, Josephine Baker... the list goes on and on. Wilde is said to have glimpsed an angel fluttering on the pavement here. In our own time, John Travolta, Shirley MacLaine, and Placido Domingo have dropped by.

But for serious bistro fare, try one of these:

Restaurant de Bourgogne
26 rue des Vinaigriers, 75010 Paris (01.46.07.07.91)
Métro: Jacques Bonsergent
Mon–Fri lunch and dinner, Sat lunch, closed
mid-July–August 21

Chez Maurice or Le Restaurant de Bourgogne is on an obscure street just off the Canal Saint-Martin, a few blocks from the République. It's a storybook-style bistro, with low ceilings, red-and-white tablecloths, and a happy buzz from the many who jam it to bursting.

Diners do not go to Chez Maurice to sample cutting-edge cuisine or to mingle with the beautiful people. You'll find inexpensive, tasty fare served in generous portions, country dishes that the typical French grandmother might have prepared. Big containers of salt, pepper, and mustard are ready on the tables, and when someone requested ketchup, the waitress cheerfully produced it.

Blackboards hanging at crazy angles give you the wine list and the three-course menu, which changes daily. Wines are mostly unknown reds, but the Côtes du Rhône we chose was a remarkably good value.

Traditional bistro fare awaits you here for prices which are hard to find elsewhere: a set menu for 13 euros in the evening? We could hardly believe it ourselves. Hors d'oeuvres included the classics: *charcuterie* (cold cured meats) and *oeufs à la mayonnaise* (egg with mayonnaise). Salads were very fresh. We remember looking at a plate of *crudités* and thinking that this would be enough by itself.

Afterward you could select from a list that includes dishes like *boeuf flamand* (beef braised in beer) and *filet de merlue à la portugaise* (hake, a type of codfish). All came with accompaniments of *frites*, *pommes vapeur* (steamed potatoes), or *pois et carottes*, and each was pronounced "Bon" or "Très bon" by our French friends who had ordered them.

The third course was a choice of cheese or dessert. Everyone in our group of five opted for the sweet finish. Desserts included *tarte aux pommes à l'alsacienne* (apple pie), judged rather too sweet, and the *crème caramel* which was successful.

❖ *Le Bourgogne: low prices, generous servings, outstanding value.*

Brasserie sous la Coupole
6th floor Au Printemps Mode, 64 blvd Haussmann
(01.42.82.58.84)
Métro: Havre-Caumartin
Open store hours, Mon–Sat 9:30 A.M.–3:30 P.M.

A lot of change has been going on: the dazzling, multicolored dome, a sight once available to any shopper, has been closed in so that it's now only visible to diners at the Brasserie. Created by master glassmaker Brière in 1923, the dome was dismantled and stored in 1939, and forgotten for decades after the war. Finally it was reassembled in 1973 by the grandson of the original glassmaker.

In our experience, the food here is not up to the level of the best bistros. Things have improved, and if you want to dine in an historic monument you can enjoy substantial *plats* like tarragon chicken and medaillons of lamb for from 20 to 25 euros. A *formule* or menu with entrée, *plat* and dessert is 26 euros. You may want to try the *salon de thé* in the afternoons.

❖ *Brasserie sous la Coupole: important for the setting. One of the sights of Paris.*

Chartier
7 rue du faubourg Montmartre, 75009 Paris
(01.47.70.86.29)
Métro: Grands Boulevards
Wheelchair access
Open daily noon–3:00 P.M., 6:00–10:00 P.M.

Chartier, an enormous and stunning restaurant with a memorable late 19th-century interior, is one of the oldest and best-known *bouillons* in Paris. It was part of a string of such places constructed around Paris, designed to provide cheap, nourishing sustenance (bouillon soup and *pot-au-feu*) for working-class people. We recall a time when the place was so informal that newcomers were allowed to stand behind tables waiting for diners to finish. Waiters would dash from the kitchen bearing 8 to 10 plates on their arms. Patrons were trusted to figure out their own bills, adding up prices on the paper tablecoverings. We improved our French by learning to order at top speed, a necessity in the frantically busy place. Chartier is still popular with Parisians and tourists alike, who come to savor its tasty food and reasonable prices in the bustling, usually crowded and still-splendid premises once frequented by Chevalier, Mistinguett, and Piaf.

❖ *Chartier: the ambience of Old Paris in a budget restaurant. Lively and still fun.*

La Grille
80 rue du faubourg Poissonière, 75010 Paris
(01.47.70.89.73)
Métro: Poissonière
Open weekdays, closed last 2 weeks in August

Years from now, when you dream about your days in France, the meals at old-fashioned bistros like La Grille will be among the experiences you'll relive with the greatest pleasure. Even if your grandmothers were French, you'd be lucky to

remember their cooking as having been as good as that served here. Happily, this is also one of the friendliest bistros in Paris. The Cullères have run this place for nearly three decades, and they bring to it the warmth of a favorite aunt and uncle.

La Grille is a proudly traditional, old-fashioned place set in two old rooms with woodwork and rooms obviously repainted many times with that special Burgundy shade of shiny enamel so popular in Paris. Traditional lace curtains are everywhere; there are also fresh flowers, an old birdcage, old oval mirrors, framed certificates, a large brass hat rack, huge plates of fruit and cheese, and even a large dog guarding the door to decide if you're worthy to come in. He always consents.

La Grille is a small bistro with only nine tables serving eighteen people, so reservations might be wise. Everything here is à la carte, but the prices are moderate considering the quality of the food.

Cooking is traditional and very good. We started by sharing an entrée of a large and very fresh salad, the *frisée aux lardons*, 9 euros, which harbored long strips of smoked bacon. Classic country dishes like *boeuf bourguignon* were on the menu for 17 euros, and the man next to us who'd ordered that seemed pleased, but we both ordered the house specialty, *turbot grillé beurre blanc*, a delicate white fish with a rich butter sauce. It's a dish served only for two, at 66 euros, with probably high caloric and cholesterol levels, but you can share your guilt as well as your pleasure and assure each other it's well worth the risk. Our wine was the Menetou-Salon Domaine de Chatenoy, a luscious white from the Loire.

At the end, a dessert of fresh berries with mango and small figs along with a small pitcher of *cassis* (blackcurrant) syrup was a perfect finish.

❖ *La Grille: a charming, country-style bistro with high quality at fair prices.*

Chez Michel
10 rue de Belzunce, 75010 Paris (01.44.53.06.20)
Métro: Gare du Nord
Tues–Sat noon–2:00 P.M., 7:00 P.M.–midnight, closed August

Chez Michel is just off the grimy boulevard Magenta near the Gare du Nord, on a relatively pleasant little street. The train station seems far away when you enter this serious restaurant, where the 30-euro menu offers a three-course meal noon and night. The chef's experience at the Crillon and the Tour d'Argent shows up in his ideas, as well as in their execution.

Dinner there recently started with an unusual *amuse-gueule*. Before we ordered we sampled a dish of *bigorneaux*, or winkles, served in their shells accompanied by mustard-flavored mayonnaise. We were given pins with which to retrieve the snail-shaped little creatures, and the hunt was worth the effort: they were delicious.

Hors d'oeuvres were of an interest and generosity one seldom sees. The crunchy Breton cakes with wild greens on top were actually little rounds of toast, still warm, with *chèvre*—goat cheese—and greens in a warm vinaigrette, all serving to accentuate the flavors. The tasty oxtail pâté would be a great hors d'oeuvre if you arrived famished; the large jar was enough for two or three people, with accompanying pickles and mustard and good *pain de campagne.*

Between courses there was time to take in the interior, which is like an old Norman farmhouse with beams and plaster. A central column with shelves built around it holds wine bottles and blackboards with the day's selections, and servers were informally dressed. Occasionally they seemed a little confused. But the service was friendly and prompt, and that was what counted.

The *dorade* (sea bass) came to the table hot on a warm plate with a topping of lamb's lettuce and little flakes of white cheddar for contrast. It was light and crisp with a flavorful purée of garlic potatoes. Very fresh and appetizing, the tuna was served on a bed of puréed zucchini.

For dessert, we chose the Paris-Brest, a pastry confection of two cream puffs stacked with a coffee cream filling, light and tasty. The coffee and cream served as admirable foils for each other.

❖ *Chez Michel: outstanding value. You'll need a reservation.*

Restaurant Julien
16 rue du faubourg St-Denis, 75010 Paris (01.47.70.12.06)
Métro: Strasbourg-St.Denis
Open daily to 1:00 A.M.
Wheelchair access

For many years the Julien was quite likely the most beautiful, the cheapest, and almost certainly the worst restaurant in Paris. We seldom dared to eat much. We would go there to admire the extraordinary Art Nouveau interior, which the Flo Group restored to its original splendor when it bought the place years ago.

When you enter this brasserie, you want to rub your eyes and wonder if you're in a peculiarly baroque sort of dream.

For the Julien can't be real—but it is. Not an easy place to
describe, because all you want to do is look, and look some
more, at the dazzling excesses of the most extravagant Art
Nouveau decor we have ever seen.

It's not just the panels of glorious, sensual women who could have walked out of a Mucha painting; it's the molding, the bas-reliefs of beneficient goddesses, smiling down from above the floral-shaped lights. They in turn are surrounded by bas-reliefs of fruit, flowers, the harvest, and everything in the curves and swirls that suggests ripeness, fecundity, abundance.

But the food—ah yes, there is the food. Some might call this *cuisine industrielle*, unvarying from day to day, but it's surprisingly satisfying. The *menu Julien* is 26 euros, but after 10:00 P.M. the more limited *Faim de nuit* 20-euro menu is available. Judging by the din, many were enjoying it. The regular menu also offers a *demi* of a Côteaux d'Aix, the *menu Faim de nuit* supplying just food.

One of us started with *soupe de melon*, little scoops of cantaloupe with grapefruit wedges and a touch of sauterne: delicious, unusual and refreshing. The other chose *carpaccio de saumon*, chopped fresh and smoked salmon with olive oil and chives. Flanked by a salad of romaine lettuce in a well-flavored vinaigrette, it was quite satisfactory, with the accompanying crusty rolls of *pain de campagne*.

Then the main course: the *magret de canard*, slices of duck breast, brown outside and red within, artfully arranged on the plate. With it an effective and unusual sauce tasting of white and yellow peaches. Served with crisp, brown *pommes sautées*, this was delicious. The *jambonnet de volaille*, a plump chicken thigh in a Creole sauce with parsleyed rice was more predictable but still successful.

Desserts, so often neglected in brasseries, were well done. One of the specialties was a *granité de pommes au vieux Calvados,* a tart green apple sherbet, cool and intense, its flavor only emphasized by the generous slosh of Calvados that our obliging waiter spilled over it. A *fondant au chocolat* was lighter-textured than most, the chocolate comple-mented by coffee-flavored *crème anglaise*.

❖ *Restaurant Julien: opulent and romantic, a sentimental favorite.*

La Marine
55 bis quai de Valmy, 75010 Paris (01.42.39.69.81)
Métro: République
Mon–Sat 8:30 A.M.–midnight

At lunch, La Marine vibrates with the energy of a young, artistic clientele. This crowded and cheerful turn-of-the-century bistro has the old bistro standards chalked up for its daily specials. Wines are available by the glass or quarter or half carafe, with most glasses 3 euros and up.

A large plate of *brandade de poisson* is served by the young waitress. The good fish in potato purée with spinach and a hint of nutmeg is filling yet subtle.

Time for dessert: the *serveuse* repeats the list and assures us, "Tout est fait à la maison" (It's all made here). We finish by going for decadence, with *gâteau au chocolat.* The cake is rich and heavy—a little *crème anglaise* would help.

Service is friendly and informal. Next to us, two artists discuss an upcoming exposition in San Francisco, reminding us again that this is indeed a small world.

❖ *La Marine: on Canal St. Martin, a stop for the young and the "in" crowd.*

Le Parmentier
12 rue Arthur Groussier, 75010 Paris (01.42.40.74.75)
Métro: Goncourt
Mon–Fri lunch and dinner, Sat dinner, closed August

It's a short walk from the canal and the Place de la République is the closest large square, but Le Parmentier's air of quiet refinement, its tasteful yet spare decor make this little restaurant seem a world away from the noisy square.

A generous two-course lunch menu is only 16 euros. Although at these prices it could be considered a budget restaurant, we were pleased to notice touches of luxury: flowers and an *amuse-gueule* of *tapenade aux olives* with toasted slices of baguette, to engage our attention while we awaited our hors d'oeuvres. Ravioli stuffed with cheese in a delicately-flavored cream sauce with a touch of nutmeg provided an unusual start. The house bread is not the usual Parisian baguette, but a good *pain de mie*, soft-crusted white bread.

Wines, mostly under 22 euros, include the recent years of small vintners. A carafe of Pays d'Oc in red, white, or rosé, large enough for two, was very drinkable at a modest 11 euros. The *dorade*, or sea bream, on a bed of fennel garnished with lime, was well-flavored, a pleasant and tasty light lunch. The *daube de boeuf,* a stew cooked in red wine, provided a hearty and substantial meal.

At Parmentier the emphasis is on flavor rather than presentation, and the artistic-appearing patrons who drift in from the untouristy 10th look as if they wouldn't have it any other way.

At Le Parmentier the *fondant au chocolat* is what other bistros call a *moelleux,* an undercooked chocolate cake, with the rich dark chocolate center oozing past the crust with a touch of the fork. Cold *crème anglaise* (custard sauce) provides a nice contrast. Tiny post-meal desserts—candied orange slices and miniature lemon tarts—go well with coffee to round out the experience.

❖ *Le Parmentier: excellent value in a setting with charm.*

Chez Prune
36 rue Beaurepaire, 75010 Paris (01.42.41.30.47)
Métro: Jacques Bonsergent
Open daily to 2:00 A.M.

The best way of describing this old Paris neighborhood now evolving into a fashionably artistic part of the city might be "shabby chic." Chez Prune is one of the most popular bistros in the neighborhood, a hot spot for young people. On warm summer nights, the crowds, mostly habitués in their twenties, line up almost onto the street trying for an evening here. Here you're facing the Canal St. Martin and if you walk a few hundred yards down the canal, you find the Hôtel du Nord, the setting for the classic film of that name.

If you can't get into Chez Prune any other time, breakfast or lunch is possible in this hangout. A shabby-chic theme is carried on in the mismatched tables and chairs, the general studied scruffiness. The young who come here love it.

This is a good place for a drink, given the variety of wines, the futuristic bar stools, and lively ambiance. Starting at 3 euros a glass, wines from the Touraine, Bordeaux, and the Rhône region might be a better bet than the harsh-tasting coffee.

A typical menu offers promising possibilities, hors d'oeuvres and a *plat* for 15 euros. One day starters included *potage du Bercy* (fish soup), *petite quiche au fromage et crevettes* (cheese and shrimp quiche). For a *plat*, there was *gratin de poisson à l'estragon* (fish gratin with tarragon), *agneau aux échalottes* (lamb with shallots), or *salade auvergnate*. But one suspects that the young people's attentions are more focused on each other rather than on the food.

❖ *Chez Prune: an "in" place for a lively, young, and artistic crowd.*

Au Rendez-Vous des Belges
23 rue Dunkerque, 75010 Paris (01.42.82.04.72)
Métro: Gare du Nord
Open Sun–Wed 5:30 A.M.–2:00 A.M., Thurs–Sat to 4:00 A.M.

Just opposite the Gare du Nord, the Rendez-Vous des Belges is a little railroad car of a café that's open almost around the clock and offers a great variety of Belgian beers on tap. While awaiting a train you may want to stop here for *steak-frites* (steak and French fries), *boeuf haché-frites* (hamburger and fries), *saucisson* (dry salami) or *omelette-frites*, all under 10 euros.

There's a coin-operated telephone in the back, useful if you haven't yet purchased a telephone card at a Tabac or post office.

The Rendez-Vous is modern and slick in its small way. A pinball machine, not quite fitting in, is obviously, noisily, there.

Shunning the fancier Terminus Nord, train conductors pop in here before their shifts start. Some of them have a word with the barman in Flemish.

❖ *Au Rendez-Vous des Belges: an authentic railroad café. Stop here before you board your train to London.*

Le Sainte Marthe
32 rue Sainte-Marthe, 75010 Paris (01.44.84.36.96)
Métro: Belleville
Mon–Sat 10:00 A.M.–2:00 A.M., Sun noon–8:00 P.M.

If you want to escape the usual tourist rounds in search of Parisian authenticity, go to the rue Sainte-Marthe, near the Belleville métro station in the 10th arrondissement. Belleville is the district of the poor and the hardworking, the ethnics who come from everywhere hoping to sink their roots in Paris. You get off at the Belleville métro station and walk through a scruffy but not dangerous area. We passed a sweatshop where young Chinese men, stripped to the waist, were pressing clothing possibly for sale in an expensive boutique. We heard several languages which were neither French nor English.

Some of the concrete apartment buildings making up the square are painted in pastels, an uncommon sight in northern France. These are not expensively-constructed buildings with stone carved facades, but functional and cheap accommodations for the poor. You may notice laundry hanging from windows. The dogs here are not pedigreed and a parked car may lack a hubcap. It all seems very Latin, very Mediterranean, and the ambiance is local, relaxed and still wildly animated. The huge *terrasse* was overflowing on a summer night, with new arrivals reluctantly having to leave the tree-shaded square and move to the hot colors of the interior.

At Le Sainte Marthe, wines are from 5 to 6 euros for a quarter *pichet*, 9 to 11 euros for a half, and 12 to 21 for a full bottle, with a selection of less-known regions, a Côtes du Tarn, for example, and a Vaucluse. We were pleased with the white we chose, a Domaine de Tarriquet.

We arrived too late to eat, but noted that hors d'oeuvres were mostly around 6, and substantial-looking *plats* from 10 to 16 euros. One of our neighbors on the little park chairs beside the green metal tables enjoyed an impressive-looking smoked salmon salad.

❖ *Le Sainte-Marthe: currently a hot spot with young Parisians and the closest thing in Paris to a small town in Provence.*

MOVING UP IN THE WORLD: THE 11TH & 12TH ARRONDISSEMENTS

That poor boulevard Richard-Lenoir! What on earth has given it that bad reputation! All right, so it does end at the Bastille. Okay, so it is surrounded by miserable slummy little streets. The whole section is full of workshops and warehouses.... Too bad for those who despise the Boulevard Richard-Lenoir.

—Georges Simenon, *Maigret's Special Murder*

The 11th and 12th arrondissements of Paris always remind us of the lower East Side of New York. Tough, authentic, direct, sometimes a little devious, maybe even cruel, they are packed with the old smells and sounds of a dozen countries. The 11th and 12th arrondissements have never been *quartiers* of choice, but places that people escaped from. Now, though, this section has become, if not a home, at least an inspiration to some of the best creative young minds in France.

The 11th district, for years snubbed by snobs and avoided by the well-to-do, has come up in recent years with the building of the new Opéra. Stretching from the Place de la Bastille to the République, up to the rue du faubourg du Temple, and east to the boulevard Ménilmontant, the 11th has no monuments to boast of, no palaces, no scenic parks.

But it has a past. Walking down the boulevard du Temple, going from the Place de la République toward the Bastille, you pass the Cirque d'Hiver, or Winter Circus. Hemingway sparred a few rounds here with some of his friends who could be persuaded to join him in boxing. Here Fellini filmed part of *The Clowns*. And who would have thought that this neglected monument, with its bas-reliefs of horses and

warriors along the top, would be the inspiration for a little boy who would become an international star?

To Maurice Chevalier, the Cirque d'Hiver was, quite simply, paradise. He was growing up in a one-parent family in the working-class suburb of Ménilmontant when he went to the circus for the first time. His mother bought the cheap, standing-room tickets which were all she could afford, and they climbed up behind the top seats and clung to the ceiling. To ten-year-old Maurice the circus and the performers were the most exciting thing he'd ever seen:

> [T]he show unfolded before us like a magic spell, an enchantment.... But it was the star tumbling act that thrilled me the most. Here a boy exactly my own age... was catapulted into the air and then caught in a perfect sitting position, hurled once more into a double somersault and caught again... The crowd would go crazy...

Later the Chevaliers waited to see the circus stars coming out onto the rue de Crussol in their ordinary street clothes. The Chevaliers followed them on foot as far as they could, thrilled to be close to such extraordinary people. Then the performers went to a nearby tavern (possibly the Clown Bar) after the evening show, and the Chevaliers walked all the way back to Ménilmontant.

Dazzled by the performances he had seen, young Chevalier decided to become an acrobat. Not especially agile, and "without the strength of a kitten in my little legs," he nevertheless kept practicing with his brother. A fall, a bloody nose, and swollen face, and he had to promise his mother he'd renounce the dream.

With acrobatics an impossibility, Chevalier started to think about other options. Perhaps he could sing for a living. Show business seemed to him his only hope for avoiding the inevitable for a poor boy from Ménilmontant, a boring life as an ordinary workman. As he wrote in *My Paris*, "The reason I became a music-hall performer is that I did not have enough skill to be an acrobat!"

Half a century earlier, Victor Hugo, author of *Les Misérables*, became involved in a real-life drama on the rue de la Roquette near the Bastille. Then as now, this street was dotted with cafés and bars. During the 1848 revolution, some revolutionaries met in cafés. The proprietor of a café on the rue de la Roquette was a man named Auguste. In June Hugo managed to save him and three of his friends from being executed for having fought on the barricades. "If ever you need me, for whatever purpose, come," said the grateful café owner. Afterward, Hugo had to take Auguste up on his promise to hide him. As a member of the outlawed National Assembly, Hugo had become a wanted man himself.

Today the rue de la Roquette is still lively and raucous at night, its tiny bistros, bars, and boutiques drawing people from the more sedate parts of the city.

The Gare de Lyon is just south of the Place de la Bastille. In this particular *gare* or train station, there is a sense of enticing possibilities. Here is a quick escape from the often gray, rainy North to the South—four and a half hours on the TGV, and you're looking at the Mediterranean.

Much of the 12th is given over to the unglamorous but necessary in life: hospitals and transportation. The hospital Quinze-Vingts, specializing in eye problems, is next to the

Place de la Bastille and behind the Opera. Just behind them lies a tangle of railway lines and broad thoroughfares.

Untouristy though they seem, these parts of Paris, particularly the 11th, account for a sizeable proportion of our recommendations. The reason is in the rents. For the 11th district a change started from 1994 to 1995, when a few bold entrepreneurs decided to take a chance. Their revolution started on the rue Oberkampf with the renovation of the Café Charbon, still the most attractive bistro in the district. Renewal has now spread to the rues Saint-Maur and Ménilmontant.

This area has great bistros—funky little bistros, late night cafés, dark little clubs featuring Caribbean music. If you ever find an old man with an accordion serenading you in a restaurant, it will most certainly be here. The area east and north of the Marais is vibrant with life, almost a new Marais, overrun with stylish shops and with-it cafés. Lower rents than elsewhere in the city encourage people who've had the dream of someday opening a modest bistro. A surprising number of the most talked-about addresses in the city are here, livening up a district that used to be very staid, dedicated to the small industries, workshops, and ateliers. When the smart young Parisian wants a night out, he won't take his girl to the Champs-Elysées or the Latin Quarter; they'll come to the 11th or possibly the 12th arrondissements.

Astier
44 rue J-P. Timbaud, 75011 Paris (01.43.57.16.35)
Métro: Oberkampf
Open Mon-Sat noon–2:00 P.M., 8:00 P.M.–10:15 P.M.,
Closed 8 days Easter, Christmas, August

We were tempted to avoid Astier, having experienced mediocre food and indifferent service there. But as we've found, Astier has changed.

We started with *coquillages et crustaces,* a generous seafood platter that included an oyster on the half shell, clams, shrimp, and whelks, served with good house-made mayonnaise and a lemon. It was fresh and good, proving that Astier has a high-quality supplier.

One of our *plats*, a *tranche de poitrine de cochon*, was a dark slice of pork served on white porcelain with an artful splash of sauce. The pork had been seared and was dark with a crisp coating. It was crunchy and delicious, enhanced by a sauce that used beets and turnips with a touch of honey for sweetness. The other *plat*, a *pintade de fermière grand-mère*, or free-range guinea hen, came hot in a Le Creuset dish. It was a leg and thigh of *pintade*, served in a well-flavored sauce involving bacon and *legumes de saison*: small mushrooms, pearl onions, carrots and parsley. The carrots, cooked separately and added at the last minute, retained a nice crispness. With the *plats* we enjoyed a dark and flavorful *pain de campagne*.

The Astier of today does desserts well. The *parfait au chocolat* was a perfect little mound of chocolate mousse, finished with a coating of bittersweet chocolate, and resting on a praline base. A delight.

Wines are available by the glass for 6.50, by the *pichet* from 19, or by the bottle from 22 euros. Most people at this lunchtime did not order wine. The clientele on a March day were almost exclusively French, in their young to middle years. It looks like an artsy crowd: at the table on our left was a man who could have played Cyrano.

❖ *Astier: the changes have made this a top bistro once again.*

La Biche au Bois
45 ave. Ledru-Rollin, 75012 Paris (01.43.43.34.38)
Métro: Gare de Lyon
Mon eve, Tues–Fri lunch and dinner until 10:00 P.M.
closed mid-July–mid-August, Dec 25–Jan. 1
Wheelchair access

If you have ever had doubts about service in French restaurants, La Biche au Bois may put an end to such concerns. Good value for money and outstanding service keep the largely business set crowding in here. The clientele are French people in their middle years. Many are regulars, and all are greeted warmly. Inside, white table linens, large

mirrors, William Morris-inspired curtains, and brown banquettes, with tables crowded together. Mirrors are placed on opposite walls, so that when you enter, you see what seems to be hundreds of people lifting their knives and forks at the same time.

There is a wide array of choices in the 33-euro menu, supplying *entrée, plat*, cheese, and dessert. Some are conservative, others more evocative of the bistro's theme— wild game and the outdoors. *Champignons à la grecque* (cold marinated mushrooms) were a tasty beginning. We chose solid bistro fare, *coq au vin*. To accompany this on a warm evening, a rosé de Tavel was just the thing.

The waiter brought a plate of tuna by mistake, and after we'd tasted our *plat* we wished we'd seized it from him. The *coq au vin* turned out to be surprisingly bland. Attractively presented in a flame-orange Le Creuset-type casserole dish, it was bubbling in a heavy brown sauce that seemed to have little to do with the flavors of either chicken or wine. Still, superb cheeses followed, and there was a range of good desserts, from the classic *crème caramel, mousse au chocolat,* and *île flottante* to fresh fruit in season and a selection of ice creams and sherbets.

❖ *La Biche au Bois: honest and authentic—we'll return.*

Au Camelot
50 rue Amelot, 75011 Paris (01.43.55.54.04)
Métro: St.-Sébastien-Froissart
Tues–Sat noon–2:30 P.M., 7:30 P.M.–midnight

Nobody goes to Au Camelot for a romantic evening. It's a long, bare, narrow room, with little tables capable of seating only 22 diners jammed together inside. Lace curtains on the windows shield you from the street. (The rue Amelot, although one of the oldest streets in this part of the city, does not look like the Paris of legend.)

Two young people preside behind the bar, right next to the door. They polish glasses, pour drinks, seat customers, and keep tabs on what's happening. At this bar, surmounted by a curious-looking lamp with a Deco base, the *serveuse* carefully poured a *kir royal* for one customer and with a flourish, produced a bottle of Coca-Cola for another. That, and a bunch of sweet peas arranged in a vase on the bar, lent a homey touch. Carrying on a conversation is a challenge at Au Camelot because of the noise created by the curious acoustics of a miniscule, lozenge-shaped room, but you hear the happy buzz of satisfied diners.

Now the menu is 32 euros and everyone enjoys the same hors d'oeuvre and *plat*, with a choice of dessert. A few wines by the glass are 4 or 5, with a carafe available for 10 to 14 euros. We chose a bottle of white Châteauneuf du Pape, about as macho as a white can get. Also available were various well-chosen smaller wines, mainly reds from Burgundy, Bordeaux, and the Southwest.

After you made your decision about dessert, a five-course meal follows: on one Saturday night, ours opened with a huge terrine of cool and refreshing gazpacho, followed by a *poêlée de girolles* (sautéed wild mushrooms) in a *mousseline d'oeuf brouillé* (scrambled egg in sauce). The gazpacho was among the best we've tasted, with a luscious flavor of home-grown tomatoes. The next dish had a base of lightly scrambled egg, with sautéed mushrooms and parsley in a cream sauce, a nice contrast of flavors and textures. Slightly salty for our tastes, but flavorful.

Then the *plat*: lasagna, with a filling of *queue de boeuf* (oxtail), like falling-off-the-bone braised beef, and caramelized onion adding depth to the sauce. A light *plat*, totally appropriate after the two hors d'oeuvres.

The cheese of the day was Camembert, and we each received a generous-sized wedge.

Desserts, which we'd chosen earlier, were light and flavorful: raspberries in a delicate warm custard; strawberries—a more typical presentation—cold with vanilla ice cream between sheets of puff pastry.

❖ *Au Camelot: excellent food without the responsibility of many choices.*

Café Charbon
109 rue Oberkampf, 75011 Paris (01.43.57.55.13)
Métro: Parmentier
Open daily 9:00 A.M.–2:00 A.M.

Artistic, young, and what used to be called hip, with a vague whiff of a counterculture—these were our first impressions of Café Charbon, the granddaddy of the currently fashionable places in the Ménilmontant area of Paris. When Maurice Chevalier grew up not far from here, this would never have been thought of as an "in" area—now it is. The people who come here are of all ages, although everyone looks at the young and slender girls.

Café Charbon looks as if it has been here dispensing coffee for hundreds of years, all the while sinking into an artistic decadence. The bistro opened a few years ago, although the building that houses it is genuinely old. Quite wisely the owners did not try to modernize what was originally a turn-of-the-century dance hall. If anything, they played up the antique features of the room: the high ceiling in an old-fashioned shade of brown and the venerable tall mirrors reflecting light from a number of chandeliers.

"C'est un brunch typiquement parisien," said a Parisian who stopped his bicycle to greet us and offer suggestions. What is a Parisian brunch? At the Charbon, on weekends, you start with yogurt, bread and pastries: after that you choose either *saumon, légumes grillés, salade, oeuf à la coque, salade de fruits*, or *saucisse, jambon, salade, oeuf à la coque*, and *salade de fruits*. In other words, salmon, grilled vegetables, salad, a boiled egg or sausage, ham, the egg, and fruit salad. All for 15 euros—reasonable in the Paris of today. Drinks are extra.

The friend's friend who'd recommended brunch had said, "Il y a les garçons de la presse là" (journalists go there), so when you do go, you may find yourself sharing a banquette with a savvy group of *intellos*—intellectuals from the area. Or possibly with people who just like the ambiance, which is very special.

What was perhaps most American at this brunch was the music. Strains of Ella Fitzgerald singing "How High the Moon," drifted over us when we first came in.

❖ *Café Charbon: good value in a fashionable place.*

Café de l'Industrie
16 rue St. Sabin, 75011 Paris (01.47.00.13.53)
Metro: Bastille
Open daily 10:00 A.M.–1:00 A.M.

If Bogart had owned a Paris café before heading off to Casablanca to take over Rick's, this would have been the one. There's something special about the Café de l'Industrie, something that draws writers and people in the film industry to this place with its retro interior of inspired disorder, which includes a rhino head not far from the entrance. "They like the peacefulness and the space where they can work," the friendly barmaid told us. In fact, Frédéric Mitterrand, the nephew of the late French president, has for some time been interviewing creative people here on Saturday afternoons.

This café, a longtime favorite in the Bastille area, is now offering substantial *plats* for from 9 to 16 euros, and reasonably-priced wines to go with them.

❖ *Café de l'Industrie: a restful haven near the hectic Place de la Bastille.*

Chardenoux
1 rue Jules Vallès, 75011 Paris (01.43.71.49.52)
Metro: Charonne
Mon–Fri noon–2:30 P.M., 8:00 P.M.–10:30 P.M., Sat eves,
closed August

Chardenoux is one of those incredibly romantic little bistros that have somehow survived the vagaries of fashion to retain the charm they originally possessed. Seated in the first room, we were well placed to study the old bar with its intricate patterns of variously-colored slabs of marble and topped with the original zinc. The dark high ceilings, in colors that suggest old worn leather, has curves and turn-of-the-century swirls around the edges. Large windows opening onto the street are covered with delicate lace. An old-fashioned wood screen with frosted glass separates the barroom from the more formal second dining room.

The wine list will please any oenophile, being a serious collection of recent vintages, many from the Loire.

Competent service is provided by two women who wait tables, open bottles, and decide where to place a table to accommodate an extra diner. Chardenoux attracts the occasional tourist, young marrieds, gourmets from the neighborhood.

Hors d'oeuvres are from 10 to 16 and *plats* from 19 to 26 euros. An hors d'oeuvre of boiled fennel was served cold in a cream dressing that tasted of orange, along with tiny crisp *haricots verts*, sprinkled with orange zest and chives.

The *plats* claimed our full attention, the *magret de canard* being the most generous portion we've seen, a piece of roast duck breast that looked like a small slab of beef, with scalloped potatoes and cooked red bell peppers. It had a rich, roasted flavor, effective with no sauce except for its own juices and a little butter. *Morue* (salt cod) was in a separate dish, sizzling hot, in a spinach and cream—*florentine*—sauce. With potatoes and a light *gratin*, or cheese topping, it was scrumptious, a happy marriage of cream, white wine, cod, and the spinach.

Dessert wasn't really necessary after such a feast, but we chose one anyway, the *fondant au chocolat aux marrons*, a very dense, creamy, cold chocolate dessert with a consistency similar to cream cheese and an intriguing undertone of chestnuts. With it was *crème anglaise*, just right with the chocolate.

❖ *Chardenoux: outstanding food in an extraordinary setting. Not to be missed.*

La Cheminée
7 rue J-P.Timbaud, 75011 Paris (01.49.23.06.76)
Métro: République
Mon–Fri noon–2:30 P.M., 7:30 P.M.–11:00 P.M., Sat dinner

La Cheminée is more slick and polished than when we first found it, but if you're in the area it's still worth stopping at this restaurant near the République, different from the fast-food chains which have taken over that historic square.

Hors d'oeuvres at La Cheminée are from 5 to 7 euros, including *poireaux* (leeks), *crudités* (raw vegetables), *salade de foie de volaille* (chicken liver salad), and a hard-to-find luxury like snails. *Plats*—and this was at night—were from 14 to 18 euros, including such possibilities as *sole meunière, rouget au beurre blanc*, and steak.

The service is deftly handled by friendly young waitresses. One also helps out in the kitchen. While we were waiting to order, we heard her say to a customer, "Ça a été?" (Was it all right?) and his response: "Super—je ne sais pas comment vous faites ça" (Great—I don't know how you do it).

Our hors d'oeuvre snails were hot, plump, and succulent in the delicious garlic and parsley butter, along with the fresh bread. The *plats* were worth the wait: the *faux filet paysanne* was a large steak with home-fried potatoes, potatoes that had been sautéed with bacon and mushrooms and were crisp, brown, and delicious. *Sole meunière* was hot and lemony, served with stewed tomatoes breaded and flavored with lemon and parsley, and white rice.

Desserts run from 4.50 to 6 euros, and include typical *crème caramel* and *pâtisserie maison* as well as complicated ice creams, most made on the premises.

❖ *La Cheminée: better than average* cuisine familiale.

Chez Paul
13 rue de Charonne, 75011 Paris (01.47.00.34.57)
Métro: Bastille
Open daily noon–2:30 P.M., 7:30 P.M.–12:30 A.M.

Go to Chez Paul and you find yourself with other people who are looking for old Paris, the sort of place you associate with beloved old movies, with gutteral-voiced intellectuals sitting up late into the night seeking to solve the problems of the world.

There's a venerable zinc bar and walls in faded ochre. Other customers there at the same time as ourselves included an *ancien soixante-huitard*, an ex-hippie, probably an original from '68, his long hair silver-streaked by the years, his companion, also long-haired, talking on and on with zest.

As the slender young waitress pointed out, there were the "grands classiques." We started with one, *oeuf à la mayonnaise,* which arrived with the egg slathered with mayonnaise. The modest little Rhône in a carafe was just right to go with a *pièce de boeuf* (steak).

My salmon was excellent, as was my companion's beef— he'd ordered medium, it turned out rare, but was succulent nonetheless. Portions were generous, the staff young and friendly. "Ça vous a plu?" our waitress asked at the end. A runny Brie de Meaux on red leaf lettuce was a fine accompaniment with the Rhône wine we'd chosen.

If you don't get a reservation for Chez Paul, your only hope is to arrive early. We heard the personnel begin turning people away at 8:15.

❖ *Chez Paul: great location, and crowded for good reasons.*

Le Clown Bar
114 rue Amelot, 75011 Paris (01.43.55.87.35)
Métro: République
Mon–Sat noon–3:30 P.M., 7:30 P.M.–1:00 A.M.,
Sun 7:00 P.M.–1:00 A.M.
No credit cards

The Clown Bar has joie de vivre and then some. The walls of this listed historic monument are covered with bright original tiles of clowns in absurd and funny postures—one shows a diminutive clown perched on the prominent paunch of another. It is this pose that the Clown Bar has chosen as its trademark.

Colorful and rare circus-related memorabilia, from clown lighting fixtures to authentic turn-of-the-century posters of clowns, brighten an already happy interior.

Prices are reasonable: a noon menu at 13.50 euros provides hors d'oeuvres and a *plat* or a *plat* and dessert, and may include *terrine maison* (meatloaf), *saucisson* (dry salami), *charcuterie* (cooked cured meats), and *rillettes d'oie* (chopped goose, cooked to a paste). *Plats*, or main dishes, go separately for 15 euros, and you could make a meal of one of these. Every day there's the *plat du jour*, as well as a cheese and dessert *du jour*.

Desserts are generous here and show more initiative than in many bistros and wine bars. Besides old favorites like *crème brûlée* and *gâteau au chocolat*, there was *délice au café*, a plate with small dishes of coffee mousse, cappuccino ice cream, and a *florentin*—a crisp, caramel-flavored wafer, a good finish for a confirmed coffee lover.

Wines by the glass are in the 3.50 to 5 euro range, with a few wines available by the half-bottle.

❖ *Le Clown Bar: a little treasure next to the legendary* Cirque d'Hiver *(Winter Circus)*.

> ### Bistrot Paul Bert
> 18 rue Paul Bert, 75011 Paris (01.43.72.24.01)
> Métro: Faidherbe-Caligny
> Tue–Fri noon-2:00 P.M. 7:30–11:30 P.M., Sat eves,
> closed August

"I couldn't think of a more French-looking bistro than this one," commented our friend, a longtime resident of Paris, as she looked around the old-fashioned interior, noticing the authentic Art Deco bar in dark mahogany, the traditional café chairs and the small tables. From where we sat we saw "Bistro à Vin" in crimson lettering on the awning. There are imaginative details, old posters, a vintage St. Raphael advertising clock in red over the bar, and lots of little *ardoises* listing wine possibilities.

Near us were business couples, retired people from the area and savvy singles. It was July, but there were few if any tourists here; possibly Paul Bert's location deep in the 11th district makes it a little out of the way.

They were missing an impressive 18-euro lunch. (At night it would be 34 euros). Ours started with *carpaccio de boeuf,* the thin slices of beef attractively presented with white radish and sprinkles of chives, all in an olive oil dressing.

We arrived too late for the *saumon mariné à l'aneth,* and none of us was tempted by the *steak tartare,* so we all chose the *sauté de veau légèrement crèmé aux champagnons.* We were pleased: the veal was tender and succulent, served with balsamic-flavored rice and a well-seasoned mushroom sauce.

Dessert was a choice between *sorbet aux fraises* or *émincé de pommes et son caramel,* and we chose the latter. It looked like a chrysanthemum, layers of apple arranged in circles with a warm caramel sauce. Rich and delicious, a perfect finish.

❖ *Bistrot Paul Bert: cuisine of creativity and finesse in an old district that's being rediscovered.*

L'Encrier
55 rue Traversière, 75012 Paris (01.44.68.08.16)
Métro: Gare de Lyon
Mon–Fri noon–2:15 P.M., 7:15 P.M.–11:00 P.M.,
Sat eves only, closed August

L'Encrier has been in its present incarnation as a bistro for only a few years. But the building dates back to about 1850, so there has been time for change. The look here is black, white, and historic. Extraordinary lights on modern wrought-iron constructions surge from the wall above the kitchen. Fan-shaped lights in a Deco style brighten the stone wall opposite.

As you enter you see a large white-tiled kitchen, open to view, where four men are working energetically, including the friendly, white-haired, jeans-and-T-shirt-clad gentleman who greeted us and was obviously in charge. We were seated at an old round oak table, reminiscent of many a farmhouse kitchen.

Overhead was the warm wood of exposed beams and beside us an historic-looking exposed brick wall.

The best thing about this space near the Gare de Lyon is its value. For 13 euros (18 in the evenings), you can enjoy a meal in a bright, attractive setting, with an honestly-priced wine to go with it.

Standards from the regular menu show the creativity of the chef, and if you want to try something à la carte, *plats* are reasonably priced. Our hors d'oeuvres were a warm *salade au gésiers* (chicken gizzard salad), tasty on a bed of romaine lettuce, with tomatoes and tiny bits of carrot for color, and a smooth and cool *fromage blanc* (white cottage-type cheese) with *fines herbes*, a savory start.

Next, perch, a large serving in a *sauce duglère*. Light and flavorful, with lemon and white and wild rice on the side. The steaks came with the crisp, thin rounds of fried potatoes that are an Encrier trademark. Unless specified otherwise, steak is served rare; you may want to say "bien cuit" if you want it thoroughly cooked.

The *tarte aux abricots* was pleasant and not too sweet, with a custard base and a crisp crust. *Gâteau au chocolat*, while tasty, was on the dry side, but a good *coulis de framboises* (raspberry sauce) and *crème anglaise* helped. A delicious fruit salad included black cherries, oranges, melon, apricots, almond syrup, and a touch of mint.

❖ *L'Encrier: great value close to the Gare de Lyon and the Bastille.*

Jacques Melac, Bistro à Vins
42 rue Léon Frot, 75011 Paris (01. 43.70.59.27)
Métro: Charonne
Mon 9:00 A.M.–5:00 P.M., Tue–Sat 9:00 A.M.–midnight,
closed August

There is a real Jacques Melac, a well-known character with a signature mustache, who always seems to be in the country when we visit his wine bar. Yet with or without the proprietor, and in spite of its location deep in the 11th district, this *bistro à vins* has become one of the most popular in the city.

After you've glanced over the lengthy list of wines available at this unique wine bar, you come to the nonalcoholic drinks. A warning is expressed before they list mineral water: "L'eau—sur présentation d'une ordonnance médicale" (water available by prescription). That sums up the jocular attitude here, where waiters wear black T-shirts with warnings against water, a suggestive remark about what fish do in it, and their trademark comment that it's only fit for cooking potatoes.

Sitting at the large bar, we saw old beams above us and almost equally impressive massive slabs of cheese in front of us. Light and delicate lace curtains separate drinkers inside from the world outside. Long doors with glass insets give a good view of the leafy foliage trailing along and down from the roof, these plants being Jacques Melac's own vines.

Most wines are about 4 to 5 euros a glass. When you order one, you notice that not only is the proprietor's name etched on it, but also his mustache, curving up like a smile. One side of the establishment is more of a restaurant, with long, heavy wood tables that have to be shared when it gets crowded—all the better for striking up an acquaintance with another wine lover.

Our barman spoke English fluently, having spent months in Chicago, which he'd loved. Between waiting on customers he took time to flirt with a departing blonde.

❖ *Jacques Melac: the selection of wines and the joie de vivre will keep us coming back.*

Le Pause Café
41 rue de Charonne, 75011 Paris (01.48.06.80.33)
Métro: Ledru-Rollin
Mon–Sat 7:30–1:30 A.M., Sun. 9:00 A.M.–8 P.M.
closed Dec. 25

The Pause Café, one of the earlier gathering spots near the now-thriving Bastille area, garnered superb publicity a few years ago with the release of a popular and romantic French film, *Chacun Cherche Son Chat*, in English "When the Cat's Away." Some scenes were shot here, and many of the Pause Café's customers look as if they forgot to leave after the filming.

This has become something of an "in" place for the young and trendy. The outdoor terrace is the main attraction; it's sunny, large, and there's an inexhaustible supply of young people who walk by or come to sit at a nearby table.

The design is scruffy post-modern, with waiters, appropriately, in jeans and T-shirts. Patrons run the gamut from young girls who may be looking for their cat to well-dressed Parisians in their 20s and 30s. Retired people come here too, many taking the time to glance at *Libération*, a left-wing daily subscribed to by the house.

Plats like *rôti de veau* (roast veal) or *travers de porc* (pork ribs) go for 12 to 14 euros. Hors d'oeuvres and desserts are in the 5 to 6 euro range, and wine is available by the glass or the half-bottle carafe.

❖ *Le Pause Café: favored by more than movie buffs.*

Le Petit Keller
13 bis rue Keller, 75011 Paris (01.47.00.12.97)
Métro: Ledru-Rollin
Tue–Sat 11:30–1:30 A.M., closed mid-July–mid-August

Just off crowded, popular rue de la Roquette, Le Petit Keller is an appealing little bistro of the type that would fit in perfectly in a small country town. Brown banquettes, yellow walls, framed paintings that owe some of their inspiration to the works of Picasso and Dali, and a large circular mirror define the main room.

When we entered around 1:00 P.M., most of the regulars—clerical and other workers from the area—had finished lunch and were calling for their *additions.*

While the decor could not be called exciting, this is a bistro that does *cuisine familiale* (home cooking) competently, with a 17-euro two-course menu. One of us chose *faux-filet,* a small steak in a mustard and pepper sauce with a baked potato garnished with sour cream; the other, stuffed peppers in salad. Both *plats* were tasty and filling. Before the main course, we enjoyed salads livened up by a Bleu d'Auvergne.

What impressed us most about this bistro was something that happened just as we were leaving. It was 2:00 P.M., the end of the lunch period, and the staff must have been tired. An elderly French couple came in, and we heard the gentleman inquire, "Could you find something to eat for Madame?" explaining that he'd already eaten but that his wife, who'd just come in by train, had not. "Yes, of course," responded the waiter, who could have mentioned the time and the end of lunch. Instead he immediately served them drinks and disappeared down the circular staircase to see what could still be rustled up from the kitchen.

❖ *Le Petit Keller: good everyday food at affordable prices.*

Le Repaire de Cartouche
99 rue Amelot, 75011 Paris (01.47.00.25.86)
Métro: St. Sebastien-Froissart
Wheelchair access
Tues–Sat noon–2:00 P.M., 7:30–11:00 P.M.

Le Repaire de Cartouche is a dark and heavy set of rooms, divided into the upstairs bistro and downstairs formal restaurant. The customer looking for a budget-friendly lunch is going to be divided from the people feasting on exotic specialities like *terrine de sanglier* in the brighter dining room below.

The 14-euro lunch offers 2 courses: we started with a *terrine de campagne*, which seemed long on grease and short on flavor. Then the main dish, *haddock aux choux rouges*—and the fish turned out to be just slightly off. We asked for a substitute, and experienced a few embarrassing moments during which we had to insist before the waiter grudgingly brought something else, *saucisse grillé* with sautéed potatoes. It was a satisfying if relatively simple *plat*.

The wine list is ambitious—cynics might say pretentious—with everything from Cotes du Rhone to Richebourg. The former, at 12 euros, was a richly-flavored wine that went well with the germanic cuisine.

❖ *Le Repaire du Cartouche: considering its reputation, a bit disappointing. A place to respect rather than love.*

Le Square Trousseau
1 rue Antoine-Vollon, 75012 Paris (01.43.43.06.00)
Métro: Ledru-Rollin
Open daily to 10:30 P.M., closed 3 weeks in August

When you walk into the Square Trousseau, you feel as if you've finally found the ultimate bistro. Here are floor-to-ceiling doors and windows in front, and high ceilings with elaborate moldings in buttery ochre. Through lace curtains of unusual delicacy you glimpse the park which gives this bistro its name. As we were glancing about, orienting ourselves to the place, two businessmen were finishing up their *crème brûlée.* "Excellent," we heard one murmur. From the conversations around us, we gathered that some of our neighbors were recognizing other customers: "Il y a des gens de la télévision ici" (people from television are here).

Lunch specials are written on *ardoises* (blackboards), with two courses for 20 and three for 25 euros. In the evenings it's all à la carte, with most plats priced between 19 and 26 euros. We elected to try the *crème de concombre à la menthe,* a delicious cold soup of cucumber with mint, and a *croustillant de chèvre aux quatre épices,* a sautéed square of goat cheese, served hot and presented on a bed of red leaf lettuce. This was followed by a *brandade de morue Benedictine,* a fish-and-potato mixture garnished with tomato sauce, and *poulet mariné au citron et coriandre* (chicken marinated in lemon juice with cilantro). Flavors were subtle and intriguing, the *brandade de morue* a light, satisfying meal.

Not quite quiet enough for an intimate lunch, Le Square Trousseau is just the sort of bistro where you'd like to invite friends. A couple near us were discussing an international conference they were attending, organized by the World Bank and the French government. Jean-Paul Gaultier is said to be a regular.

❖ *Le Square Trousseau: "Vous ne serez pas déçu," (you won't be disappointed), said a departing Parisian when we sat down. He was right.*

Au Trou Normand
9 rue Jean-Pierre Timbaud, 75011 Paris (01.48.05.80.23)
Métro: République
Open daily noon–2:00 P.M., 7:30–11:00 P.M.

For years Au Trou Normand was a working-man's restaurant on the edge of the 11th district, an area that has gone upscale. Here they served simple food to hungry locals. Maggy, the previous proprietress, "ran the place for 30 years," recalled a fog-voiced old hand. Now with a change in management, the Trou looks better, serves better food, and keeps surprisingly reasonable prices. A 12.50-euro lunch menu gave us each two substantial courses, and the desserts that followed were beyond our expectations. At night, *plats* are available for between 8 and 18 euros.

❖ *Au Trou Normand: an authentic working-class bistro with good cuisine familiale at low prices.*

Le Viaduc Café
43 rue Daumesnil, 75012 Paris (01.44.74.70.70)
Métro: Ledru-Rollin
Open daily 9:00 A.M.–4:00 A.M.

If the food were as lovely as the girls serving the drinks, the Viaduc Café would be heavenly. Unfortunately it's not—most people find the fare rather standard. Of course, what's average in Paris might be exciting in Amarillo.

Still, this is perhaps the most attractive café we've ever seen near a large railway station. It's smartly designed, *branché*, or hip, and attracting a crowd of beautiful people. About two blocks from the Gare de Lyon, the viaduct transports you into another world, that of the arts. When you go to the Viaduc Café you feel as if you could be in a design studio, with the immense ceilings formed by the viaduct overhead, the exposed stone on the walls, and the charming wood bar with Second-Empire lines. You sink into one of the old-style sofas or armchairs in cherry-colored wood and admire the view onto the terrace outside.

A great deal of attention has been paid to style here; the seating has been selected for comfort as well as attractiveness, the staff are young, friendly, and attractive, flitting about like birds.

You can enjoy a meal here at fair prices—lunches at 16.50, an evening menu for 20.50 euros, with starters like gazpacho, *tartare de saumon*, or green salad, *plats* like *osso buco*, *le burger de Viaduc*, and *demi poulet braisé*. There's a good wine list, with some offered by the glass from 4, or by the carafe for 11 euros. In this setting near the artists' studios under the viaduct, the food seems a particular treat.

❧ *Le Viaduc Café: a good place—quite unlike the grubby cafés usually found near railroad stations. For a more over-the-top experience, try Le Train Bleu (picture below) in the Gare de Lyon for a drink or Sunday brunch.*

Le Villaret
13 rue Ternaux, 75011 Paris (01.43.57.89.76)
Métro: Parmentier
Mon–Fri noon–2:00 P.M., 7:30 P.M.–midnight, Sat eves;
closed August

If you're a serious admirer of French cuisine, the classics interpreted with untraditional flair, you should make a trip deep into the 11th arrondissement. The rue Ternaux is a street that houses secondhand stores, a dark-looking laundromat, and forlorn little cafés. Go past them to Le Villaret.

There's nothing remarkable about Le Villaret's decor—a stone wall behind the bar, pleasantly muted earth tones elsewhere, fan-shaped lighting on the walls. But the food is special. At 21 or 26 euros, depending on whether one chooses two or three courses, the lunch offerings at Villaret are a good value—at dinner it's à la carte, except for the 50-euro tasting menu. The wine list is serious but a nice half-liter of Chablis in a *pichet* was just about right for two.

The *crème fraiche de rougets et petits croutons* was an intensely-flavored fish soup, reminiscent of some we've consumed with relish much closer to the Mediterranean. Our Parisian friend's *tartare de saumon fumé* was smoked salmon served with a crisp wafer, a rose-like tomato, and sprinklings of chives. She pressed samples upon us: "The smoked salmon is really good." Tasting it, we concurred.

Following were *calamars à la crème*, well-seasoned in a rich sauce, a generous helping on white rice. Roast chicken came was served with a scrumptious cream sauce.

Only one of us had enough appetite left for dessert, the *poêlée de cerises*, cherries lightly sautéed with port and served with gingerbread-flavored ice cream.

"There's a real chef in that kitchen" we agreed as we left Le Villaret, each of us separately plotting return visits.

❖ *Le Villaret:* cuisine raffinée—*refined cuisine, a treat for the gourmet. Worth searching out.*

LEFT BANK SOUTH:
THE 13TH & 14TH
ARRONDISSEMENTS

The Dôme soon expanded from a bistro to a big, garish café with rows and rows of tables... toward evening it was impossible to find a seat.... Around you people milled in a slow-moving stream. They were a motley crowd—tall, raw-boned Swedes, sleek Russians and Spaniards, noisy Americans, self-conscious English, anxious or portly French, all intent on their own affairs.... Women dressed in the height of fashion rubbed elbows with shabby models or gaudy prostitutes....

—Jimmie Charters, *This Must Be The Place*

If the 6th arrondissement is the quarter of artists and writers, then the 14th cannot be far behind. The 13th and 14th arrondissements run directly south and under the more famous 5th and 6th districts on the map of Paris, but they do not have the same spirit about them. In the 5th and 6th, you have the feeling that these neighborhoods, however reluctantly, are hosting a perennial fair. People jostle one another along narrow, twisted streets, peer at the street performers giving spontaneous concerts, toss coins to streetside beggars as they make their way to museums by day, to theaters and cafés by night. More sedate in its nature, the 14th, dividing up the boulevard du Montparnasse with the 6th district, still retains some of the famous bistros which lined that street during the Jazz Age.

The so-called "American cafés," which started in the 1920s, are part of every book about the bistros of Paris. With the 6th and the 14th joined at the boulevard like Siamese twins, you have La Rotonde and Le Sélect in the 6th district, and their competition across the street, La Coupole and Le

Dôme in the 14th. Since these bistros were just across from one another, people would go from one to the other in their nightly search for entertainment.

Ernest Hemingway wrote about how it used to be. He was sitting at the Dôme when he described to Sherwood Anderson a night in December 1921:

> *We sit outside the Dôme Café opposite the Rotonde that's being redecorated... and it's so damned cold outside.... And when it's a cold night in the streets of Paris and we're walking home down the Rue Bonaparte we think of the way the wolves used to slink into the city and François Villon and the gallows at Montfauçon. What a town.*

It was easy to get caught up in the bistro routine. Canadian writer Morley Callaghan, in *That Summer in Paris*, described the summer of 1929 and his friendships with Hemingway and Fitzgerald. Starting in the 14th arrondissement, Callaghan and his wife would move on to bistros in the 6th and even across the river in the 8th and 9th districts: "We would... walk slowly over to the Coupole, have a little lunch on the terrace, then go across the river to the American Express to inquire for mail. Sometimes we loafed around the Right Bank for hours, having a drink at some café by the Opéra, or the Madeleine."

Now the bistros on the boulevard are quieter than they were, the 13th and 14th arrondissements—the 13th with the Gobelins, the 14th with the catacombs at Denfert-Rochereau—relatively peaceful. There's a cluster of hospitals at the northern edge of the 14th and a cemetery, the Cimetière de Montparnasse, nearer its center. Probably the most famous among the hospitals is La Pitié-Salpetrière, on the boulevard de l'Hôpital, in the 13th district. Founded as a workhouse for orphans, it became a center specializing in the treatment of mental illness. Freud himself spent six months observing and working there, and in our own time, Princess Diana was brought there after the fatal crash in the tunnel near Alma-Marceau.

Below Denfert-Rochereau is the Cité Universitaire, founded in the 1920s to provide students with reasonable lodgings. Several of the pavilions were designed by noted architects, the Swiss and Brazilian ones by Le Corbusier. A stay at the Maison des Etats-Unis years ago gave us an idea of what the Cité is like: comfortable housing, but with a feeling of isolation, so far from the center.

In some ways those Parisians who live in the 13th and 14th districts are fortunate. Although their quarters may look desolate in places, they are out of the noisy hubbub and crowds of the Latin Quarter. They have the jewel-shaped park, the Jardin du Luxembourg, stretching down toward them. And they have some of the most notable bistros in today's Paris.

Some of these bistros are:

> ### *L'Avant-Goût*
> 26 rue Bobillot, 75013 Paris (01.53.80.24.00)
> Métro: Place d'Italie
> Tue–Sat noon–2:00 P.M., 8:00 P.M.–11:00 P.M.,
> closed August

L'Avant-Goût attracts people who love food. You will not travel there for the setting, nor for the welcome, which was correct but not warm.

If you want dinner you'll have to reserve; we saw a gentleman being turned away at only 8:30 P.M. The 31-euro menu suggested why enthusiastic diners were crowding in: good variety, with *champignons à la grecque* (mushrooms stewed in olive oil with tomato and lemon), *langue d'agneau* (lamb's tongue), *bouillon de pot au feu au cochon* (pork stew) offered as starters, followed by possibilities like *maigre bar poelé, risotto aux crustacés* (lean sautéed European sea bass, risotto with seafood), *cocotte de caille* (quail in casserole), and *filet de canard griotté aux poivrons* (duck filet with sour cherries and peppers).

A Côte du Rhône from Domaine Rabasse was a sturdy accompaniment to the food. The soups we chose were both light and flavorful, one a fish broth with croutons of *rouille* (garlic and olive oil mayonnaise) and tapenade, the other a savory pork. Both were garnished with watercress and olives.

Service was competent without being particularly friendly. Dress is relatively informal: a teenager at a nearby table was in T-shirt and jeans, the universal costume at McDonald's. Being at l'Avant-Goût and being French, he knowledgeably ordered *langue d'agneau rôtie* (roast lamb's tongue) and downed it with relish.

If more than one diner orders the *pot-au-feu* (beef stew), it comes to the table in a cast-iron casserole, the stew garnished with new potatoes and olives.

A large portion of *bar* with a crisp cake of fried rice was dramatically displayed on what looked like squid or octopus ink. The *magret de canard* was rich and flavorful on a bed of peppers and tomatoes with a light cream sauce.

Fraises façon tiramisù and *moelleux de chocolat* were a satisfying finish, the *moelleux* a partly-cooked cake with melting, warm bittersweet chocolate in the center and vanilla ice cream lending a contrast.

❖ *L'Avant-Goût: exceptional cuisine in an unlikely setting.*

Chez Gladines
30 rue des Cinq-Diamants, 75013 Paris (01.45.80.70.10)
Métro: Corvisart
Open daily noon–3:00 P.M., 7:00 P.M.–midnight,
closed August
No credit cards

It's a slice of old Paris begging to be remembered in black and white. It's an old corner bistro dating from the early twentieth century, half-heartedly modernized, with some crazy Deco trim from the 1930s, topped off with a formica bar after World War II and then essentially unchanged. You might not manage to see much of this, however, since Chez Gladines was packed tighter than any place we've seen.

We found this bistro blocked by young people when we elbowed our way inside. In minutes, we were seated at one of the long tables covered with faded red-and-white checkered oilcloth, like an old farmhouse kitchen. We were elbow-to-elbow with students, many of them wolfing down salads from dishes of a size customarily used as mixing bowls. Service was a bit primitive but charming, and provided by a hardworking girl with a diamond in her nose.

Chez Gladines bills itself as a Basque restaurant, specializing in a cuisine of simple and hearty food. We tried a dozen *escargots* as an hors d'oeuvre, hot and flavorsome in parsleyed butter. Following that there was *canard sauce roquefort* (duck in Roquefort sauce) and *cassoulet*, both only 11 euros and both delicious, although the duck was overcooked. It was accompanied by a huge serving of fried potatoes. *Cassoulet* filled a heavy iron casserole with generous amounts of duck, sausage, and bacon, classic *cassoulet* ingredients along with the white beans. A farmhouse version of the dish but very satisfactory.

We chose a half-liter of the Madiran, a big macho red from the South which balanced the *cassoulet*.

In any case it was difficult to concentrate on food with so many young people around joyously celebrating—what? It wasn't the end of the week. Possibly they'd passed their exams. The feeling of Chez Gladines was happy, exuberant, crazy, and crowded with young life. The hormones were running wild, the flirting was outrageous, and, except for us, there wasn't anyone there over the age of 25.

A young man who could have been actor Gérard Départieu's younger brother asked to borrow our pen. This happened twice and was not surprising, given the informality of the place. Complete strangers said "Goodbye" to us as they left.

❖ *Chez Gladines: If you think the French are reserved, formal, even stuffy, take a look at them here.*

Le Havane
70 blvd Auguste Blanqui, 75013 Paris (01.43.37.48.64)
Métro: Porte d'Ivry
Open daily 9:00 A.M.–3:00 P.M., 6 P.M.–11:00 P.M.

What brightness this corner of an otherwise dreary boulevard has is supplied by a warm and cheerful bistro. Le Havane is a few meters away from the headquarters of *Le Monde*, the most prestigious newspaper in France. *Le Monde* journalists have made Le Havane their canteen, and the famous cartoonist who signs his works "Plantu" is seen lunching there almost every day.

Our experience is that the food at Le Havane ranges from average to fairly good. On one day we tried a pork stew with lentils, rabbit in mustard sauce, and cod with puréed potatoes. All three *plats* were reasonable but none stood out as something justifying a trip to the 13th arrondissement.

❖ *Le Havane: unexceptional cuisine, but a chance to mingle with the people who write the news.*

Hawai
82 ave. d'Ivry, 75013 Paris (01.45.86.91.90)
Métro: Porte d'Ivry
Open daily 10:30 A.M.–3:00 P.M., 6 P.M.–11:00 P.M.

This is a book about French bistros and restaurants, places where you can enjoy French cuisine. But one night when Parisian friends offered to take us to a true remnant of colonial France, we could not refuse.

"Little Vietnam" is what our French friends call Hawai and the area around it, and that's what it seems to be. In Hawai there's no attempt at decor: the look is basic, even brutal. Cheap paper covers formica tables, the walls are lined with ordinary-looking mirrors, a piece of hollowed-out bamboo holds spoons and chopsticks on each table. Plastic-coated menus are thrust at you briefly before being grabbed away: you're expected to make choices in seconds.

Food is slapped down in front of you and, if you're lucky, you might get a thin paper napkin.

Yet Hawai is full of noisy, happy diners, French as well as Asian. Why? It's authentic. Hawai is to Vietnamese restaurants in Paris what Katz's Delicatessen is to New York. Our Parisian friends joked that some of the food must have a taste of *pouce de serveur* (waiter's thumb), so slapdash is the service. The same friends come here in the morning and see people consuming bowlfuls of nourishing soup, a typical Vietnamese breakfast.

If you want soup, it starts at 6 euros for the one most people order, *soupe aux boulottes de boeuf*. A spring roll is 4

euros—and it is good, delicately flavored with shrimp, rice noodles, a little lettuce, and mint. There are *brochettes de crevettes* (shrimp on a skewer) for 8 euros, and a dish of *pate imperial "nem,"* or crunchy, greasy little rolls, fried with a filling of ground pork and served with *nuoc-mam,* a dipping sauce, for 6 euros. One friend ordered the *riz au porc grillé,* grilled pork ribs with rice and carrots, with a light coating of flavorful sweet-and-sour sauce.

The highlight of our meal was when the bowl of soup was served, or, one should say, slammed down unceremoniously in front of us. The *plat de résistance,* which almost everyone orders, looked like a gallon of flavorful beef broth with thin slices of beef, noodles, sliced onions, and cilantro. "Une nourriture très parfumée" (very savory food), commented our friend, finding the soup appetizing but in such an impossibly large quantity that he could only finish half of it.

❖ *Hawai: like something from the back streets of Saigon.*

Au Petit Marguéry
9 rue du Port-Royal, 75013 Paris (01.43.31.58.59)
Métro: Gobelins
Open Tues–Sat noon–2:15 P.M., 7:30–10:15 P.M.
Closed in August

Entering Au Petit Marguéry is like walking into an old sepia photograph from the turn of the 20th century. This is not and never was a student restaurant, or even a worker's canteen: it's serious, conservative, and very middle class. Most of the patrons are older men. These are people who are used to good cuisine and are willing to pay to get it.

The colors around you are old-fashioned and somber. The tablecloths are white, the mirrors clean, the glasses sparkle and the bar has received many coats of paint through the decades. You notice small ferns sprouting from clay pots, the kind of plant your grandmother in the country might have had. Here they look right.

The food is old-fashioned but very good, and the portions generous. At noon 23.50 and 25-euro menus are available. We opted for solid, substantial fare on a winter afternoon: foie gras followed by *canard* for one of us, *terrine de poisson* and *filet de rouget au beurre blanc* (red mullet in wine-and-butter sauce) for the other. The foie gras at Marguery is superior, rich and delicious. It was followed by *aiguillettes de canard* (slices of duck breast). Served in a meaty sauce with *girolles,* they filled a platter-sized plate. The *daurade au safran* (sea bream with saffron) had enough eye appeal to rate a photograph. It also had great delicacy of flavor. When it came to the *rouget au beurre blanc*, we expected to be disappointed, having spent summers in the Loire Valley area, where this sauce is a speciality. We have never tasted a better example of it than here.

Au Petit Marguéry makes several wines available by the half bottle. A pleasant Côtes du Rhône complemented the duck and the fish. Both of us chose the soufflé Grand Marnier for dessert. It was creamy with a very moist filling, a fitting conclusion to a very successful lunch.

❖ *Au Petit Marguéry: one of the better bistros in Paris.*

La Régalade
49 ave. Jean Moulin, 75014 Paris (01.45.45.68.58)
Metro: Alésia
Mon eves, Tue–Fri noon–2:00, 7:00–11:00 P.M.,
closed August

Way off in a remote corner of the city, near the end of the métro line going into the southern reaches of the Left Bank, there's a restaurant where it's almost impossible to get reservations. With some luck, we finally achieved a 7:00 P.M. booking. We were seated with other foreigners and found ourselves in a corner near a man from Texas with the girth and dramatic presence of an Orson Welles. He was already tucking into a *pigeon rôti* and a bottle of Côte Rôtie.

La Régalade has a simple bistro interior. It's small and has a homey look, with huge loaves of bread and bottles of wine clustered around a pillar in the center of the room. The service was warm and friendly, the waitresses ready to translate or explain the menu.

This is one of those rare places where you have the feeling that all you have to do is sit back, fasten your seatbelt, and see what the person behind the scenes will do to amaze you. When our gazpacho came to the table, we were presented with a large plate bearing a small, icy *sorbet de tomate* in the center. We looked at it aghast. Was this evening going to be an experience of nouvelle-cuisine-type deprivation? But no—next the waiter brought a huge terrine of green gazpacho, composed of *morue* and *cresson* (salt cod and watercress) to surround the icy sorbet and to feast on almost indefinitely. The other hors d'oeuvre was a delicately-flavored *foie gras de canard en gelée*, beautifully presented with portions of prunes and currants surrounding the foie gras for added flavor contrasts, all in a lightly flavored aspic.

One main dish, *lieu* (pollock) came in a rich sauce with *girolles* (wild mushrooms). The other was a perfectly cooked *pièce de boeuf*; this is a place that takes your order about how you want your steak cooked seriously. An unusual sauce of *anchois, pommes et girolles* (anchovies, apples, and wild

mushrooms) heightened the flavor. For wine we chose a Côtes de Roussillon, a rich red from the South, which went nicely with both meals.

While tasting these rare dishes we were entertained by our neighbor. A born raconteur, he was enjoying a *hachis parmentier boudin noir* (meat loaf of blood sausage and potatoes). With a little encouragement, he went on in detail about a character he'd worked with, the great Texas criminal lawyer Racehorse Haynes: "He could do anything he wanted with a jury," he said, adding a little ruefully, "The only thing he couldn't pass on was his talent."

Then came puffed and golden Grand Marnier soufflés, a perfect conclusion to a memorable meal. But La Régalade hadn't quite finished with us: a small basket was delivered to our table.

In it, two madeleines (shell-shaped cakes). In Shakespeare's England, rosemary is for remembrance. In Proust's Paris, it's the madeleines.

❖ *La Régalade: still, with a new owner, one of the best bistros in Paris.*

Le Temps des Cerises
30 rue de la Butte aux Cailles, 75013 Paris
(01.45.89.69.48)
Métro: Place d'Italie
Mon–Fri noon–3:00 P.M., 7:30 P.M.–11:00 P.M.,
Sat eves only

Le Temps des Cerises is popular. Too popular. A look inside and we knew we had a problem. The place was hectic, earsplitting, and jammed; we edged our way in and were told it would be at least a half-hour wait for the three of us. French families with children were crowded at the long tables and heaping plates of *crudités*—raw vegetables, a popular starter—were being carried past.

We noticed that the 15-euro menu featured *boudin* and *androuillette* (blood and chitterling sausage), but at 18 euros there were other possibilities. This menu offered good hors d'oeuvres: the *saumon* was an impressive plate, with large slices of smoked salmon, *crème fraîche*, black olives, tomatoes, sliced cucumbers, and, a surprise, little slices of fresh mango. *Tarte à l'indienne* was a cooked vegetable tart (eggplant, zucchini, onion, etc.) with a dash of curry, served with a large lettuce salad. The *féroce de morue* was a small dish of cod, with chopped parsley, black olives, basil, and *crème fraîche*. Avocado was used to bind the mixture and a touch of hot pepper added piquancy.

Huge plates of *filet mignon de porc* (pork filet) came with giant helpings of crisp gold French fries, the pork with an artichoke-and-cream sauce, cooked perfectly, moist, tender, and delicious. Little quails—*caille aux cerises*—had a flavorful sauce strongly imbued with the flavor of black cherries. Desserts were brought, one of us getting a cheese plate, another *bavarois aux framboises* (raspberry bavarian) in a *coulis* of raspberries.

❖ *Le Temps des Cerises: in a down-to-earth setting, food of surprising subtlety.*

PRIVILEGE & PROSPERITY: THE 15TH & 16TH ARRONDISSEMENTS

Neither the working class nor the poor have any place in this perpetual garden party which goes on year in year out between the place Victor Hugo and the Seine. All the ceremonial occasions of Passy-Auteuil see the same troop of guests... they confer on the social events of the seizième arrondissement a slight air of comic opera which is not without charm.

—Léon-Paul Fargue

The 16th arrondissement is richer in fine apartments and great mansions than it is in bistros. Although it is home to some of the great and famous, a curious dullness pervades the area. You can walk for blocks without finding an inviting café or a newsstand. Wealth acts as a shield, insulating the denizens of the 16th from dirt, noise, and the unexpected, but also from the excitement and stimulus of the outside world. Cars disappear into underground lots, nannies appear at regular intervals to walk dogs and children, and a heavy Sunday silence lingers over all.

People who live in the 16th always seem to mention it in much the same way that Harvard graduates will casually slide their schooling into a conversation. Both the 15th and 16th seem more spacious, more private in a sense than other districts, and both feel like a newer part of Paris. There are good bistros here, but considering the wealth of the population, fewer than one might expect. Rents are high and young chefs struggling to develop a clientele usually can't afford them.

Writer Julien Green remembered growing up in Passy, a suburb in the 16th district just west of the Eiffel Tower.

He found the old townhouses with their gardens enchanting. But he remembered another section of Passy less favorably: "The other Passy, the prosperous Passy, I loathed even as a child. There was a kind of wealth that made me want to weep because of a certain quality of severity and arrogance in those strutting balconies, unwelcoming carriage entrances, and sumptuous porter's lodges."

Like the 16th, the 15th district is not an area for pleasure-seekers. There's nowhere in the area to go for fun. Quiet and bourgeois, with a few small parks (the French call them "squares"), the odd hospital and several schools, the 15th is not a quarter you're likely to frequent unless you're visiting a friend or making an effort to go to a favorite restaurant. It's a pleasant part of the city in which to live but not especially memorable for the visitor.

Some dining possibilities in an expensive area:

Bélisaire
2 rue Marmontel, 75015 Paris (01.48.28.62.24)
Métro: Convention
Mon–Fri noon–2:00, 8:00 P.M.–11:00 P.M., Sat eve only,
closed Sun and August

We'd already been let in on the secret about Bélisaire: it's a favorite of some top officials at the nearby Cordon Bleu, the famed cooking school. When we went there to try out this little bistro on a side street, it was not hard to understand why aficionados might want to keep it quiet.

Small, rustic— welcoming is the feeling at Bélisaire. Good smells waft from the kitchen as you enter this friendly place, and you know you've come to the right spot.

The 20-euro lunch menu changes daily, and a recent one promised intriguing starters: *gratin de moules aux épinards* (mussels with spinach), *poêlon d'escargots à la crème* (sautéed snails with cream), *crème glacée de poivrons verts* (cold green pepper soup). An evening menu is available for 30, and a Saturday evening *menu dégustation* (tasting menu) for 35 euros.

Crème glacée de poivrons verts was a delicately-flavored, cold cream soup made from green bell peppers and potatoes, but with a refined aspect that didn't seem to owe its origins to either of these humble ingred-ients. *Gratin de moules,* served hot in a small cast-iron dish, was intense and satisfying, with flavors of mussels and cheese.

The *dos de saumon* on a bed of zucchini and eggplant came with an artistic dusting of pepper. An intriguing treatment of a classic: *dos de saumon* prepared with care and imagination, the first-rate salmon hot on its bed of vegetables. The *bavette sauce au poivre* for the meat-eater in the party was a flavorful steak with a good sauce, accompanied by a ramekin-shaped mound of scalloped potatoes.

Dessert was similarly above our expectations. We chose an *entremet poire-caramel*, layers of pear, *génoise*, and caramel. Accompanied by a caramelized wafer, it was an assembly of the luscious flavor of fresh pears at their peak of ripeness with fine-textured white cake and a caramel glaze.

A young and gifted chef, Matthieu Garrel, is responsible for the culinary surprises emerging from the kitchen of this small bistro. He likes to cook with seafood and is intent on pleasing his clientele, a combination that's sure to earn him a reputation.

❖ *Bélisaire: cooking in the great tradition of old France.*

Le Bistro d'Hubert
41 blvd Pasteur, 75015 Paris (01.47.34.15.50)
Métro: Pasteur
Mon–Fri 12:30–2:30 P.M., 7:30–10:30 P.M., Sat eve
Wheelchair access

The setting chez Hubert is attractively simple, like Martha Stewart's idea of a Provençal kitchen. Old armoires in dark wood display antique porcelain canisters, jams, and *eaux de vie*, along with strings of garlic, old *madeleine* molds and bright red peppers.

The ambiance is at once relaxed and busy: the clientele are, for the most part, casually-dressed French people. The staff are kept busy running to the open kitchen where you watch energetic young cooks at work.

A 26-euro noon menu weekdays at noon offers no choices; a larger menu is available weekday evenings at 34 euros. Our friendly server brought us a pre-starter of duck pâté with slices of toasted baguette. Following was a *gâteau de crabe,* flanked by hearts of palm and little slices of sweet red pepper, drizzled with a vinaigrette and topped with chives. The *carpaccio de taurillon argentin* (smoked beef from Argentina) was attractively presented but tasted curiously bland. A comment brought a salmon mousse layered with onion and tomato, as delicious as it looked.

Main dishes were mostly fish, and were tasty and appealing: a *pavé de thon* (sautéed tuna) looked like beef filet on a bed of spinach, surrounded by an artistic sprinkle of a sweet sauce made from balsamic vinegar, with zucchini and carrots in a dish on the side. A generous portion of *morue* (salt cod) was topped with crisp fried sprouts and slivers of crisp onion, all in a delicately-flavored sauce.

Desserts were equally imaginative, and we left Hubert's in a good mood.

❖ *Bistro d'Hubert: imaginative offerings for a largely BCBG (yuppie) crowd.*

Café Dapper
Musée Dapper, 35 rue Paul Valéry, 75116 Paris
(01.45.00.31.73)
Métro: Victor Hugo
Open daily 11:00 P.M.–7:00 P.M.

The Musée Dapper is Paris's museum of African art. The museum is well worth seeing, but the café downstairs is interesting in its own right: it's sleek and modern. On our first visit here we noticed the tables swinging about on ball bearings.

This café offers appetizing, low-priced lunches. A typical lunch might be salad, with small salads at 5, and larger ones for 11 euros.

Food here is reliably good, and inexpensive for the 16th arrondissement. Lunch *formules* or fixed-price menus allow you a quiche-and-salad lunch for as little as 11 euros. Wine is available by the glass, and bottles are fairly priced.

❖ *Café Dapper: good food and reasonable prices in a sophisticated setting.*

Cafe du Musée d'Art Moderne de la Ville de Paris
11 ave du President Wilson, 75016 Paris (01.53.67.40.47)
Métro: Alma Marceau
Tue–Fri 10:00 A.M.–5:30 P.M., weekends to 7:00 P.M.
No credit cards

This is a museum for the more radical experimental artists. Constructed in 1938, the building is probably as interesting as the often incomprehensible art inside. The former café of this modern art museum is now a snack bar.

There's a fancier restaurant upstairs, but we like the informal snack bar. You'll sit in adult versions of children's colorful kindergarten chairs, and you'll see beautiful young people near vast abstract fantasies. You could have a drink—coffee is 3 euros—but if it's lunchtime, you may want to try a sandwich or salad before you explore the Champs-Elysées or check out the Eiffel Tower.

❖ *The Café du Musée de l'Art Moderne: for a light snack in a pricey district. Open on Sunday.*

L'Os à Moëlle
3 rue Vasco da Gama, 75015 Paris (01.45.57.27.27)
Métro: Lourmel
Wheelchair access
Tue–Sat noon–2:00 P.M., 7:00–11:00 P.M., closed August

L'Os à Moëlle attracts the inquisitive gourmet in each of us. How many times have you wanted a hint of novelty, a subtle surprise? L'Os will give you that and more, in numerous courses.

The 38-euro tasting menu changes daily and offers the diner many small dishes, the creations of Thierry Faucher, the gifted chef. We started with *amuse-gueules,* small cheese-flavored cream puffs—light and tempting. We went on to taste a cold soup, savoring the sweetness of summer cantaloupe at its peak, with shreds of ginger and ham to accentuate the flavors.

Next three succulent oysters, lightly cooked and served on the half shell with herb butter. A third course had us baffled at first: *moelleux de homard à la pommes écrasées et sa crème* was a light fluff of whipped potatoes in the middle of a lobster-colored cream sauce, the potatoes concealing chunks of lobster.

The main dish was *suprême de canard poêlé au miel et épices,* a little piece of duck served hot on a sizzling platter with allspice, honey, and sauerkraut. The duck was good, but slightly underdone for our tastes. (Sharper knives would have helped.)

Then the cheese course: a round of white *fromage fermier* accompanied by a few leaves of lettuce—tasty with the accompanying *pain de campagne* (country bread).

Desserts are a speciality, and this is why you're asked to make your choice when you first arrive. We had ordered *quenelles au chocolat* and *baba au rhum.* The *quenelle* was a large shell-shaped serving of chocolate mousse on *crème anglaise*, with a light sifting of cocoa and a few caramelized almonds on the side. Rich and delicious. Rum babas were tiny, served with strawberries, blackberries, and a puff of whipped cream, an appealing combination.

❖ *L'Os à Moëlle: a place to sample the creative ideas of a dedicated chef.*

Le Petit Rétro
5 rue Mesnil, 75016 Paris (01.44.05.06.05)
Métro: Victor Hugo
Mon–Fri lunch and dinner, Sat dinner only, closed 2
weeks in August

Le Petit Retro was recommended by a friend who lives in the 16th. "They have lovely *langoustines*," she said. They weren't on the menu when we went there, but we did like Le Petit Retro's ambiance.

The first thing you notice here are the tiles, stylized Art Nouveau poppies on old tiles on the walls and ceiling of the front room. Apricot petals and dark-green leaves with burgundy touches swirl with a grace and a freedom that Mucha himself might have approved, all against the background of white and yellow.

Intensely-flavored cold cucumber soup was a promising start: a generous serving came with color added by a garnish of cherry tomatoes and flat-leafed parsley. The scorpion fish or *rascasse* had been cooked in olive oil and was served with a large helping of ravioli and bright touches of tomato and scallions. The piece of fish was undersized, the pasta bland. Lamb chops in puffed "beignet" coatings were more successful. They had good flavor, the crisp coating giving added interest to this dish. An unusual *clafoutis*, made not with the usual cherries but with apples and bananas on a bed of *coulis de fruits rouges,* appeared for dessert. A satisfactory conclusion.

❖ *Le Petit Retro:* cuisine familiale *in an attractive setting.*

Le Scheffer
22 rue Scheffer, 75116 Paris (01.47.27.81.11)
Métro: Trocadéro
Mon-Fri noon–2:30, 7:30–10:30 P.M. Closed weekends,
2 weeks August

Le Scheffer's interior with its delicious clichés could well serve as a movie set. It's all here: the lace curtains, the red-checkered tablecloths, the tile floor, the posters of distilled spirits and champagne, the watercolors of indifferent quality.

We saw waitresses handing out well-filled plates and a sophisticated-looking crowd devouring the fare with relish. Hearty *plats* include the old bistro standards. We chose *haddock sauce royale* and *steak-frites*. Both were most satisfactory, the haddock in a delicious *beurre blanc*, the steak with a good grilled flavor and plenty of hot crisp fries.

As we left, we mentioned to the proprietor how much we'd enjoyed the haddock. "We've had the same supplier for over 21 years," he said. "The haddock he sends us comes in thick slices, so it's not dried out and tough like some. We have people who come in again and again just for that." We understand why.

❖ *Le Scheffer: you'd like to have this bistro near you.*

Le Tie Break
36 rue de Danzig, 75015 Paris (01.45.31.07.99)
Métro: Convention
Mon–Fri noon–2:00 P.M., 7:30 P.M.–10:00 P.M., Sat eve,
closed August

"Eating here could be as cheap as eating at home," reports Katherine, who lives in the area and put us on to this budget find. A 14-euro evening menu gives you a two-course meal and a quarter carafe of rosé or red wine, beer or mineral water.

Our *cabillaud* (fresh cod) was in a good sorrel sauce with white rice and green beans. Properly cooked, it was served in a generous portion: an outstanding meal for the money. An *escalope de dinde* was a tasty turkey cutlet in a cream sauce.

Desserts at Tie Break are impressive: we savored a *gâteau au citron et framboise*, a Bavarian cream with layers of lemon and raspberry on a cake base.

❖ *Le Tie Break: real food at minimal prices.*

Le Troquet
21 rue François Bonvin, 75015 Paris (01.45.66.89.00)
Métro: Cambronne
Tue–Sat noon–2:00 P.M., 7:30 P.M.–11:00 P.M.

At Le Troquet the chef, Christian Etchebest, is a hefty fellow who looks as if he'd be more at ease behind the wheel of a semi than dabbling in the culinary arts. But Etchebest, who worked with Christian Constant at Le Crillon, creates a refined and innovative cuisine that has people coming from all over to this little bistro on a side street in the 15th district.

A long, rectangular room with tables around the edges filled with BCBGs (yuppies) in animated conversation, Le Troquet has high ceilings and Lalique-style light fixtures, no two alike, suspended from the ceiling.

One day the fixed-price menu choices were *gaspacho façon Troquet, marbré de sardines avec péquillas* (gazpacho with slivers of sardine and peppers) followed by *morue façon Bascayenne* (salt cod Basque-style), *caille façon crapaudine* (breaded and grilled quail), and cheese or dessert. Lunch is 24 euros for three courses, and dinner for 28 or 38 euros.

Starters were excellent: lightly spiced gazpacho with tiny diced vegetables, colorful and crunchy textures, the flavor of tomato enhanced with a little balsamic vinegar. The *marbre de sardines* was marinated sardines cleverly presented as a *roulade*, rolled with sweet red bell peppers and tiny diced vegetables, all bound by thinly sliced zucchini, presented with a garnish of lightly sautéed greens.

Morue façon Bascayenne was cod served on a purée of tomatoes, rich and concentrated; the *caille façon crapaudine* was crisp portions of quail on a sauce of a pleasing intensity with touches of sweetness, complex and scrumptious, with potatoes, peas, and carrots in a separate ramekin.

Desserts looked like something from *Gourmet Magazine*: a *compôte de rhubarbe* was stewed rhubarb with citrus undertones, topped by a *quenelle* of strawberry sorbet and encircled by a rhubarb-flavored syrup. The whole was a more delicious rhubarb dessert than one could ever have imagined. The other dessert was a large almond-flavored macaroon filled with vanilla cream—surely some real vanilla beans featured in its creation—served on crunchy, lightly grilled apricots. A delightful finish.

Chatting with the chef afterwards, we brought up the subject of bistros, and he generously recommended some of the stars of this collection, the bistros of other chefs trained by Christian Constant at Le Crillon. Constant and others like him have inspired the young chefs who have revolutionized the bistro scene in Paris.

❖ *Le Troquet: Exceptional cuisine at reasonable prices.*

Café Le Victor Hugo
4 place Victor Hugo, 75016 Paris (01.45.00.87.55)
Métro: Victor Hugo
Open daily 6:00 A.M.–2:00 A.M

The 16th is a posh, sometimes resented part of the city where apartments are often large and always expensive. It's old ladies from old families. Young blonde wives. Kids in 200-euro jeans. Not many bookshops. No vibrant street life either.

In this expensive part of the city, Le Victor Hugo may be the most comfortable and least expensive bistro. This is not a destination for hard-core foodies. You will not be competing for a table with Patricia Wells, or spotting reviewers from the *Times* or the *Washington Post.*

Still, in this prosperous enclave on the Right Bank, so close to the Arc de Triomphe and the Champs-Elysées yet bourgeois as only the 16th district can be, a café like Le Victor Hugo is a breath of fresh air. With its noon menu at less than 20 euros, its wines offered by the carafe, its hearty snack choices available late into the night, Le Victor Hugo might be just what you've been looking for.

A popular choice here is *moules-frites*, hot mussels served with a large portion of piping hot fries. Or you might try a meal of one of the large puffy omelets, served with a small salad or fries. Traditional café fare is offered here, variations on the *croque-monsieur*, from 7.50, or the old-fashioned sandwich for 4.50 euros.

❖ *Le Victor Hugo: dependable value in a high-priced neighborhood.*

ESCAPE FROM CONVENTION: THE 17TH & 18TH ARRONDISSEMENTS

Night is coming on, the night of the boulevards, with the sky as red as hell-fire and from Clichy to Barbès a fretwork of open tombs. The soft Paris night, like a ladder of toothless gums and the ghouls grinning behind the rungs.... It's in the night that Sacré-Coeur stands out in all its stinking loveliness. Then it is that the heavy whiteness of her skin and her humid stone breath clamps down on the blood like a valve.

—Henry Miller

Look up toward Sacré Coeur, rising like a white exclamation point into the northern sky, and you're looking at Montmartre. Unlike its sister districts, Montmartre is an area apart, a hill where narrow streets circle around, dilapidated buildings remain standing, where the poverty that has clung to the hill would inspire an Aristide Bruant to celebrate the unfortunate, the little, forgotten people of Montmartre in his songs. Here in the stillness of the side streets you can imagine that on some parts of the hill there are still clusters of windmills turning in the wind of early dawn, instead of the two which survive to our day.

Rue Lepic runs around the slope, with the more famous windmill, the Moulin de la Galette, at number 77. This former cabaret, immortalized by the Impressionists, can best be glimpsed from rue Tholozé. Just south of the other remaining mill, Moulin Radet on the rue Lepic, is the Place Emile-Goudreau. At number 13 of this Place was the Bateau Lavoir, which once sheltered Picasso, Max Jacob, Juan Gris, Georges Braque, Guillaume Apollinaire, and others. Here in

1906 Picasso started his own revolution by creating the first Cubist work, *Les Demoiselles d'Avignon.*

Montmartre has remained a village unto itself, somehow resisting being drawn into the city. There's a vast tolerance here, tolerance even for the sleaze of Pigalle and the hucksters on the Place du Tertre, where the price of a cup of coffee can equal that on the rue St. Honoré or at the Café de la Paix.

Outside of the turbulent Place du Tertre, Montmartre keeps its own special and distinctive character. Go farther

away from the Place and you will see what we mean. The sense of being in a town rather than a capital city is palpable around the Lapin Agile, that picturesque old cottage, where you can imagine young Picasso paying his way with a Harlequin painting to gain entrance to the singing and revelry within.

> *The Place des Abbesses with its Métro station, the théâtre de l'Atelier, which looked like a toy or a stage set, and its bistros and small shops, seemed to the inspector far more the genuine working-class Montmartre than the Place du Tertre, which had become a tourist trap...*
>
> —*Georges Simenon, Maigret & the Saturday Caller*

If you admire Art Nouveau, a good approach to Montmartre is by métro to Abbesses. You emerge into daylight at one of the best preserved of Hector Guimard's remaining métro entrances. In the same square you can study an Art Nouveau church, St. Jean-L'Evangéliste.

On the lower slopes of Montmartre, the little bistros and restaurants retain the ambiance of local hangouts possibly not unlike those in your own neighborhood; the proprietor greets you with a warmth that does not seem feigned, and you find yourself in a milieu that you would enjoy going back to.

What is there to see at the top? Sacré-Coeur, of course; the Place du Tertre that gives the visitor struggling through the loud and frenzied crowds a good opportunity to discover how masochistic he or she can be; the Lapin Agile; possibly the Musée de Montmartre; a few artists' addresses; and, other than that, the whole city of Paris, spread out before you in all of its splendor when you stand near Sacré Coeur looking down the hill.

> *Around ten thirty a drumroll announced the floorshow. The lights went out, the projectors focused on the dance show, which was then invaded with a triumphant yell by the cancan dancers in a flourish of flying skirt....*

> —Georges Simenon, *Les Anneaux de Bicêtre*

The Moulin Rouge is no longer the last word in anything, but its eye-catching facade with neon lights and posters of the latest attraction liven a part of the boulevard de Clichy that is dedicated mostly to drab sex shops and bars. But William Faulkner thought differently, finding it "The last word in sin and iniquity," in a letter written in 1925, explaining, "It is a music hall, a vaudeville, where ladies come out clothed principally in lip stick."

In the 1920s, some of the residents of the 18th district all seemed to know each other. Toulouse Lautrec and Aristide Bruant were friends. Salvador Dali lived at 7 rue Becquerel with Gala, the wife of the surrealist poet Paul Eluard. When Dali first came to Paris in 1927, he met Pablo Picasso and Joan Miró. Dali was friends with the Spanish filmmaker Luis Buñuel.

A cousin to the 18th district is the 17th, on the western side of Montmartre. Part of the 17th has something of the same character as the 18th: part of it is more chic, with neighborhoods good enough for anyone and better than most of us are used to, near the Arc de Triomphe. We have seen elegant apartments in the 17th with high ceilings, parquet floors, and the elaborate carved wood panels that the French call *boiserie*. But for us the 17th is associated with our memories of the modest *quartier populaire*, with street markets and a large immigrant population buying and selling merchandise near the Place de Clichy and La Fourche.

A professor who still lives near the Place de Clichy would joke about the increasingly colorful character of her area. "Il y a des travesties qui sortent la nuit," she remarked. "On peut les voir vers minuit" (Transvestites go out at night—you can see them around midnight). She kept a large black dog of indeterminate origin which she referred to as her "grosse bête"—large beast. He was, we suspect, kept more for company than to ward off transvestites or anyone else. His black coat stood out in the apartment which she had painted white even to the floorboards.

With the village feeling, the narrow, cobbled side streets and the well known nightclubs of "Gay Paree," the 17th and 18th districts are a study in contrast. They are also places where working artists continue to exist. If the nightlife, so well documented in the paintings of Toulouse-Lautrec and the Impressionists, still continues to thrive, might not the creativity be still alive in countless little ateliers?

When most people think of Montmartre their images are of mysterious windmills and can-can dancers in nightclubs, bad painters and areas of kitsch crammed together in the Place du Tertre. They might remember Sacré Coeur, the smelly tourist buses clustered near the Moulin Rouge, and maybe even Picasso and Utrillo. But there's another Montmartre, a part of Paris that's residential, middle class, very respectable, and surprisingly quiet. It's a place where people don't drive like madmen and the painter is probably someone who comes by to touch up the doors and windows.

If you're looking for the "real" Montmartre, try these bistros:

L'Eté en Pente Douce
23 rue Muller, 75018 Paris (01.42.64.02.67)
Métro: Anvers
Open daily noon–midnight

If you've ever trudged through the tiresome parts of tourist Montmartre, pushing through crowds and stepping past the sidewalk artists who insist on painting your portrait, L'Eté en Pente Douce will be a breath of fresh air. It's halfway up on the lesser-known eastern slope of the hill. On the day we went there with a friend, we found a charming café in green and white with a glassed-in terrace and small green tables and chairs within and without. Little mosaic tiles cover part of the walls with a design of cherries, flanked by borders of retro green. Above is a remarkable ceiling with vintage tiles.

Here substantial *plats* start at 12 euros. Ours, *pintade* (guinea hen) with sautéed potatoes and a salad, was 14.50 euros. Otherwise there was a vegetarian quiche, *saumon fumé*, and *filet mignon* (a pork filet). Large salads, available for 12 to 13 euros, also offer vegetarian choices.

Servings were large: a quarter of *pintade* was accompanied by an abundance of potatoes and a salad involving greens,

carrots, celery, and beets. "Very French and very delicious," as our friend remarked. The bread, a *pain de seigle*, was dark and substantial. Here they bake their own in a baker's oven from the 19th century.

❖ *L'Eté en Pente Douce: good cuisine familiale in a part of the real, untouristy Montmartre.*

L'Etrier Bistro
154 rue Lamarck, 75018 Paris (01.42.29.14.01)
Métro: Guy Moquet
Tue–Sat noon–2:00 P.M., 7:30 P.M.–10:30 P.M., closed August

This is a quiet, classy little bistro, with whitewashed walls, white floor tiles, and framed botanical prints of fruit above the bar area. Huge windows, too large for traditional café curtains, are covered by an expanse of light, gauzy fabric, swept up by ties of raffia. A nice touch is the small bunch of flowers at each table.

This little restaurant offers a refined and inventive cuisine. A set lunch or *formule* is at 20 euros. At night there's a 35-euro *prix fixe* menu.

The *escabèche de thon* hors d'oeuvre was unbelievably good, made with fresh tuna combined with dried tomatoes, onions, and served on little toast rounds with salad greens; one serving would be enough for two diners. A *polenta d'aubergine et courgette* was a light, warm, and tasty appetizer, the vegetables layered in polenta and served with crisp greens.

Parmentier de haddock was fish combined with puréed potatoes, with diced parsley and chives contributing color and flavor. This was in a rich and delicious *beurre blanc* sauce. Roast chicken was well flavored and accompanied by small roast potatoes.

Desserts were good too: a *fondant d'amandes et citron*, an almond-studded cake, was pleasantly light and served with *crème anglaise*. A *tarte aux abricots* had an intense fruit flavor, complemented by the custard sauce.

❖ *L'Etrier Bistrot: for good cuisine in a romantic setting.*

Aux Négociants
27 rue Lambert, 75018 Paris (01.46.06.15.11)
Métro: Lamarck-Caulaincourt
Mon–Fri lunch, Wed–Fri dinner, closed weekends, August

If you think that this *bistro à vins* looks vaguely familiar, it very well could be. It's long been a favorite of Paris-based photographers and journalists, and the walls are covered with extraordinary photographs taken here, some of them by well-known people. This is Montmartre, but it's the more authentic and less touristy part behind the hill. Almost everyone who comes in is a regular and the clientele look interesting even for Paris. A film director might reject some of them as being too exaggerated in appearance.

Who are they? Workers from the area, intellectuals, and wine-lovers. Some of the people look very intriguing—a lanky brunette in black posed against the bar and a white-haired, mustachioed gent near us chatted with the proprietor about a certain vineyard. There were cluckings of tongue and shakings of head over the news that it had recently been sold—"Vendu—il fait la retraite" (Sold—he retired). Evidently they don't feel they can rely on a newcomer to produce the same quality product.

Aux Négociants is one of the city's best wine bars. Proprietor Jean Navier knows his wines, as you gather from spending some time here.

A few *plats* are available for people requiring more sustenance than the grape. On a recent visit, we chose *saumon aux courgettes*, a light and pleasing combination, with salmon making up the center and grated zucchini the outside of a terrine that included homemade mayonnaise; the dish was perfect on a warm day, and just right with the hearty *pain de campagne*, supplied in generous quantities. Accompanying it was a salad of lettuce and tomato with a light vinaigrette.

Plats are generous: a large quarter of chicken came with yellow beans and an enormous amount of flavorful rice. The emphasis is less on presentation than on flavor, and a discriminating crowd leaves well pleased with what they get.

The wine list emphasizes wines of the Loire, with prices running from 3 to 5 euros a glass. Most are available only by the glass or the bottle.

Dessert, *tarte maison aux abricots*, was very popular. Someone asked Navier what was in it. He responded with typical, poker-faced humor: "Tu veux l'essayer? Risqué. Impossible à décrire" (You want to try it? A risk. Impossible to describe).

Risky or not, the man's pretty companion consumed it with gusto.

❖ *Aux Négociants: honest food at good prices in authentic bistro surroundings.*

Le Nord-Sud
Place Jules-Joffrin, 79 rue du Mont Cenis, 75018 Paris
(01.46.06.02.87)
Métro: Jules-Joffrin
Open daily 6:30 A.M.–2:00 A.M.

A vivacious young Parisienne who works at the world-famous Cordon Bleu cooking school in the 15th district likes this brasserie near her home in the 18th. "It's typical," she said. "The cuisine is O.K. Everybody gets the *steak-frites*."

A heaping plate of the *steak haché-pommes frites* (hamburger and fries) she mentioned is 13 euros now, and *francfort* (hot dog) or ham with fries 7.50 euros.

We were impressed to find the Nord-Sud usually open and packed with happy diners. There are staid-looking older French people from the neighborhood, the odd tourist, the young mothers coping with children or dogs or sometimes both.

This is no designer café. The look here is flashy, with brass and plastic imitating burled walnut. Incongruous paper tablecloths in pale pink clash with everything in sight. Mirrors, lights, loud music, photos in gaudy frames—the Nord-Sud has it all.

❖ *Le Nord-Sud: plain food but decent value in a simple neighborhood brasserie.*

Le Petit Caboulet
6 Place Jacques-Froment, 75018 Paris (01.46.27.19.00)
Métro: Guy-Môquet
Mon–Sat 11:30 A.M.–2:00 A.M., closed 1 week August
Wheelchair access

The first thing that catches your eye at Le Petit Caboulet are the bright, vintage advertising signs all over. Signs like "Dunlop—Pour Aller Vite," "Byrrh: l'apéritif" and the cobalt-blue and white, "Chocolat Menier."

There's no set lunch menu, but attractive salads like the plate of *crudités*, with red and green bell pepper, beet, and avocado on a base of green and purplish lettuce is 6.50 euros. Hot *plats* like *cabillaud* (cod) are 13.50. The fish came with pasta in a light butter sauce, garnished with red bell peppers and chives. Delicious!

The house red, or *pot lyonnais*, was modestly priced if rather rough. Better-known varieties are available. There are several tables outside, and "On peut manger dehors?" (Can we eat outside?) is a question one hears repeated often.

❖ *Le Petit Caboulet: good value in an attractive bistro.*

Au Relais
48 rue Lamarck, 75018 (01.46.06.68.32)
Métro: Lamarck-Caulaincourt
Tue–Sat lunch and dinner, closed 2 weeks in August

When most people think of Montmartre, their images are of mysterious windmills, can-can dancers, and nightclubs like the Moulin Rouge. But there's another Montmartre— middle class, respectable, and surprisingly quiet.

Some small bistros are here, places where people go for good food and not necessarily a culinary vision. A favorite is Au Relais, a family-run bistro. Recently it has changed hands, and the former owners Edouard and Marie-Jeanne Martinez are enjoying a well-deserved retirement.

Au Relais still offers a bargain 11-euro *entrée-plat* or *plat- dessert* weekday lunch menu. Wines are available by the bottle from 16.50 euros. There's a good selection of the wines of Bordeaux, with some wines available by the carafe.

Desserts are a specialty: Au Relais has a better-than-average dessert list. We saw two svelte Parisiennes digging avidly into large plates of dessert. One enjoyed *profiteroles*, the other a sundae garnished with lashings of dark chocolate.

The clientele who come in regularly from the 18th district include individuals from show business, as well as literary and professional people.

❖ *Au Relais: a charming neighborhood bistro with good, sustaining food.*

La Renaissance
112 rue Championnet, 75018 Paris (01.46.06.01.76)
Métro: Jules-Joffrin
Mon-Sat 10:00 A.M.–midnight

A large bistro from the Art Nouveau period, La Renaissance caught the eye of Robert Abbas. He told us he had been working in the fabric business, but when he saw a "for sale" sign in front of this historic bistro, he kept thinking about it. Finally La Renaissance won: Abbas made a momentous decision to change careers and make this bistro his own.

It's not surprising that movies and television specials have been shot in this interior, with its swirling curves of carved wood and etched frosted glass. Most of the clientele attracted to this historic place are young. Many are in the music business. Vincent and Benoit told us they drop by regularly for the good food, the informality, and the girl watching. Like them we ordered salads, and a *pichet* of white wine. The *salade paysanne* with sautéed potatoes and bacon was particularly delicious. Near us others were tucking into a hot daily special, *hachis parmentier*, the ground beef crowned with fluffy potatoes.

Before leaving we asked if we could take a last photo, in the dining room this time. Monsieur Abbas looked uneasy. "Better not," he said, adding with a conspiratorial smile, "I think there could be people here who are not with their wives."

❖ *La Renaissance: Old Paris in Montmartre.*

Le Sancerre
35 rue des Abbesses, 75018 Paris (01.42.58.08.20)
Métro: Abbesses
Open daily 7:00 A.M.–2:00 A.M.

The blues thunder overhead and the tang of strong espresso fills our nostrils as we enter this old bar. We've climbed up to the rue des Abbesses, a street and a world away from the sleaze and the neon lights of Place Pigalle. We're seated at a long wraparound *zinc*, with young barmen in front of us in perpetual motion and the lowest-priced coffee we've seen this year. There's emphatic decoration—black walls emphasizing a bright mural in oils, a huge mermaid in paper maché improbably suspended above us: this is not your usual neighborhood bar.

Le Sancerre is a favorite with locals who come in for the well-made *plats*, the *pavé de colin beurre blanc* (hake in white wine and butter sauce) at 12.40 euros or a *pot-au-feu* (beef stew) at about the same price. Burgers with fries are popular. Large salads go for 10 or 11 euros and wines by the glass for 3.50 to 5 euros or 11 for a carafe.

Dark red banquettes near the windows support young people, a few with laptops taking advantage of the free Wifi connection. Others, more wisely, focus their attention strictly on each other. It's crowded, casual, noisy, and friendly.

❖ *Le Sancerre: a lively bar with particular appeal to the young.*

Wagon Bleu
7 rue Boursault, 75017 Paris (01.45.22.35.25)
Métro: Rome
Mon–Sat noon–3:00 P.M., 7:00 – 11:30 P.M. Closed Sunday

Fed up with the usual? Then head north to métro stop Rome, west of the Place de Clichy, to experience something very different. The first thing you see upon entering is a bar with highly colored walls. But the second room is special: an authentic *wagon*, a train car from the Orient Express of

1925, with polished mahogany woodwork and a feeling of the gilded age. Have you ever read Agatha Christie's *Murder on the Orient Express?* That's what we're talking about. It's not the Jazz Age that's evoked in this old train car, but the richness of the early 20th century, Edwardian elegance in warm woods, heavy brass luggage racks, curving ceiling, and charming alcoves. Adding to the ambience are sounds of real trains, en route to Normandy.

Once a bar with a simple menu, the Wagon Bleu has gone upscale, with substantial food, lunch *formules* at 24.50, 30 euros and more.

❖ *The Wagon Bleu: if you're a railway buff or a fan of murder mysteries, this unique bar-restaurant is for you.*

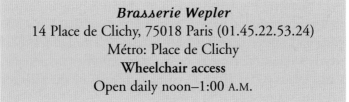

Brasserie Wepler
14 Place de Clichy, 75018 Paris (01.45.22.53.24)
Métro: Place de Clichy
Wheelchair access
Open daily noon–1:00 A.M.

Henry Miller was an old habitué, but one cannot imagine him in the splendid marble-and-glass interior of Le Wepler in our time. (On the other hand, one can picture him on the plainer brasserie side.)

Inside are warm colors and waiters hurrying to and fro. It's an elegant interior, with large globe-shaped lights in brass fixtures. On the terrace, a number of businessmen enjoy an animated lunch.

A light lunch, the *midi-express* at 20 euros, offers an entrée and *plat* or *plat* and dessert. Three courses are 26 euros, and wines are available by the glass from 3.80 or by the carafe from 10 euros. This is a seafood brasserie, but classics include sauerkraut.

Service is efficient and professional, correct but not particularly friendly. The food makes up for any deficiencies. It starts with a *salade de pêcheur*, an imposing plate with mussels, shrimp, black and green olives, tomatoes, and frisée

lettuce artistically arranged. In the salad there's a generous quantity of seafood with good-tasting vinaigrette liberally laced with lemon.

The *plat* is a large portion of hot *julienne* (sea burbot) with fresh pasta on the characteristic Wepler plate. Accompanied by sauce Béarnaise, it is satisfying, warming, and delicious. A couple near us are served a large, impressive platter of *langoustines*, beautifully presented. "Formidable," murmurs one of them.

So if you're in the shabby, rather sordid area of the Moulin Rouge, you have only a short walk to the Place de Clichy and the Wepler.

❖ *Brasserie Wepler: a landmark, with sustaining brasserie fare in an elegant setting.*

11

OUT OF THE LOOP:
THE 19TH & 20TH
ARRONDISSEMENTS

From the top of our hill in Ménilmontant we could
look down on the heart of Paris, as if we had seats in
the highest balcony of a theater.... This distant world
seemed to us... like the private paradise of the
bourgeoisie, the rich, the aristocrats and all their
grand doings. It was the Paris of History. We others
were actually like the peasants of the capital, humble
and self-effacing, and as if held apart, kept in our
places on the fringe.

—*Maurice Chevalier, My Paris*

The 19th and 20th arrondissements are an outer ring of districts, made up largely of Belleville, Charonne, and Ménilmontant. These villages became part of Paris only in 1860, when people dispossessed by Haussmann's new boulevards crowded into the outer suburbs. Much was lost in the transition. There had been cabarets and *guinguettes*, cafés with music and dancing, and people in the neighborhoods tended to know one another. Now the area took on some aspects of a slum, infested with thugs who called themselves "apaches." In recent years these districts have been a place for modern architects and their experiments.

Maurice Chevalier and Edith Piaf came from Ménilmontant, a place of stories, songs, and sad memories. Chevalier recalled that his mother, the family's sole support, had to work hard as a seamstress, sewing all day and sometimes through much of the night. This gave young Maurice freedom to explore the area and to get to know the local merchants who would sometimes give him a treat, a croissant or even a slice of horsemeat sausage, when he went out to buy the family's food.

He remembered the area with affection. It was not central Paris, it was not at all glamorous, but the town hall looked imposing and the church beautiful in the eyes of a child. Sundays were special occasions when his mother would take her sons to a café near Place Gambetta, and all would share French fries and a small beer. Afterward on the walk back, they would find something to admire about the Père Lachaise Cemetery, which they passed on their way.

Still, Chevalier admitted that life in this district was far from easy:

> In these rough, crowded, vital districts, peopled by hard-working and hard-living Parisians of every degree of human decency, I came to learn, just like a boxer, how to dodge, to guess, and to avoid as many knockouts as possible.... from my surroundings in Paris when I was a little street kid, I formed a very good idea of everything I came to know later as a performing artist and even more as a citizen.

When he was relating his memories of a childhood in the early part of the twentieth century, Chevalier could see that his neighborhood was changing and becoming unrecognizable. He was doubtful about what was happening to the streets he knew so well, noting, "A new architecture has moved in and... it begins to reject any memories of the past."

> Whenever you leave Paris for a few months, you invariably find on your return that it has been brutally improved here and there, with the modernizing of some old façade or with an entire edifice replaced by a huge hole, indicating one more skyscraper to come or an altitudinous new apartment house of the type the French call "de grand standing," meaning luxury flats.

—Janet Flanner, *Paris Journal*

Whether you like the changes here depends on your attitude toward modern architecture or possibly your capacity for accepting change. The 19th arrondissement has been a fertile ground for enthusiasts of modern design. Here the Cité des Sciences et de L'Industrie was created. The most eye-catching feature of this whole complex designed by the architect Adrien Fainsilber is the Géode, an enormous shiny ball, its triangular steel plates casting strange reflections.

The Parc de la Villette was once one of the city's main stockyards. Now it has an extraordinary science museum, with interactive exhibits on astronomical and ecological themes, talking robots, a planetarium, and more. The area outside is dominated by large structures designed by Swiss architect Bernard Tschumi. Some of them are called "follies." These structures start with red three-story cubes of ten meters square and emanate out from that. It takes more of a stretch of the imagination to see the follies at the Parc as part of our conventional picture of Paris. The paved expanse with red follies, bridges, and slides has become a gigantic playground for children, who love the color and the novel experience of unlimited room to run about under the watchful eyes of their parents.

If you are drawn to this part of Paris, a place to stop for refreshments could be:

La Boulangerie
15 rue des Panoyaux, 75020 Paris (01.43.58.45.45)
Métro: Ménilmontant
Mon–Sat noon–2:00 P.M. 8:00–11:00 P.M.

Ménilmontant has always been considered one of the poorest parts of Paris. Maurice Chevalier came from here. So did Edith Piaf. Most of the people who lived in the neighborhood were on the lower rungs of the working class, some of them not too securely. It's an area comparable to the East End of London or the Lower East Side of New York. In the dark and grubby northeast reaches of the city, one little expects to come upon one of the nicest low-cost bistros in Paris.

Originally a bakery, La Boulangerie has evolved into a most attractive little restaurant, with *ardoises* on the bright, walls, and extraordinary tiles on the floor.

To start we were given complimentary *amuse-gueules*, pork terrine in small earthenware pots. After that we enjoyed a salad of freshly grated carrots with sesame seeds.

The *plats* that followed were serious food, not the sort of thing you'd expect in a bargain lunch. The *dorade* was lovely and light, superbly sauced with olives and accompanied by a cake of polenta. The pork cutlet was served with tiny caramelized onions and a square of sautéed fries. With the *plats* we drank a Sauvignon de Touraine 2004, at 12 euros a good and fairly-priced accompaniment. Several other wines here are less than 20 euros a bottle.

A light and elegant rhubarb dessert was presented in a glass with whipped cream and little caramel wafers. The flavor might have been a little tart for some palates, but to us it was just right.

❖ *La Boulangerie: outstanding value in a part of Old Paris.*

Le Café de la Musique
Place de la Fontaine aux Lions, 213 ave. Jean-Jaurès, 75019
Paris (01.48.03.15.91)
Métro: Porte de Pantin
Open daily 8:00 A.M.–2:00 A.M.

If you like modern design, and still haven't recovered from the razing of the first Café Costes near the Pompidou Museum, you might want to visit the Café de la Musique. This highly-styled café from the Costes brothers is another of their experiments in world-class sophisticated design.

At Le Café de la Musique colors are muted: inside are pale wood tables and a matching floor. You're seated in a large elegant room done in cool colors—grayish-green velvet chairs, greenish glass, a skylight over the modern bar. Outside, the old gray cobblestone terrace supports rows of chrome and wicker chairs around circular steel tables. One looks out over one of the bleakest vistas in Paris, the intentional abrasiveness of modern architecture, but crowds come here because of La Villette.

In the Café, hors d'oeuvres, including salads, are 9 to 14 euros. *Plats*, which include ground round steak, tuna and salmon, are between 15 and 25 euros. Drinks start at 5 euros.

When we visited the café it was almost deserted, with just a trio of elegant designer types, in jacket and tie and blue jeans, sipping beer a short distance away. Outside some of the local people were there with small children, a situation made more understandable with all of La Villette's playgrounds nearby.

❖ *Le Café de la Musique: sleek, modern and overpriced.*

Lou Pascalou
14 rue des Panoyaux, 75020 Paris (01.46.36.78.10)
Métro: Ménilmontant or Père Lachaise
Open daily 9:00 A.M.–2:00 A.M.

Lou Pascalou is a café off Ménilmontant. It's also a joyous romp into the past.

To get here you'll have to walk down boulevard Ménilmontant, a lively and untidy street lined with all sorts of ethnic restaurants. Ordinary people live out here. Dogs bark. Children cry. Old ladies lug their packages out of the Arab grocery across the street. There is life and vitality here, even late at night, that you can't find in the more exclusive parts of Paris.

On the way we pass old dilapidated apartments with no balconies, just a rail in front of the window, and others which lack even that. Just as the search seems fruitless, we spot rue des Panoyaux, and a little way along see how this small street, with an exaggerated curve and V-shaped *placé*, becomes a haven, with lively-looking restaurants and bars.

Lou Pascalou is one of the best. The inside of the large old café has been painted in deeply warm colors suggestive of the late 19th century, the red earth tones of terracotta, the faded browns of the South, the richness of old varnish. Along one wall is a long rounded bench with dark wooden slats, reminiscent of seats in the old Métro. A strangely curved wooden bar balances the othe side of the room, and a pressed tin ceiling remains from another era. Strange spidery metal chandeliers cast a golden glow through the large windows.

Drinks here are fairly priced: wines 3 to 4 euros a glass. Even in the evenings coffee is only 2 euros, with soft drinks a little more. An impressive list of beers is available, as well as the usual French apéritifs like pastis, Ricard, Pernod, and Suze. If you need more sustenance, simple café food is available day and night: sandwiches starting at 4.50 euros include *jambon* (ham), Gruyère, Camembert, and *saucisson.*

The regular clientele are young professionals of the artistic variety, including people working in television and the film industry. People go to Lou to relax; we heard lots of laughter on the welcoming terrace. So if you're in the 20th to pay your respects to Oscar Wilde, Jim Morrison, or just to scope out the neighborhood, Lou Pascalou is a good stop.

❖ *Lou Pascalou: well worth a trip to the 20th.*

Le Petit Belleville
12 rue des Envierges, 75020 Paris (01.44.62.92.66)
Métro: Jourdain
Mon–Fri lunch, Tue–Sat dinner

Entering the Petit Belleville is like taking a trip back in time. Accompanied by two French architects, we found ourselves in a *café-chantant* from the past. Upon entering we saw a long, narrow room lined with tables pushed back against the walls— the reason for their placement became apparent later. Dark cream walls are covered with momentos of "greats" from the area: well-worn record jackets from old Edith Piaf and Maurice Chevalier albums, framed black-and-white photos of the same. It's a modest little hangout which on weekends is transformed into a joyous old-time *café-chantant,* where local residents celebrate the end of the work week.

The food at Le Petit Belleville is on the *cuisine familiale* level. A decent meal can be made from a *plat,* preceded, if you wish, by a *salade parisienne* with ham, or perhaps a *salade auvergnate.*

The friendly proprietor, who enjoys practicing his English, came by to answer questions about the menu and to welcome us to his bistro. When we entered the Belleville at

7:45 P.M., he suggested that we come back later, as the music doesn't get started until after 9:00 p.m. on Friday and Saturday nights.

And what a show there was! Dressed in a costume of quirky individuality, the accordionist—a perky blonde—filled the bistro with her voice and music. First she made sure everyone could join in, handing out photocopied sheets of words. Most were for songs from long ago, ballads with catchy tunes and bawdy lyrics that the strait-laced-looking locals bellowed with gusto.

A few people got up and danced: most stayed where they were, singing, laughing and eating, ordering dessert or more wine. Loud, raucous music filled the air; conversation became impossible, and we were swept up in the mood, singing with the accordionist and guessing at the naughty nuances in the songs.

❖ *Le Petit Belleville: a look at old times. Family-style cuisine and great fun.*

Le Saint-Amour
2 ave. Gambetta, 75020 Paris (01.47.97.20.15)
Métro: Père Lachaise
Open daily to 10:30 P.M.

We first heard about the Saint-Amour years ago in the course of researching a book about Paris cafés. This bistro was warmly recommended by an intellectual Parisian with a profound knowledge of his city. It seemed an unlikely choice. Nothing about the exterior of Le Saint-Amour is particularly appealing, and the interior is even worse, recalling a garish New Jersey diner, or possibly the studied kitsch of a restaurant scene in a gangster movie.

But low prices combined with the quality of first-rate produce from the Auvergne gives this brasserie serious appeal. Budget-minded travellers will go for the express menus at 10 and 12.50 euros, and served until 9:00 P.M.

The 12.50-euro menu offers hors d'oeuvres and *plats,* typically a choice of a specialty of Auvergne. Dessert in the set menu offers bistro classics like *mousse au chocolat* and *crème caramel* as well as *tarte aux pommes maison* (homemade apple pie). With the three courses this menu offers a quarter bottle of rosé, Pays du Var, red wine from Castalou, or mineral water. Jean-Louis Rouchet, the proprietor, has a particular interest in wines of the Southwest, and offers a carefully chosen variety.

Since the hour was late, we took just a *salade Auvergnate* and an *assiette de charcuterie*. The salad was large and very good, a platter heaped with *jambon du pays* (cured country ham), Cantal cheese, walnuts, hard-boiled egg, and boiled new potatoes on a bed of greens. The *assiette de charcuterie* (plate of cured meats) was fresh and tasty with ample quantities of pâté, *saucisson* (dry salami), thin slices of the excellent country ham, and pickles. Both choices gave us a taste of excellent produce from Auvergne, and were an exceptional value.

The *tarte bourdaloue* was a fine example of Auvergnate pastry. It involved layers of thinly-sliced pears with almonds on pastry, served warm with a dark chocolate sauce. A sublime and satisfying dessert.

❖ *Le Saint-Amour: good food in an unlikely-looking setting.*

12

MAIGRET'S BISTROS

> *...the thing that strikes me most is the bond that is formed between the policeman and the quarry he has to track down.... the prostitute on the Boulevard de Clichy and the policeman who is watching her... both have aching feet from trudging along miles of asphalt. They have to endure the same rain, the same icy wind.*
>
> —*Georges Simenon, Maigret's Memoirs*

Paris reveals itself to Maigret. It shows itself in bistros and brasseries, by chance encounters and strange coincidences. This was the discovery of Georges Simenon's brilliant Chief Inspector. For Maigret, the background checks and surveillance that are standard procedure often started in bistros. There was nothing self-indulgent about Maigret's frequenting them, although the amount of alcohol that he put away would have provoked a *crise de foie* in a lesser man, and in his later years became a cause for alarm in his good friend Dr. Pardon.

The secrets of Paris were accessible from the bar of a bistro. From his first case onward, certain police procedures came more easily to Maigret in the relaxed ambiance of a local hangout. And the description of the café or bistro he patronizes during a case can lend a fine exactness to the locale. We picture the Marais and the Place des Vosges, delineated for us by the mention of three familiar drinking-places in *L'Amie de Madame Maigret*: "In a square that everybody knew, there are the three cafés, one on the corner of the rue des Francs-Bourgeois, the Grand Turenne opposite, and, about 30 meters away, the Tabac des Vosges."

No longer called the Tabac des Vosges, the bistro on the

corner could still be considered one of Maigret's because of its close identification with the Chief Inspector of Simenon's stories. Now known as Ma Bourgogne, this warm and venerable watering place with the massive beams overhead dominates a corner of the Place des Vosges, a square even more fashionable than in Maigret's day. Privileged people can be victims of crime, just like anybody else, and his work would take him into districts like this, where someone might exact payments for concealing damaging information, or try to hasten the demise of a wealthy relative.

In certain of Maigret's adventures, the great detective gives such attention to the *cuisinier's* and sommelier's arts that one wonders how he could keep a clear head for solving the crimes. England's Sherlock Holmes was lean and spare, leading a Spartan regime, paying little attention to what or if he ate—most of Mrs. Hudson's scones were consumed by Watson. Holmes's French counterpart recognizes the importance of the table. And Sherlock had no wife, no kindly Madame Maigret to welcome him with a bistro-type dish simmered all morning, its aroma wafting down the stairs to welcome him when he would come home.

The Maigrets' tastes on the occasions when they dine at home together run to the *cuisine grand-mère* that makes up classic bistro food. In *Maigret and the Loner*, Maigret goes home for lunch to find that his wife had made *coq au vin*, one of his favorite dishes. In another story, a day off on a weekend is made special by the food: Madame Maigret has prepared a beef stew. It is simmering in the blue-tiled kitchen, making their apartment fragrant with the scent of herbs. Old-fashioned dishes are perceived as best, and for a dinner with their friends the Pardons, Madame Maigret made an excellent *boeuf bourguignon* which became the center of conversation.

> *Maigret had been only a detective when he had made a sally that was often repeated to newcomers to the Quai des Orfèvres. Told to watch a banker... he had said to his chief: "To understand how his mind works I must breakfast with financiers."*
>
> —Georges Simenon, *Maigret Has Doubts*

Trying to understand the thinking of all types of suspects and victims, whether financiers, racketeers, petty criminals, or call girls, the whole gamut of society that becomes mixed up in murder, Maigret's investigations familiarize him with all of Paris and he patronizes bars and bistros throughout the city. His local bar near work is the Brasserie Dauphine in the Place of the same name. He sends down to the Brasserie for beer and sandwiches when he's conducting the marathon questioning of a suspect which often leads to a confession and terminates his work on a case.

When he has more time, he can savor the simple cuisine there: he remembers that the brasserie has distinctive odors and in *Maigret and the Headless Corpse,* identifies the dominant ones as the smell of Pernod around the bar and *coq au vin* simmering in the kitchen. On another day he perceives a scent of wines from the Loire Valley, and an aroma of herbs, particularly tarragon and chives.

A case on the rue St. Dominique in the 7th arrondissement brings Maigret closer to the seat of power; with Janvier, he picks a restaurant on the rue de Bourgogne, patronized by officials from nearby ministries. Here they start a meal with asparagus and proceed to ray in brown butter. Near the Parc Monceau in a rich *quartier* he remembers walking with Madame Maigret not long after their marriage, looking at the elegant houses overlooking the park. The young Maigrets imagined the privileged way of life that went on behind those façades.

Other stories take Maigret to the seamier parts of Paris, in particular the 18th district. In *Maigret Has Scruples,* he notices a pimp waiting in the detention center and thinks that he "had Place Pigalle written all over him." He remembers working on the boulevard de la Chapelle, where, beneath the elevated métro, night after night there were "familiar shadows." Maigret thought he knew what the women were doing, waiting around there, but that it was much more difficult to work out what reasons such men could have for hanging about doing nothing, men of all races and ages, who came out in the evenings when it was dark and cold.

Closer to home Maigret frequents a bistro on the Place de la République, near the family apartment on boulevard Richard-Lenoir in the 11th district. In *Maigret's Little Joke*, he decides to spend his vacation quietly in Paris while spreading the word that he and Madame are enjoying the beaches at Les Sables d'Orlonne. He starts to follow a murder case, reading the morning papers on a relatively deserted café terrace on the Place.

In the course of the Maigrets' Paris vacation, they make their way to Montmartre and stop for a drink at the Place du Tertre. There they notice three cafés dominating the square. Maigret notices that the square had changed since he was young, that it still seemed amusing, like a fairground, but more vulgar than ever.

Starting with his first case, Maigret acquired the habit of dropping into a bistro wherever his work might take him. Often his purpose was to gather information. In *Maigret's First Case*, young Maigret is trying to observe the activity in a building where he thinks a murder has been committed. He spends hours trapped in a bistro called the Vieux Calvados, feeling that he has become the victim of a generous or sadistic proprietor who keeps pouring him glasses of Calvados, the Norman liqueur of almost lethal potency. He is tormented by doubts, asking himself if it is worthwhile "to hang around all day in a bistro, in order to watch a house where nothing happened?" Maigret could not foresee that some day, although chief of the special squad with police officers under his command, he would continue to do lookouts himself, following a suspect through the streets and waiting in small bistros for hours on end.

> Having crossed Place de la Bastille, he was passing a little bistro on his way down Boulevard Henri IV.... As he went past... Maigret's nostrils were assailed by a gust of fragrance which was forever to remain with him as the very quintessence of Paris at daybreak: the fragrance of frothy coffee and hot croissants, spiced with a bit of rum.

—Georges Simenon, *Maigret and the Spinster*

Caught up in an investigation, Maigret considers ordering sandwiches from the Brasserie Dauphine, but decides instead to try the Henri IV, a little bar opposite the statue, where he orders a ham sandwich and is recognized by the waiter. Later on the same day he makes do with a sandwich and beer at La Coupole, a famous brasserie on the boulevard du Montparnasse, while he ponders the case.

In the evening, a little self-conscious now at being shadowed by Spencer, an American criminologist who has come to Paris to study his methods, Maigret finally stops to eat in a bistro near the Porte d'Orléans, with a zinc counter, a few marble-topped tables, and sawdust on the floor. The proprietor, a pleasant man with a blotchy complexion, comes and shakes hands with Maigret. His wife Mélanie produces a substantial meal, starting with *cèpes à la bourdelaise,* the mushrooms fresh from the country, and proceeding to *coq au vin.* With it, the proprietor suggests, "Your usual Beaujolais, Superintendent?" and Maigret accepts.

The young American questions Maigret to learn his views on the psychology of murderers, and is surprised by his thinking on the question. Maigret asks whether he is talking about murderers before or after they've committed the crime, because before it they're not yet guilty, and they might live 40 or 50 years of their lives behaving just like everyone else:

> *"What makes you think, Monsieur Spencer, that just killing one of his own kind should change a man's character from one minute to the next?"*

> *"So what it comes down to," said the American, "is that a murderer is a man like any other."*

After they've found the murder victim's cache of thousand-franc notes and Maigret is fairly sure of who the murderer is, he receives a lesson in the differences between himself and the congenial American. Maigret suggests that they drop into a nearby bistro for a glass of something while they're waiting for their streetcar:

"I'll have a Calvados. What about you?"

"Would they have such a thing as a glass of milk, I wonder?"

Maybe that explained how a man of thirty-five had managed to retain a complexion as rosy as the muzzle of a young calf.

Sometimes a bistro or brasserie is crucial to the plot of a Maigret story. La Coupole, on the boulevard du Montparnasse, is almost a character itself in *Maigret's War of Nerves*. The story begins with a prisoner escaping from the maximum security section of the Santé prison. The escape is secretly engineered by Maigret, who has been convinced for some time that the wrong man was condemned to die for murdering a wealthy American woman. A day before his execution, Joseph Heurtin finds his cell door open and the guard nowhere near. A note had appeared in his food two days before, suggesting that escape would be possible at 2:00 A.M., when a rope ladder and a disguise would be at hand.

Maigret's unconventional approach to trying to solve the crime is put to the test when an article appears in *Le Sifflet*, one of the evening newspapers, exposing his carefully planned scheme and stating that it was the police officials themselves, along with the judicial authorities, who presided over this "pseudo-escape."

Who could have leaked the information? Maigret finds that the editors at *Sifflet* had received a letter written on stationery from one of the cafés. He narrows the source down to the Coupole.

To solve this case, Maigret has to spend time at the Coupole. He is intrigued by the brasserie, so different from the bistros he usually frequents. His observations give us an excellent description of many Parisian brasseries today:

> *The place was writhing with humanity.... Four waiters were all shouting at once, accompanied by the clatter of plates and tinkling of glasses. Snatches of different languages broke out on all sides. Yet somehow the whole scene—customers, barmen, waiters, the room itself—gave the impression of a homogeneous whole.*

A wealthy and socially prominent American couple, Mr. and Mrs. Kirby, enter. The arrival of these people in their luxurious sports car with their other signs of conspicuous wealth makes Maigret think of the escapee Heurtin, that pathetic figure, the strange-looking young man who was somewhere in the city with just over twenty francs in his pocket.

Further work on the case leads Maigret again to the Coupole, to the Pelican, a small bar on the rue des Ecoles, to other bistros on the boulevard du Montparnasse, and, finally, to the house where the murder had been committed and where the real murderer gives himself away.

Some of Maigret's time in bistros, when he isn't actually questioning a barman or a proprietor about a suspect, a victim, or possible witness, is spent getting a "feel" for the place. In *Maigret's Memoirs*, the great detective relates his ideas on the subject: "You have to know. To know the milieu in which a crime has been committed, to know the way of life, the habits, morals, reactions of people involved in it, whether victims, criminals, or merely witnesses. To enter into their world without surprise, easily, and to speak its language naturally."

This is why Maigret feels that the police are not wasting their time when they spend years pacing sidewalks. Theirs is the serving of an apprenticeship, different from other apprenticeships because it goes on for a lifetime, as the variety of settings in Paris is almost infinite.

Maigret's patronage of bistros allows us insights into the man himself: he can manage to keep going on beer and sandwiches—how many beers and sandwiches has he had sent up from the Brasserie Dauphine during the course of an interrogation? But he prefers home cooking: used to Madame Maigret's *cuisine familiale* at home on boulevard Richard Lenoir, he is able to appreciate good food when he finds it.

The pleasure of the ordinary bistro, its sights, sounds, and smells, are celebrated in *Maigret Bides his Time*. Inside Chez l'Auvergnat, an old-fashioned bistro with a zinc counter and a jovial, mustachioed owner, Maigret notices sausages and gourd-shaped cheeses. Hams with grayish rinds hang from the ceiling, and there are enormous flat loaves of bread from the Massif Central. Cooking is done by the owner's wife. The lunch menu changes daily, chalked on a slate blackboard. This day Maigret samples *rillettes du Morvan, filet de veau, fromage,* and *tarte tatin,* served by the owners who are clearly proud to entertain such a famous customer.

Maigret's bistros still exist in Paris. Some of them are easy to find: obvious, well-known, named in the books. Others need a little searching out, but are worth the effort for Simenon enthusiasts and on their own merits:

Le Bar du Caveau
17 Place Dauphine, 75001 Paris (01.43.54.45.95)
Métro: Cité
Mon–Sat 8:30 A.M.–6:30 P.M. May–Sept; Mon–Fri.
Oct–April

Situated in the Place Dauphine behind the Palais de Justice, this is almost certainly the original of the Brasserie Dauphine patronized so often by Maigret. Here are old stone walls, venerable beams, an old oak bar, brass-edged marble café tables, and charm. The clientele are mostly French: two men standing and talking at the bar looked to be almost caricatures of middle-aged French government officials. High above them was a shelf with numerous carefully arranged bottles, conveying the fact that this is a wine bar with serious wines. They are available by the glass, the *demi,* and the full bottle.

Small basic lunches are served at low prices, lunches like tabouli, salad, and *crème caramel. Tartines* (open-faced sandwiches) on *pain poilâne* are from 4.50 to 7 euros. Wine by the glass ranges from 4 to 6 euros.

While eating we had a chance to appreciate the quiet refinement of this little bistro tucked away into one of the most coveted parts of the great city. An oil painting, large enough to be a mural, conveys the feeling of what life by the Seine must have been like years ago. Old wooden boxes contain glossy magazines about food, wine, and the good life in general; the daily newspapers hang near the door. The dour barman did not affect anyone's pleasure at being in this idyllic retreat.

Ma Bourgogne
19 Place des Vosges, 75004 Paris (01.42.78.44.64)
Métro: Bastille
Open daily 8:00 A.M.–1:30 A.M.

Originally called the Tabac de la Place des Vosges, Ma Bourgogne has a warm and welcoming interior. Prices reflect the important location, but a drink at the bar is still a bargain. Avoid peak times, when it's next to impossible to get near the bar. A coffee and croissant on the *terrasse* is a nice beginning to a day in Paris. This bistro is specifically identified in *L'Amie de Madame Maigret.*

La Coupole
108 blvd du Montparnasse, 75014 Paris (01.43.20.14.20)
Métro: Vavin
Open daily to 2:00 A.M.

Dining at La Coupole is, for better or worse, one of the quintessential experiences of being in Paris. It's an institution, a legend, an artistic memory, an historic monument, and it's a restaurant where everybody goes. It has a midtown Manhattan sort of flavor. It's festive, it's fun, it's bright, it's glossy and glittery. It's also noisy, swarming with Parisians and tourists alike, and it virtually shouts, "I'm important and famous!" Everybody has been here, and it's no use listing their names.

La Coupole is not a bistro, but a brasserie important enough to come up in several mysteries. Also La Coupole has been an historic writers' and artists' gathering place from its beginnings in 1927. It quickly became a favorite of the American expatriates. The main floor was a brasserie and thirty-some artists, Léger included, contributed their skills to the decoration of the huge room. Since 1988 it has belonged to the Groupe Flo.

La Coupole is a vast space, generally believed to be the largest restaurant in all of France, with high ceilings, elegant lighting, and a remarkable floor in Deco-patterned tile. The interior is broken up by pillars and banquettes. There are suspended Deco light fixtures, Deco curves in the molding around the ceiling, and a ceiling the color of a pale *café crème*.

The food is sometimes described as *cuisine industrielle*, but in our experience, the Groupe Flo food, while never very creative, can be surprisingly good. A lunch *formule* is 24 euros, and when we went there on a Saturday night with friends, there was a 32-euro menu of three courses with wine or mineral water. Starters were *foie gras*, oysters, or *carpaccio de tomates*. In our party of six, somebody ordered each of the possibilities, and they were all good: the *foie gras de canard* delicious with accompanying cubes of aspic, the *carpaccio de tomates* a dish of tomatoes covered with a round of *fromage blanc,* with green pesto sauce and chives.

For *plats,* the well-flavored salmon on a bed of cooked red and green peppers was served hot in an ironware dish with little boiled potatoes. *Canard confit* (literally "preserved duck") was duck cooked a long time; it tasted delicious, the meat falling off the bone. The *rumsteak* was tasty in a rich brown sauce with mushrooms. Desserts included a spectacular *soupe aux fraises,* a bowl of strawberries sliced in half, in a strawberry purée, topped with a scoop of strawberry ice cream.

All of us were satisfied. Flo cuisine pleases most people: it provides consistency and a certain level of competence. It's an institution. You've been dining at a legend, and it's not bad. It's glitzy, glossy, and fun.

La Patache
60 rue de Lancry, 75010 Paris (01.42.08.14.35)
Métro: Jacques Bonsergent
Open daily 5:00 P.M.–2:00 A.M.
No credit cards

Almost certainly the "dingy-looking bar" described in *Maigret and the Headless Corpse.* "The ceiling was low and blackened with smoke, and the walls were grimy. Indeed, the whole place was murky, except for faint patches of sunlight here and there."

This bar is an old photographic postcard brought to life. It had a reputation for boisterous patrons, mediocre folk music, and, some might add, 19th century sanitary conditions. The latter have been improved under a new owner, and now food, cheese, and plates of *charcuterie* are available. Worth seeking out, especially if you want to see what an old-fashioned *café-bougnat*, a place that sold drinks and coal, looked like.

Au Pied de Fouet
45 rue Babylone, 75007 Paris (01.47.05.12.27)
Métro: Sèvres-Babylone
Mon–Fri noon–2:30 P.M., 7:00 P.M.–9:30 P.M.,
closed August

A different location, but similar in spirit to the little restaurant on the rue de Miromesnil described in *Maigret Hesitates* as a relic of former days. The menu was chalked up on a slate, and "Each of the regulars had his napkin in a pigeonhole and frowned when someone took his seat."

Le Royal Turenne
24 rue de Turenne, 75004 Paris (01.42.72.04.53)
Métro: Chemin Vert
Open daily 7:30 A.M.–midnight

This is the café mentioned in *L'Amie de Madame Maigret* as "Le Grand Turenne." The Royal Turenne gives you a superb people-watching vantage point, something Maigret would need. During the few minutes we were there, slender young Parisiennes moved past like silent deer and a bald gentleman wearing a business suit and carrying *Le Monde* rounded the corner on rollerblades and then whirled down the street.

Here are the venerable brass-edged café tables, the old bar and exposed stone, and a good view of the café L'Escurial across the way. In fact, under the blue-and-white striped parasols of Le Royal Turenne, you have a choice spot for reconnoitering the whole neighborhood.

Here you can stop for an espresso or a *croque monsieur*. Times have changed, and now you can even get Coca-Cola and hot dogs. But Maigret was not a person to be disturbed by change; he had travelled, he'd been to New York and enjoyed the pubs of London, so a few American innovations would not be likely to upset him. Still, his favorite *consommation* at Le Royal Turenne would most likely be a beer, at 5, or possibly a glass of wine, at 3 euros.

If it's around lunchtime, a *plat du jour* could be an economical meal.

Le Sélect
99 blvd du Montparnasse, 75006 Paris (01.42.22.65.27)
Métro: Vavin
Open daily 7:00 A.M.–3:00 A.M.

One of the most historic of the literary cafés, this name comes up several times in the Maigret mysteries, notably in *Maigret Mystified* when Nine, the murder victim's mistress, waits in vain for him to keep a rendezvous with her there, not knowing that the wealthy man who's supported her is dead. Typically, Maigret is more sympathetic with her than with the victim's other associates and even lends her money for a taxi. Le Sélect is described elsewhere on pages 73–75.

Taverne Henri IV
13 Place du Pont-Neuf, 75001 Paris (01.43.54.27.90)
Métro: Pont-Neuf
Mon–Fri noon–3:00 P.M., 6:30 P.M.–8:30 P.M.,
closed August

A famous winebar on the Ile de la Cité with a notoriously grumpy proprietor. Noted for the variety of its wines and for the good sandwiches on *pain Poilâne*. Worth a visit. Here Maigret goes for a ham sandwich during a rainy day in *Maigret and the Spinster*. It was a day when he felt the need to get out of his office and the usual sandwiches ordered up from the Brasserie Dauphine just wouldn't do.

13

ROMANTIC BISTROS

"Oh! To wander Paris! Such a lovely, delectable experience!"

—*Balzac*, La Physiologie du Mariage

It should always be seen, the first time, with the eyes of childhood or of love.

—*M.F.K. Fisher*, The Gastronomical Me

It must be something about the light in Paris: something rather unusual, a softness, an ethereal, diffused quality, a glow that illuminates faces and flowers and creates a mood. Alone among cities, Paris is still associated with romance, love for the young and the not-so-young, where the beauty all around hints at romantic possibilities.

Magic exists here, and not only in the great places of recognized importance, the palaces and mansions and exclusive haunts of the privileged. It can be elusive, but is to be found as surely in the perfume from a shower-sprinkled flower, a view of the Seine from one of its bridges on a cloudy day, the sinuous curvings of a métro entrance or a wrought-iron balcony, an expanse of chaotic grass with violets competing with the orderly rows of trees in a park.

Under the spell of Paris things said and felt take on a greater significance. Life is charged with a particular energy, an intensity not to be found in any other place. Stay in Paris for a week, and, while time races relentlessly on, as it does everywhere, you are left with the sense that you've lived and felt much more than the experience of a few days.

Paris is a special place for lovers, too, who flock everywhere in this great city. They meander hand-in-hand along the narrow streets, they embrace beside the Seine, they exchange long, soulful glances across rooms and at train stations. (Increasingly, too, when apart they shout sweet nothings at each other over cell phones.)

But there remains something reassuringly old-fashioned about romance. The most modern Parisian bride is choosing to be wed in a Victorian froth of white lace and silk; she has no doubt been courted across the tables of traditional family bistros, familiar haunts that lure one with their promise of cozy intimacy.

Picasso celebrated love in many of his paintings. An American reporter found that he had something eloquent to say about it, too. Janet Flanner, Paris correspondent for the *New Yorker*, remembered seeing Picasso during her first years in the city. He too was an habitué of the bistros: "After 1945 he began coming to the Café de Flore at night. He always sat at the second table in front of the main door, with Spanish friends. I would sit where, without seeming to, I could view his remarkably mobile face with its amazingly watchful eyes."

In the mid-1950s Flanner happened to be in Cannes. She met the artist son of an old friend and learned that Picasso had given the young man a gift, a sketch of his infant son. He had promised to sign and dedicate it if the father stopped by. They went to the great artist's villa, and Flanner, not wanting to intrude, stayed behind in the car. Summoned twice to come in, she told of walking into the art-crowded salon and being recognized by Picasso:

> ... *with a loud cry of astonishment, [he] shouted: 'You! Why didn't you ever speak to me in the old days at the Flore? For years we saw each other and never spoke, until now. Are you just the same as you were? You look it!* By now he had his arms around me and was thumping me enthusiastically on the shoulders. *"You look fine, not a day older,"* and I said *"Nor do you,"* and he said, *"That's true; that's the way you and I are. We don't get older, we just get riper.... Tell me, do you still love the human race, especially your best friends? Do you still love love?"* "I do," I said, astonished at the turn the monologue was taking. "And so do I!" he shouted, laughing. "Oh, we're great ones for that, you

and I. Isn't love the greatest refreshment in life?" And
he embraced me with his strong arms, in farewell.

Flanner and Picasso are gone now, but like them, you can still find the romantic Paris that remains to be enjoyed.

Start with morning coffee with croissants in an historic café—we might pick the unspoiled Sélect; walk on the historic Ile Saint-Louis or the Ile de la Cité, indulge in a ride around Paris at off-peak hours, not with tourists in a group but with Parisians on a regular bus route that's special—we like the 29, which sweeps past the Café de la Paix and the old Opéra, and the 96, with its views of Notre Dame, the Marais, and the Place Saint-Sulpice. Along the way, spot the small streets and little galleries which you wish to return to and explore on foot together; share a boat trip on the Seine; pick up a snack from a vender or at a boulangerie, and take it to enjoy in a green place, perhaps the Jardin du Luxembourg; indulge in hot chocolate or tea and a pastry in the afternoon in the gilded luxury of a good *salon de thé*; explore the stalls of the *bouquinistes* along the Seine, and find a postcard or print of old Paris that's good enough to be a special keepsake; finally, walk near the river when the lights begin to glow all over the city at twilight.

"A walk through the Paris streets was always like the unrolling of a vast tapestry from which countless stored fragrances were shaken out," wrote Edith Wharton. You will sense the romance in these narrow streets with the cobblestones underfoot and the sky above, the fanciful Old-World façades of countless little shops shining, a painter's palette of deep and luscious tones—cobalt blue, hunter green, umber, burnt sienna. And there are endless surprises along the way: a massive brass door knocker in the shape of a lion, an unexpected niche in an old wall with an unlooked-for saint or Virgin and Child, a morning splash of color in a market vender's stall, the oranges, reds, and yellows of artfully piled fruit in a marvel of balance and symmetry, a glimpse of a courtyard with trees and flowers, an old-fashioned bistro with its original zinc bar and an affable proprietor.

When you leave the modern noise and nervous intensity of the tourist world and turn into the Place Dauphine, you'll hear birds singing and leaves rustling. It's an exquisite place, almost unnaturally quiet and unhurried, a part of Paris most visitors never enter. Though a few feet away you glimpse tourists searching for Notre Dame and the Conciergerie, here it's like finding yourself in an especially quiet provincial town on a lazy Sunday afternoon.

There are several restaurants on the Place: our favorite is not a restaurant but a wine bar, the **Bar du Caveau**, at 17 Place Dauphine. Inside is a room of real charm, where you sit on a classic bentwood chair at a marble-topped, brass-rimmed café table. You brush against ancient stone walls and notice on one side a Romantic-influenced oil painting of early Paris by the Seine. It's a special place for drinks and low-priced lunches in an enchanting corner of the city. (Further details in "Maigret's Bistros.")

If you were going by the **Bistro du Peintre**, not far from the Bastille at 116 avenue Ledru-Rollin, 75011 Paris, you'd almost certainly say to your partner, "Remember where we are—we've got to come back here sometime." This bistro recalls the Paris of romantic legend, the Belle Epoque with Toulouse-Lautrec and Sarah Bernhardt. Large swirling Art Nouveau-shaped windows cover the front and massive oak cabinets carved into quasi-organic floral forms are punctuated by highly polished brass. It's a charming place with cuisine that is honest, basic, and good. *Pichets* of the house wine are more than adequate. *Plats* around 11 euros might include simple bistro fare like *brandade de haddock* or a *pot au feu* (stew). In the afternoon you can enjoy this setting for the price of a cup of coffee or a glass of wine. It's open every day until 2:00 A.M. except for Sunday, when it closes at 8:00 in the evening.

To get a feeling for the 9th arrondissement, leave the department stores and take the bus or métro to the métro stop Grands Boulevards. Walk up the rue du faubourg Montmartre, stopping at **Chartier**, number 7, located at the end of a courtyard. An old-fashioned *bouillon* from the Belle Epoque, Chartier was originally founded to give working-class people a place whre they could afford to eat simple low-priced meals, often soup, hence the name. High ceilings and elegant but not

especially elaborate moldings give a turn-of-the-century flavor that belies the modesty of Chartier's origins.

Sometimes romance has little to do with appearances. Consider the **Café les Deux Moulins**, open daily at 15 rue Lepic, 75018 Paris (01.42.54.90.50), Métro: Abbesses. The look of this café is shiny, glitzy, and cheap—no aspiring young actresses or lanky long-haired models lurk about here. But this was the locale for the movie *Amélie*, in French *Le Fabuleux Destin d'Amélie Poulain.* It's the story of a French girl who works in a drab little café and spends her spare time trying to do good things for people. On the way she falls in love with a rather ordinary boy. The Café les Deux Moulins is in a part of Montmartre where tourists seldom go, a rather crowded and intense working-class area without much of the usual Parisian charm. But young, impressionable tourists now flock there

from all over, to photograph each other in the café where Audrey Tautou, the star, worked as a waitress in the film. (Sometimes they even leave graffiti in the washroom—little notes for "Amélie" telling how she has touched and inspired them.) While many of the tourists are Japanese schoolgirls, some are also Europeans and Americans.

The Café les Deux Moulins is memorable, yet plain. A dramatic neon tube zigzags above the bar. Tables are unabashed formica. The real barmaid is an unsmiling blonde of a certain age, tending bar with a lean French waiter. No one courts the late afternoon crowd with Amélie charm, but the Deux Moulins still gets more than its share of customers. If you have wine or a beer at an inside table it's about 3 euros; a coffee in the same place would be 2. Fair prices for a neighborhood hangout that made it into the big time.

Would you like to dine in Victorian splendor? You'll find the real thing at **Gallopin**, 40 rue Notre-Dame-des-Victoires (01.42.36.45.38), right behind the Bourse. Here is a setting with all of the richness and elegance of the late 19th century. Gustave Gallopin was an Anglophile: he not only married an English woman, he created this, the ultimate Victorian restaurant, in all of its extravagance. Here is fine mahogany woodwork, a veritable wall of stained glass, an elaborate ceiling and ornate fixtures, all made by English craftsmen in London and reassembled in Paris in 1876.

Gallopin is a favorite with young couples out for a romantic evening. If you go for one of the *formules*, between 24 and 35 euros, you just might find yourself next to celebrities: Gallopin has long been frequented by the beautiful people, politicians, writers, journalists from Agence France Presse, and actors including Jane Birkin and Gérard Depardieu.

It may be that the most romantic spot in Paris to sit and sip coffee is by the outdoor café, **Café Les Gaufres**, at the northern end of the Luxembourg Gardens. The nineteenth-century style metal and glass building looks like nothing more than a large gazebo, with olive chairs and tables spreading out around it. In the summer, you'll sit somewhere outdoors at a table under a tall tree, watching the dusky light filter down through layers of translucent green foliage. On even the warmest summer days the breezes feel cooler here.

Our server was clad in the garb of the classic French waiter, even down to the corkscrew emerging from his pocket. He might have been an old actor hired for the role. The 2-euro coffee is drinkable if not special, and if you wish to spend more than your day's allowance, they can bring you champagne.

In an unlikely location just off a busy boulevard, there's a place of unusual charm. **Le Clown Bar** (see pages 145–146) is a small *bistro à vins* between the République and the Bastille. Here you can raise a glass of simple country wine, taste a snack, or enjoy a full meal right next door to the Cirque d'Hiver (Winter Circus), where Hemingway would sometimes practice boxing with his friends. We like to think that afterwards his bruised fists might have cradled a drink at the Clown Bar, although it's not exactly his sort of place. Too much charm.

The walls in the two small rooms are covered with spectacular old tiles from 1919, many of them depicting clowns in assorted comic poses. They remind one of pictures in old children's books, especially those illustrated by Kate Greenaway. Original vintage posters of clowns and other circus memorabilia complete the picture. At night during warm weather, the doors open and a young crowd spills over onto the sidewalk, but inside the low lighting and lovely setting suggest romance.

L'Etrier Bistro (see pages 187–188), is an almost ideal neighborhood bistro in the less-visited part of Montmartre. It's small, bright, and intimate, a light and airy place offering delicious cuisine, which is not surprising since the owner once worked at the Élysee Palace. Developed from what was once a storefront with only ten small tables, L'Etrier is cleverly decorated with white walls, white floor tiles, and fine lace curtains tied back with raffia. Flowers adorn each table and classical music plays softly in the background.

One of Paris's prettiest little bistros is tucked away in a lovely residential area near the Ecole Militaire, not far from the Eiffel Tower. The **Fontaine de Mars** at 129 rue St. Dominique was named for the old fountain beside the outdoor terrace. On warm summer days most visitors choose tables there, but the room inside has a radiance born of many years of service. Highly polished nineteenth-century oak cabinets, antique brass, and simple plaid curtains suggest an old-fashioned local bistro. It's a quiet and civilized setting suitable for romantic conversations. Patrons tend to be well-tailored and soft-spoken. It's an especially likeable little bistro.

Le Restaurant Julien is a glorious Art Nouveau brasserie in a grubby district. Go anyway for its fabulous interior and a feeling of Parisian life in the early 1900s. More details on page 125–127.

Very few tourists come to the 10th arrondissement. But romantic couples are drawn to walk beside the Canal St. Martin, and go to the most famous café along its banks: the **Hôtel du Nord**, at 102 quai de Jemnapes, 75010 Paris (01.40.40.78.78.) Made famous by Marcel Carné's film, *L'Hôtel du Nord*, the café-bar retains much of its mystery. One can imagine the film's star, Arletty, there—she lived in an apartment overlooking the canal.

Le Temps des Cerises in the 4th district is the perfect Parisian bistro, a little gem hidden away in the touristy Marais. Its popularity with the locals makes Le Temps too chaotic to be romantic at lunch, when people from the quarter flock there for the daily specials in the ambiance enhanced by the friendliness of the proprietors. But Le Temps is perfect for a mid-afternoon pick-me-up, or for a drink and a snack to sustain you in your meanderings through the picturesque 4th arrondissement. It is described in more detail earlier in this book on pages 41–42.

A hundred and some years ago, Montmartre was a small village just north of Paris, known for its bawdy entertainment and artistic freedom. Today the town looks much the same, but it has been almost taken over by foreign tour groups. The center of this frenzied activity is the Place de Tertre, a small-town square now completely jammed with restaurant tables, itinerant artists, and bewildered foreigners milling about, trying to make sense of it all.

Le Vieux Chalet is everyone's idea of a typical French restaurant. Somehow it survives in the most unlikely location, near sidewalk artists and souvenir stands. From the Place du Tertre go along the rue Norvins. At number 4 you'll find the Old Chalet. Waves of people surge past, but in this restaurant with its dark beams, whitewashed walls, and red-and-white checkered tablecloths, you feel secure. The menu

is simple, with starters like pâté, sardines, minestrone, and *salade de tomates*, followed by reliable classics like steak, pork chops, and roast chicken. And the surprise was not the menu but the prices—even on a Saturday night, the 15-euro menu was in force.

A tureen of steaming minestrone and a plate of sardines, garnished with tomatoes and lemons were satisfying beginnings, followed by roast chicken, hot and crisp, with sautéed potatoes and a large steak, with a good smoky flavor of the grill.

Service is friendly and attentive; the manager-owner speaks fluent English, and enjoys chatting about the Vieux Chalet. "It's over a hundred years old," he told us. So this restaurant was here in this village when Utrillo painted his views of the streets and when Picasso went by on his way to the Lapin Agile.

The wine list is surprising. There are some perfectly decent wines for from 9 to 12 euros, and a few very unexpected bottles—a Lafite Rothschild, a Cos d' Estournel, all from good years. When we asked about this, the manager mentioned that he had bought up several private wine cellars.

A final word:
As you go through our pages, you'll realize that a separate chapter about romantic restaurants wasn't really necessary: there are so many of them, thanks to the genius of the French for creating places where one is made to feel special. So whether you like the old stones and weathered beams of historic drinking-places, prefer quiet garden retreats that seem to have been created especially for you, or love the flamboyant decor of a great brasserie, you can find just what you've been looking for in Paris.

BIBLIOGRAPHY

Angelou, Maya. *Singin' and Swingin' and Gettin' Merry Like Christmas*. New York: Bantam Books, 1989.

Beauvoir, Simone de. *The Prime of Life*. Cleveland and New York: World Publishing Company, 1962.

—. *After the War: Force of Circumstance, I 1944–1952*. Trans. Richard Howard. New York: Paragon House, 1992.

Baldwin, James. "Equal in Paris." in *The Price of the Ticket: Collected Nonfiction, 1948–1985*. New York: St. Martin's Press, 1985.

Boyle, Kay, and Robert McAlmon. *Being Geniuses Together, 1920–1930*. San Francisco: North Point Press, 1984.

Campbell, Barbara-Ann. *Paris: A Guide to Recent Architecture*. London: Ellipsis London Ltd., 1997.

Charters, Jimmie. *This Must Be The Place: Memoirs of Montparnasse*. As told to Morrill Cody. New York, London: Collier Books, 1989.

Chevalier, Maurice. *My Paris*. Photographs by Robert Doisneau. New York: Macmillan Co., 1972.

Courtine, Robert J. *Madame Maigret's Recipes*. Trans. Mary Manheim. New York: Harcourt, Brace Jovanovich, 1975.

Ducongé, Ada Smith, and James Haskins. *Bricktop*. New York: Atheneum, 1983.

Fabre, Michel. *From Harlem to Paris: Black American Writers in France, 1840–1980*. Urbana: Univ of Illinois, 1991.

Flanner, Janet. *Darlinghissima: Letters to a Friend*. New York: Random House, 1985.

—. *Paris Journal, 1965–1971*. New York: Viking, 1972.

—. *Paris Was Yesterday 1925–1939*. New York: Viking, 1972.

Green, Julien. *Paris*. Trans. J.A. Underwood. New York: Marion Boyers, 1991.

Haine, W. Scott. *The World of the Paris Café: Sociability among the French Working Class, 1789–1914*. Baltimore and London: Johns Hopkins UP, 1996.

Hansen, Arlen J. *Expatriate Paris*. New York: Arcade Publishing, 1990.

Himes, Chester. *The Quality of Hurt*. New York: Thunder's Mouth Press, 1971.

—. *My Life of Absurdity*. New York: Thunder's Mouth Press, 1976.

Hughes, Langston. *The Big Sea.* New York: Thunder's Mouth Press, 1940.

Lamar, Jake. *Ghosts of Saint-Michel.* New York: St. Martin's Minotaur, 2006.

Littlewood, Ian. *Paris: A Literary Companion.* New York: Harper and Row, 1988.

Marshall, Paule. "Chez Tournon: A Homage," in The New York Times Oct. 18, 1992.

Miller, Henry. *Letters to Anaïs Nin.* New York: G. P. Putnam's, 1965.

Morton, Brian N. *Americans in Paris.* Ann Arbor: The Olivia and Hill Press, 1984.

Russell, John. *Paris.* New York: Harry Abrams, 1983.

Schlosser, Eric. *Fast Food Nation.* New York: Houghton Mifflin, 2001.

Shirer, William L. *Twentieth-Century Journey: A Memoir of a Life and The Times, 1904–1930.* New York: Simon and Shuster, 1976.

Simenon, Georges. *Maigret and the Black Sheep.* Trans. Helen Thomson. New York and London: Harcourt Brace Jovanovich, 1976.

—. *Maigret and the Headless Corpse.* New York: Hamish Hamilton, 1955.

—. *Maigret and the Spinster.* New York: Harcourt Brace Jovanovich, 1977.

—. *Maigret's First Case, in Maigret Cinq.* Trans. Richard Brain. New York: Harcourt Brace Jovanovich, 1977.

—. *Maigret Hesitates.* New York: Harcourt Brace Jovanovich, 1970.

—. *Maigret's Memoirs.* Trans. Jean Stewart. New York: Harcourt Brace Jovanovich, 1985.

—. *Maigret Mystified.* Trans. Jean Stewart. Middlesex, England: Penguin, 1964.

—. *Maigret's War of Nerves.* Trans Geoffrey Sainsbury. New York: Harcourt Brace Jovanovich, 1940.

Stein, Gertrude. *Paris France.* New York: Liveright, 1970. First published in 1940.

Stovall, Tyler. "Harlem-sur-Seine: Building an African Diasporic Community in Paris." Stanford Electronic Humanities Review 1997. vol. 5.2 (1997).

Wright, Richard. "There's Always Another Café." Kiosk, vol. 10, 1953.

GLOSSARY

Useful terms: the following does not pretend to be an exhaustive list of the foods you'll find in bistros, simply a few basics that will help to get you started comprehending French cuisine.

l'addition: the bill
agneau: lamb
ail: garlic
amande: almond
amuse-gueule: cocktail snack
anchois: anchovy
ancienne, à l': in white sauce
andalouse, à l': garnish of squid, tomatoes, peppers, eggplant
andouille, andouillette: cooked tripe sausage
aneth: dill
asperge: asparagus
assiette: plate
avocat: avocado

baba: rum-soaked sponge cake
bar: sea bass
barbue: brill, flat sea fish
basquaise, à la: with tomatoes, peppers, garlic, and cured ham
basilic: basil
batavia: type of lettuce
bavarois: Bavarian cream dessert
bavette: beef flank steak
Béarnaise: Hollandaise sauce with tarragon, spices, and shallots

Belle Hélène: pear with ice cream, topped with chocolate sauce
beignet: doughnut or fritter
beurre : butter
beurre blanc: sauce flavored with white wine, shallots, vinegar, and fish stock
bien cuit: well done
bière: beer
bifteck: beef steak
bisque: thick soup
boeuf: beef
boeuf bourguignon: beef stew
boudin: blood sausage
bouillabaisse: Mediterranean fish soup of various fishes, tomatoes, garlic, etc.
brouillé (oeuf): scrambled eggs

cabillaud: fresh cod
caille: quail
Calvados: apple brandy
canard: duck
carafe: decanter, pitcher
carafe d'eau: tap water
carotte: carrot (*rapée*: grated)
carpaccio: appetizer of slices of raw cured beef
carte: menu

cassis: black currant

cassoulet: white bean stew with duck, lamb, or sausage

cèpe: type of wild mushroom

chantilly: whipped cream

charcuterie: cured meats

Charlotte: creamy fruit dessert made with gelatin

chèvre: goat (*fromage de chèvre*: goat milk cheese)

choux-fleur: cauliflower

choux: cabbage

coeur: heart

contre-filet: upper filet of sirloin steak

coq: rooster

cornichon: pickle

côte: rib of beef or pork

courgette: zucchini

crème brûlée: custard dessert with caramelized topping

crème caramel: caramel custard dessert

cresson: watercress

crevette: prawn or shrimp

croque-madame: open-faced toasted ham-and-cheese sandwich topped with fried egg

croque-monsieur: toasted ham-and-cheese sandwich

cru: raw, uncooked

crudité(s): raw vegetables

daube: meat stewed in red wine, onions, and herbs

daurade, dorade: sea bream, a white, delicate fish

de campagne: country-style

dinde, dindon: turkey

eau: water

échalotte: shallot

émincé: thinly sliced

entrecôte: beef ribsteak

entrée: hors d'oeuvre, starter

épinard: spinach

erable: maple

escargot: snail

espadon: swordfish

estragon: tarragon

faisan: pheasant

faux-filet: sirloin steak

fermier: farm; free-range

feuilleté: puff pastry

fines herbes: mix of herbs including chives, parsley, tarragon, and chervil

flan: tart made with eggs and milk, sweet or savory

foie: liver

foie gras: fattened goose or duck liver

frais: fresh, chilled

fraise: strawberry

framboise: raspberry

frit(e): fried

frites: fried potatoes, French fries, chips

fromage: cheese

fumé: smoked

galette: pancake

garni: garnished, usually with vegetables

gaspacho: cold soup made with tomato, cucumber, onions, and sweet pepper

gâteau: cake

gaufre: waffle

génoise: sponge cake

gésier: gizzard

gibier: wild game

gigot: lamb

girolle: apricot-colored wild

mushroom

glace: ice cream

gratin dauphinois: scalloped
potatoes, sliced, with
cream cheese

grenouille: frog

griotte: sour cherry

grondin: gurnard, a marine fish
used in bouillabaisse

groseille: currant

haché: chopped, minced

hareng: herring

haricot: bean; *haricots verts:*
green beans

huile: oil

île flottante: dessert of caramel
coated egg whites in custard

jambon: ham

joue: cheek

jus: juice; *au jus:* in its cooking
liquid

kasher: Kosher

lait: milk

langoustine: large prawn

langue: tongue

lapin: rabbit

lard: bacon

laurier: bay leaf

légume: vegetable

lotte de mer: monkfish

lieu: pollock

loup: European bass

macédoine: mixture of diced
vegetables or fruit

mâche: lamb's lettuce

madeleine: small shell-shaped
cake

madère: Madeira

magret (de canard): duck breast

maître d'hôtel: head waiter;
sauce maître d'hôtel: butter and
lemon sauce

mangue: mango

maquereau: mackerel fish

marc: brandy

marchand de vin: sauce with
red wine and shallots

marron: chestnut

médaillon: small round slice

menthe: mint

menu: a set-price menu, as
opposed to the *carte*

mer, fruit de: seafood

meunière: sautéed with lemon
juice and parsley

miel: honey

millefeuille: puff pastry; a
Napoleon filled with custard

moëlle: bone marrow

Mont Blanc: chestnut cream
dessert

morille: morel mushroom

morue: salted cod

noix: walnut, nut

nouilles: noodles

oeuf: egg

onglet de boeuf: similar to flank
steak

osso buco: veal shin braised in
white wine with tomatoes,
garlic, and onions

pamplemousse: grapefruit

paincomplet: whole-wheat
bread

pan bagnat: round sandwich
with tuna, anchovies, and
olives

Parmentier: potato-based dish

Pastis: anise-flavored, before-
dinner drink

pâte: pastry
pâté: seasoned, cooked meat
pâtisserie: pastry
pavé: thick slice
pêche: peach
pichet: pitcher or jug for wine
pintade: guinea fowl
pistou: Provençal sauce of basil, garlic, and olive oil; also a rich bean soup
plat: main course, dish
poire: pear
pois: peas
poisson: fish
poivre: pepper
poivron: bell pepper
pomme: apple
pomme de terre: potato
porc: pork
poulet: chicken
praline: caramelized sugar with almonds
pression: draft beer
prix: price
prix fixe: fixed-price menu
quart: quarter
quatre-quarts: pound cake
quenelle: dumpling
queue: tail
quiche: tart with eggs

raifort: horseradish
radis: radish
raie: ray fish
raisin: grape
râpé: grated
rascasse: scorpion fish, used in bouillabaisse
rillettes: meat, often pork
ris: sweetbreads
riz: rice
rognons: kidneys
rognon blanc: testicles

rosbif: roast beef
rôti: roast
rouget: red mullet
rumsteak: rumpsteak

sabayon: frothy sauce of white wine, egg, and sugar
sablé: sweet biscuit or shortbread
safran: saffron
salade: lettuce
salé(e): salted
Salers: highly regarded beef from Auvergne, also cheese
sang: blood
saucisse: sausage
saucisson: dried salami-type sausage
saumon: salmon
sauvage: wild
sec, sèche: dry
seigle: rye

tartare, steak: raw ground beef
tartine: open-faced sandwich
terrine: dish used for prepared meat, seafood & vegetables
thon: tuna
truffe: truffle
truite: trout

vacherin: meringue cake w/ice cream & whipped cream
viennoiserie: pastries
vin: wine
vinaigre: vinegar

xères: sherry

yaourt: yogurt
zeste: outer peel of citrus fruit, zest

INDEX